the STORY of the WORLD

Volume 1: Ancient Times

ALSO BY SUSAN WISE BAUER

The Story of the World
History for the Classical Child
(Well-Trained Mind Press)

Volume 2: The Middle Ages (revised edition 2007)
Volume 3: Early Modern Times (revised edition 2019)
Volume 4: The Modern Age (revised edition 2020)

The History of the Ancient World
From the Earliest Accounts to the Fall of Rome
(W.W. Norton, 2007)

The History of the Medieval World
From the Conversion of Constantine to the First Crusade
(W.W. Norton, 2010)

The History of the Renaissance World
From the Rediscovery of Aristotle
to the Conquest of Constantinople
(W.W. Norton, 2013)

The Well-Educated Mind
A Guide to the Classical Education You Never Had
(W.W. Norton, 2nd edition 2015)

The Great Shadow
A History of How Sickness Shapes What We Do, Think,
Believe, and Buy
(St. Martin's Press, 2026)

WITH JESSIE WISE
The Well-Trained Mind
A Guide to Classical Education at Home
(W.W. Norton, 5th edition 2024)

www.susanwisebauer.com

the STORY of the WORLD

History for the Classical Child

Volume 1: Ancient Times

From the Earliest Nomads to the Last Roman Emperor

25th Anniversary Expanded Edition

by Susan Wise Bauer

illustrated by Jeff West

WELL-TRAINED MIND PRESS

Charles City, Virginia

Well-Trained Mind Press

2006 Cover design by AJ Buffington and Mike Fretto.
2026 Cover design by Mehreen Fatima.
Book design by Itamar Katz. Composed in Plantin MT Pro.

Names: Bauer, Susan Wise, author. | West, Jeff, illustrator.
Title: Ancient times : from the earliest nomads to the last Roman Emperor / by Susan Wise Bauer ; illustrated by Jeff West.
Description: 25th anniversary expanded edition. | Charles City, Virginia : Well-Trained Mind Press, [2026] | Series: Bauer, Susan Wise. Story of the world ; v. 1. | Interest grade level: 1-4. | Summary: For 25 years, The Story of the World has helped millions of children fall in love with history. Now, the Expanded 25th Anniversary Edition brings the sweep and drama of the human story to a new generation of readers. Susan Wise Bauer has updated and expanded this history, while retaining the engaging and accessible style that made the original so beloved. From the pyramids of Egypt to the palaces of China, from the rise of the first cities to the fall of the Roman Empire, The Story of the World will captivate your child. — Publisher.
Identifiers: ISBN: 9781944481834 (hardcover) | 9781944481827 (paperback) | 9781944481841 (ebook)
Subjects: LCSH: World history—Juvenile literature. | Civilization—Juvenile literature. | History, Ancient—Juvenile literature. | Nomads—History—Juvenile literature. | BISAC: JUVENILE NONFICTION / History / Ancient. | EDUCATION / Schools / Levels / Elementary. | EDUCATION / Teaching / Subjects / Arts & Humanities.
Classification: LCC: D20 .B35 2026 | DDC: 909—dc23

The translation of “The Great Hymn to the Aten” on page 112 is used by permission of The University of California Press.

welltrainedmind.com

Contents

Foreword

I started writing the *Story of the World* series back in 1999, right after finishing the original edition of *The Well-Trained Mind.* In that book, my mother Jessie Wise and I had recommended two principles for the study of elementary history: first, that history be studied by period, not by country (so that young readers can see what's going on all across the world at the same time); and second, that history be told as the fascinating, engaging story that it is.

Unfortunately, we couldn't find a single elementary history that followed these principles. The available books were either encyclopedias (nice pictures, boring disconnected snippets of text), or if they were told as narratives, they focused in on the history of a single country; and that country was almost always America, with little attention to the rest of this very large world.

So I decided to write my own.

It's hard to understand, at the beginning of a big project, just what you're letting yourself in for. At first, telling the story of the entire world for young readers seemed like a fun and necessary enterprise. But it didn't take me long to realize how difficult it would be to choose, out of more than four thousand years of recorded history, exactly the tales and characters that would bring the past alive— and also give my budding historians the important pegs of information that they would need to help them make sense of future studies of the past.

I believe that the first edition of *The Story of the World*—a narrative, big-picture, chronological world history—succeeded in this. The books have been enjoyed by hundreds of thousands of young readers and their families. They have learned about parts of the world that they never knew existed, delighted in the stories of past heroes, discovered how the ancient past still speaks to us today, and (let's not forget) they've mummified quite a few chickens.

I also heard from hundreds of readers who wished I'd done it differently: highlighted lesser known cultures, taken an alternative point of view, included a national hero that didn't make it into the original pages. In many cases, I had to sigh and say: "Well, if I only had another hundred pages or so..." But I also listened, and this anniversary edition takes that feedback into account. It is more strictly chronological, adds more non-Western history, and includes ten new profiles of history-makers, lesser-known characters from the past who nevertheless changed their countries, and deserve to be better known. They add even more layers to this story of our world.

Twenty-five years on, I constantly meet adults who say, "Oh, I LOVED *The Story of the World* when I was little!" The series opened their eyes to the size of the world, the beauty of other cultures, the enduring puzzle of human motivations, and the sheer fascination of the past (as Leslie Hartley famously observed, the past is a foreign country; they do things differently there). I believe that this anniversary edition will continue on in that tradition.

Susan Wise Bauer
Charles City, Virginia

Introduction
How Do We Know What Happened?

What Is History?

Do you know where you were born? Were you born at a hospital, or at home? How much did you weigh when you were born? What did you have to eat for your first birthday?

You don't remember being born, do you? And you probably don't remember your first birthday party! So how can you find the answers to these questions?

You can ask your parents. They can tell you about things that happened long ago, before you were old enough to remember. They can tell you stories about when you were a baby.

These stories are your "history." Your history is the story of what happened to you from the moment you were born, all the way up to the present. You can learn this history by listening to your parents. They remember what happened when you were born. And they probably took pictures of you when you were a baby. You can learn even more about your history from these pictures. Did you have hair? Were you fat or thin? Are you smiling or frowning? What are you wearing? Do you remember those clothes?

You have a history—and so do your parents. Where were they born? Were they born at home, or at a hospital? Where did they go to school? What did they like to eat? Who were their best friends?

How can you find the answers to these questions? You can ask your parents. And if they don't remember, you can ask *their* parents—your grandparents.

Now let's ask a harder question. Your grandmother was once a little girl. What is her history like? How much did she weigh when she was born? Did she cry a lot? When did she cut her first tooth? What was her favorite thing to eat?

You would have to ask *her* mother—your *great*-grandmother. And you could look at baby pictures of your grandmother. But what if you can't talk to your great-grandmother, and what if you don't have any baby pictures of your grandmother? Is there another way you could find out about your grandmother's history?

There might be. Perhaps your grandmother's mother wrote a letter to a friend when she was born. "Dear Elizabeth," she might have written. "My baby was born at home on September 13. She weighed seven pounds, and she has a lot of fuzzy black hair. She certainly cries a lot! I hope she'll sleep through the night soon."

Now, suppose you find this letter, years later. Even though you can't talk to your great-grandmother, you can learn the *history* of your grandmother from her letter. You could also learn *history* if your great-grandmother kept a diary or a journal, where she wrote about things that happened to her long ago.

In this book, we're going to learn about the *history* of people who lived a long time ago, in all different countries around the world. We're going to learn about the stories they told, the battles they fought, and the way they lived—even what they ate and drank, and what they wore.

How do we know these things about people who lived many, many years in the past? After all, we can't ask them.

We learn about the history of long-ago people in two different ways. The first way is through the letters, journals, and other written records that they left behind. Suppose a woman who lived in ancient times wrote a letter to a friend who lived in another village. Her letter might say, "There hasn't been very much rain here recently. All our crops are dying. The wheat is especially bad. If it doesn't rain soon, we'll have to move to another village!"

Hundreds of years later, we find this letter. What can we learn about the history of ancient times from this letter? We can learn that people in ancient times grew wheat for food. They depended on rain to keep the wheat healthy. And if it didn't rain enough, they moved somewhere else.

Other kinds of written records tell us about what kings and armies did in ancient times. When a king won a great victory, he often ordered a monument built. On the monument, he would have the story of his victory engraved in stone letters. Or a king might order someone in his court to write down the story of his reign, so that everyone would know what an important and powerful king he was. Thousands of years later, we can read the stone letters or the stories and learn more about the king.

People who read letters, journals, other documents, and monuments to find out what happened in the past are called *historians*. And the story they write about the past is called *history*.

What Is Archaeology?

We can learn about what people did in the past through reading the letters and other writings that they left behind. But this is only one way of doing history.

Long, long ago, many people didn't know how to write. They didn't write letters to each other. The kings didn't carve the stories of their great deeds on monuments. How can a historian learn the story of people who didn't know how to write?

Imagine that a whole village full of people lived near a river, long ago. These people don't know how to write. They don't send letters to their friends, or write diaries about their daily life. But as they go about their duties every day, they drop things on the ground. A farmer, out working in his wheat field, loses the iron blade from the knife he's using to cut wheat from the stalks. He can't find it, so he goes to get another knife—leaving the blade on the ground.

Back in the village, his wife drops a clay pot by accident, just outside the back steps of her house. It breaks into pieces. She sighs, and kicks the pieces under the house.

Her little boy is playing in the dirt, just beyond the back steps. He has a little clay model of an ox, hitched to a cart. He runs the cart through the dirt and says, "Moo! Moo!" until his mother calls him to come inside. He leaves the cart where it is and runs into the house. His mother has a new toy for him! He's so excited that he forgets all about his ox and cart. Next day, his father goes out into the yard and accidentally kicks dirt over the clay ox and cart. The toy stays in the yard, with dirt covering it.

Now let's imagine that the summer gets drier and drier. The wheat starts to die. The people who live in the village have less and less to eat. They get together and decide that they will pack up their belongings and take a journey to another place, where there is more rain. So they collect their things and start off down the river. They leave behind the things that they don't want any more—cracked jars, dull knives, and stores of wheat kernels that are too hard and dry to use.

The deserted village stands by the river for years. Slowly, the buildings start to fall down. Dust blows overtop of the ruins. One year, the river floods and washes mud over the dust. Grass starts to grow in the mud. Eventually, you can barely see the village anymore. Dirt and grass cover the ruins from sight. It just looks like a field by a river.

But one day a man comes along to look at the field. He sees a little bit of wood poking up from the grass. He bends down and starts to brush dirt away from the wood. It is the corner of a building. When he sees this, he thinks to himself, "People used to live here!"

The next day he comes back with special tools—tiny shovels, brushes, and special knives. He starts to dig down into the field. When he finds the remains of houses and tools, he brushes the dirt away from them. He writes down exactly where he found them. And then he examines them carefully. He wants to discover more about the people who used to live in the village.

One day, he finds the iron knife blade that the farmer lost in the field. He thinks to himself, "These people knew how to make iron. They knew how to grow wheat and harvest it for food. And they used iron tools to harvest their grain."

Another day, he finds the clay pot that the farmer's wife broke. Now, he knows that the people of the village knew how to make dishes from clay. And when he finds the little ox and cart that the little boy lost in the yard, he knows that the people of the village used cows, harnessed to wagons, to help them in their farm work.

He might even find out that the people left their village because there was no rain. He discovers the remains of the hard, spoiled wheat that the people left behind. When he looks at the wheat, he can tell that it was ruined by lack of rain. So he thinks to himself, "I'll bet that these people left their village during a dry season. They probably went to find a place where it was rainy."

This man is doing history—even though he doesn't have any written letters or other documents. He is discovering the story of the people of the village from the things that they left behind them. This kind of history is called *archaeology*. And historians who dig objects out of the ground and learn from them are called *archaeologists*.

Chapter One
The Earliest People

The First Nomads

Where do you live? Where do you sleep? Do you sleep in the same bed every night, or do you move into a new house every week?

Thousands and thousands of years ago, families didn't live in houses and shop at grocery stores. Instead, they wandered from place to place, looking for food and sleeping in tents or caves. Ancient families who lived this way were called *nomads*. Nomad means "a person who wanders or roams around." In some parts of the world, nomads still wander from place to place today!

Nomads gathered their food from the land around them. They ate plants that they picked, roots that they dug out of the ground, and nuts and berries that they gathered from bushes and trees. When they had eaten most of the food in one place, they would move on to another place. Women and children had the job of digging up roots; picking nuts, berries, and plants; and collecting other kinds of food—eggs, wild honey, and even lizards and snakes. Men hunted for meat with spears, bows, and arrows. If the nomads camped near a river or lake, the men and women would both fish, too.

After the nomads had hunted in one area for a while, all the animals would move away from them. When that happened, the nomads would pack up and follow the game. They would keep wandering and moving on.

In warm places, nomads built tents by stretching animal hides over wooden frames. They could take these tents with them when they moved. Nomads who lived in colder, rocky places used caves for shelter. We know that they lived there because they painted pictures of animals on the walls of the caves; we can still see these pictures today.

TARAK IS A SEVEN-YEAR-OLD GIRL WHO LIVES with her family in the days of the nomads. She likes warm weather the best, because she can sleep out in the open and look at the stars until she falls asleep.

One warm morning, Tarak gets up when the sun comes up. She is sleeping outside, so all she has to do is pick up the piece of animal skin she sleeps on and take it to her mother. She wears the same clothes all the time, so she doesn't even have to change out of her pajamas.

In the middle of the nomads' camp, the fire is still burning from the night before. Tarak's uncle and some of the other adults have taken turns staying up through the night, watching the fire and keeping it burning. They heard a wildcat screaming in the night and wanted to keep it away from the camp. Tarak's uncle says that the wildcat has already frightened away the flocks of small deer that the hunters were tracking. There's no meat for breakfast this morning. If the hunters don't shoot any deer today, the whole group of nomads will pick up their tents and skins and begin to walk towards a new place to hunt.

Tarak doesn't like the grain that her mother offers her for breakfast, so she decides to wait and eat when she goes out to gather food. Every morning, Tarak and her brothers go out with their mother to look for plants and berries. But they've been gathering food in the same place for a long time, and they've already picked most of the leaves that are good to eat. They've already scraped all the honey out of the wild bees' nest that her younger brother found in the crack of a rock. And they've taken the eggs from all the nests that they can climb up to.

She and her younger brother get their game bags—small bags made out of skin—and start out to look for food. "I'm going to find another bees' nest," brags her brother. "Then we can eat honey again."

"I'm the best lizard catcher in the family," Tarak retorts. "I bet I can find a lizard before you can find a bees' nest."

Sure enough, as they walk out of a patch of woods into the sunshine, Tarak sees a lizard dart away into the crack of a log. She leaps on the log and turns it over. Three lizards try to scurry away from her, but in a moment, she has scooped them up and dumped them into her bag. There isn't very much meat on a lizard, but her mother is a wonderful cook; she can stew the lizards in boiling water until every shred of meat has come off the bones, add herbs and roots, and serve a good filling stew to the whole camp. All the way back to the nomad camp, Tarak can feel the lizards squirming in her bag. It makes her hungry. She can't wait to taste her mother's lizard stew.

The First Nomads Become Farmers

One of the best places for nomads to live was in an area called the Fertile Crescent. It was called a *crescent* because it was shaped like a crescent moon— like this:

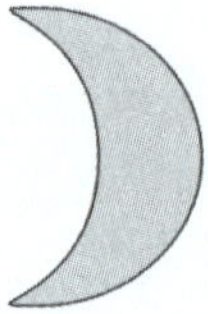

And it was called *fertile* because two rivers, called the Tigris and the Euphrates, ran through it. Rich grass, wild barley, and wild wheat grew in the damp soil of the riverbanks.

When nomads wandered through the Fertile Crescent, they saw herds of animals feeding on the grass. They saw grain that they could harvest, and wide rivers where they

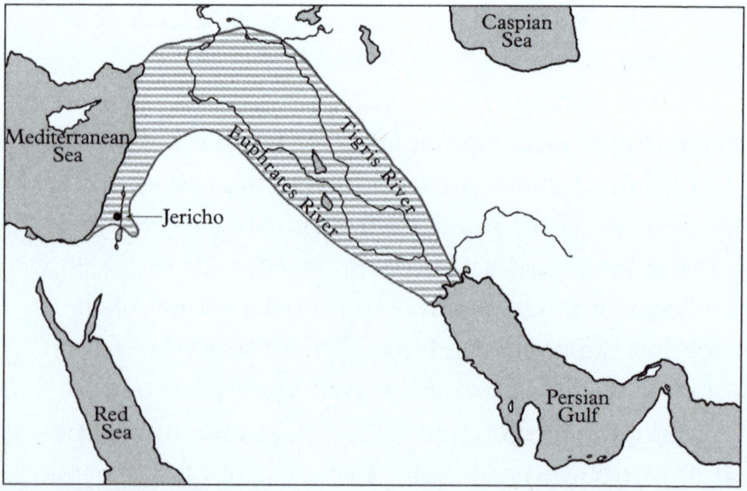

The Fertile Crescent

could fish and get fresh water to drink. Because it was so easy to find food, nomads returned to the Fertile Crescent again and again. Some of these nomads began to live near the two rivers all year long, instead of wandering from place to place in search of food.

Nomads who settled in the Fertile Crescent couldn't just pick leaves, nuts, and berries to eat. Since they weren't moving on, they would soon run out of wild plants to harvest. Instead, they had to begin to plant grain for themselves. The nomads of the Fertile Crescent were turning into farmers.

These new fields of grain needed extra water to flourish. The land near the rivers was damp enough to make growing easy. But it didn't rain very much in the Fertile Crescent, and farther away from the shores, the land was dry for much of the year. So the farmers learned to dig canals from the rivers out into their fields. That way, even if it did not rain, they could bring water to their crops.

Today, irrigation machines are enormous metal sprinklers, higher than a house and longer than three or four semitrucks. They pump water out of lakes and spray it over entire fields. But long ago, farmers had a simpler machine to get water out of the canals and onto their crops. This machine was called a *shaduf.* Early farmers balanced a pole lengthwise on top of a pillar. They tied a weight to one end of the pole, and attached a leather bucket to the other. Then the farmers lowered the bucket into the canal, raised the bucket by pushing down on the weight, and then swung the bucket around to pour the water on the crops. The shaduf was one of the first farm machines.

A farmer with a shaduf

Farmers had to tend their crops every day for months. So they began to build houses that would stay in one place, instead of living in tents that could be moved every few days. They used whatever materials were around them. Farmers who lived near the river built houses out of reeds, or out of bricks that were made from mud and left to dry in the sun.

Soon, farmers discovered that it was best to build houses close together so that they could help each other to water and tend their fields. These were the first villages. The farmers also learned that they could tame animals such as sheep and goats, feed them grain, and then use them for meat. This was easier than hunting wild animals! Villages were often built around a central pen or field where the tame animals were kept.

Some villages were very successful in growing grain and raising sheep and goats. They even grew rich by trading grain, sheep's wool, and animal skins to others for metals, pottery, wood, and other goods. Because they were afraid that they might be attacked and robbed by bandits, they built stone walls around their villages.

These were the first cities.

One of the earliest was the city of Jericho. Jericho had one of the thickest, strongest walls of the ancient world. It was made of stone, and it was ten feet thick and thirteen feet tall, with a circular tower on one side so that village lookouts could see enemies approaching. The tower was at least twenty-eight feet high—taller than a two-story house!

NOT LONG AFTER THE DAY THAT TARAK catches enough lizards for her mother's lizard stew, Tarak and her family wander into the Fertile Crescent, searching for food. They find plenty of roots, nuts, and berries to eat. Tarak's uncle is excited because he sees large herds of horses and small deer to hunt.

But the most exciting thing Tarak sees is a huge river, flowing by right at her feet. She has never seen so much water in one place in her life. Usually, her family and the other nomads only find small pools of water, or tiny streams trickling through the rocks. They need this water for drinking—so Tarak has never been swimming. As a matter of fact, she has never had a bath in her whole life. Now, she can walk right into the water up to her chin.

At first, Tarak and her brother are afraid to get into the water. They just squat on the shore and splash each other. But slowly they put one foot, and then the other into the water. Tarak wants to show her brother how brave she is, so she wades out almost to her knees. She hears her brother wading in behind her. He splashes her all over, so she turns around and dunks his head under the water. He comes up spluttering and yelling. He's never been under water before.

Tarak and her brother spend the whole morning in the river. When they get out, Tarak notices that her brother smells much better than he used to.

That night at dinner, there is horsemeat to eat. Tarak's uncle says, "I met other men a little farther down the riverbank. But they weren't hunting. They were putting seeds into the ground. They told me that if we put seeds into the ground too, grain would grow right here where we are. We could pick it, and we wouldn't have to keep looking for new fields to gather food in. I think we'll stay here for a while and watch what they're doing."

Tarak grins at her brother. She likes living on the bank of the river; she likes eating horsemeat instead of lizards; she likes the idea that she won't have to go searching for roots every day. And most of all she likes swimming.

Note: Nomads roamed through the Fertile Crescent from at least 9000 BC/BCE. The stone wall at Jericho dates to around 8000 BC/BCE.

Chapter Two
Egyptians Lived on the Nile River

Two Kingdoms Become One

Tarak could go swimming almost any day she wanted to, because the Tigris River was full of water all year round. But the farmers who lived along the banks of the Nile River had a very different kind of river to deal with. Sometimes the river was very low—so low that you could almost see the bottom. Other times, it was so full that it flooded all over their farmland.

The Nile River is a long river in Africa. At the top, it splits into several different little rivers and runs into the Mediterranean Sea. This area is shaped like an upside-down triangle. The Greek letter for *D*, *delta*, is shaped like a triangle too. So this part of the river is called the Nile Delta, after the Greek letter of the alphabet.

Every year, the Nile flooded. During rainy seasons, water would fall on the mountains in the south, where the Nile River begins. The water would pour down the mountains, into the river, and run down towards the delta. So much water poured into the Nile at once that it overflowed its banks and spread all over the farmland on either side. The wettest place of all was the Nile Delta—all the little rivers ran over their banks and spread out so that the whole delta was underwater.

Would you like to live on the banks of the Nile? Do you think it would be a good place to build a house? What would happen to your house?

If a farmer had a river flood all over his crops today, he'd think it was a disaster. It would wash his crops away. But the farmers who lived along the Nile liked to see the river flood. The river flooded at the same time every year, so they were ready for it. When the water came up out of the river, rich dirt from the bottom of the river came with it. This dirt was called *silt*, and it was full of good vitamins and minerals for plants. The floodwater would

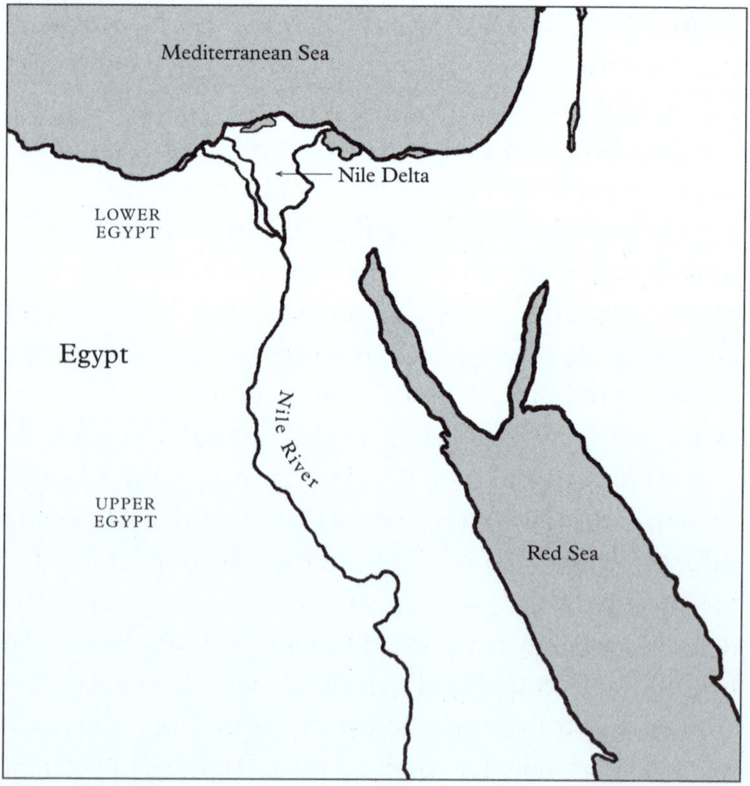

The Nile Delta

spread the silt all along the edge of the river, and then the water would recede—go back into the river until the next year. Then the farmers, who lived a little ways away from the riverbank so that their houses wouldn't flood, would come out and plant their crops in the rich silt. They learned to dig canals leading away from the river, so that floodwater would run into their canals. Then they would block the ends of the canals so that the water couldn't run back into the river. They could use the water in the canals during dry seasons.

The people who lived along the Nile were called *Egyptians*. Early in Egypt's history, there were two Egyptian tribes who lived along the Nile. The Egyptians who lived in the north, in the Nile Delta, were called the "Lower Egyptians." The Egyptians who lived along the straight part of the river, further south, were called the "Upper Egyptians."

When you look at a map, "north" is usually at the top and "south" is usually at the bottom. So it might seem to you that the Nile Delta should be "Upper Egypt." After all, it's on the upper part of your map.

But the ancient Egyptians didn't think about the world in that way. The Nile River flowed from the mountains in the south, down to the delta in the north. So the ancient Egyptians thought about the southern part of their country, Upper Egypt, as "up the river," and the northern part, Lower Egypt, as "down the river." If you turn the map at the top of this page upside down, you'll see the world as the Egyptians did.

The Lower Egyptians were ruled by a king who wore a red crown, and the Upper Egyptians were ruled by a king who wore a white crown. Both kings wanted to rule over all of Egypt. So for years, the White Crown King and the Red Crown King fought with each other, and the Upper Egyptians and the Lower Egyptians sailed up and down the Nile and fought with each other too.

Finally, the two kings fought one great battle to settle, once and for all, who would rule Egypt.

The Upper Egyptian king, the White Crown King, was named King Narmer. Around five thousand years ago, King Narmer defeated the Red Crown King and took his crown away. Then he put the red crown overtop of his own white crown and announced that he was the king of all Egypt.

From now on, the king of Egypt would wear the Double Crown of Egypt, which had a white spike at the center and a red band around the outside. This showed that he was the ruler of the entire country—both Upper and Lower!

Gods of Ancient Egypt

Now that the Egyptians were all part of one country, the king of Egypt became known as the *pharaoh*. He carried a shepherd's crook to show that he was supposed to lead and take care of all the Egyptian people, just like a shepherd takes care of and feeds his sheep. Soon, the Egyptians began to think that the pharaoh was actually a god. They believed that he was able to make the Nile

overflow its banks every year so that their crops could grow. The pharaoh got more and more powerful, because no one wanted to make a god angry!

The pharaoh wasn't the only god the Egyptians worshipped. Ra was the god of the sun. He was the chief god; other gods were part of his family. Osiris was the god who judged the dead and decided whether they had been good or bad. Isis was Osiris's wife, and the mother of Horus, who was the god of the sky.

Egyptian stories about the gods often tried to explain why the Nile overflowed every year. One Egyptian story, or *myth*, tells about Osiris and his brother, Set. Here's the myth of Osiris as an Egyptian child might have heard it from his mother, long ago.

ONCE UPON A TIME, THE GREAT GOD OSIRIS and his wife Isis were ruling over the whole land of Egypt. Osiris went on a trip around the world and left Isis in charge of the kingdom.

But while he was gone, Osiris's evil brother Set decided that he wanted to be king. When Osiris came back from his trip, Set invited him to a great feast with all the other gods. "Dear brother," he said, "come to my house so that we can celebrate your safe return!"

Isis was afraid that Set wanted to harm Osiris, but Osiris laughed at her fears. "He's my own brother!" he said. "Why would he want to hurt me?"

So they went together to the feast. After all the gods had eaten until they were full, Set said, "Look what I have found!" He brought out a beautiful coffin, all carved and decorated with gold and pictures. When the gods all admired it, Set said, "I will give this beautiful coffin to whichever god fits into it the best."

The gods didn't know that Set had ordered the coffin made so that it would only fit Osiris. One by one, they lay down in the coffin. But all of the gods were too large or too small—until Osiris got in, and found that the coffin fit him perfectly. Osiris was so pleased that he lay all the way down in the coffin. "Look!" he said. "I've won the coffin!"

But as soon as he lay down, Set slammed the coffin closed and threw it into the Nile, where it floated away. "Now I'm the king of the gods, because Osiris has drowned!" Set announced. He took over the throne and began to rule Egypt.

But Isis went on a long journey down the Nile to find the coffin. Finally she discovered it, caught in the reeds beside the Nile's bank. She opened it, but Osiris had drowned.

Isis sat down and wept and wept for grief. Even the Nile cried over the death of Osiris, so that the river ran dry and all the Egyptians were desperate for water.

Finally Isis wrapped Osiris's body in linen—so that he became the first mummy. But as soon as she wrapped him in linen, he came back to life again.

The whole earth was glad to see Osiris alive again! The Nile filled back up and overflowed its banks, so that all the Egyptians had water to drink, and their crops began to grow again. And that's why the Nile overflows every year—because it remembers that Osiris came back to life.

Note: The Upper and Lower Kingdoms were united around 3000 BC/BCE. King Narmer is also known as King Menes.

Chapter Three
The First Writing

Hieroglyphs and Cuneiform

The Egyptians were among the earliest people to use writing.

Why do you think it's important to be able to write things down?

Suppose I write a message for you on a piece of paper and put it on the table. Then I leave the room. If you look at the paper, you'll know what I wanted to say to you—even though I'm nowhere around. That's one reason writing is important. Once the Egyptians learned to write things down, they could send messages from one part of their kingdom to another.

What if you found my message a year after I wrote it? You would still be able to "hear" my words—even though I had written them down long before. That's the second reason that writing is so important. The Egyptians could write down the important events that happened during their lifetimes, and leave them for their grandchildren and great-grandchildren to read.

The Egyptians used pictures to write with. We call these pictures *hieroglyphs*. The pictures stood for certain words. The Egyptians used to carve these hieroglyphs into stone tablets.

The stone tablets lasted for a very long time—but they were heavy to carry, and carving the pictures into stone took weeks of work.

Another country near Egypt had a better idea. They carved their pictures into tablets of wet clay instead.

This country was called Sumer. Sumer was in the Fertile Crescent, between the Tigris and Euphrates rivers. The place between the rivers is called Mesopotamia. The word *Mesopotamia* means "between two rivers." Do you know what the word *hippopotamus* means? *Hippo* means "horse," and *potamus* means "river." A hippopotamus is a "river horse"! In Mesopotamia, we can see the word *potamus* again, only this time it has a different ending. *Potamia* means "rivers," and *meso* means "between."

The Sumerian picture writing was called *cuneiform*. Because the Sumerians lived between two rivers, they had plenty of damp clay. Instead of carving their cuneiform onto stone, they would mold this clay into square tablets. Then, while the clay was still wet, they would use a sharp knife or stick to make the cuneiform marks. After the message was carved into the clay, the Sumerians could either wipe it out and write another message (if the message was something unimportant, like a grocery list), or else bake the clay until it was hard. Then the message would last for a very long time.

Writing in clay is easier than carving stone. But even clay tablets can be heavy. And clay tablets are thick; if you want to store a whole lot of them, you need a lot of space—whole buildings full of rooms for even a small library.

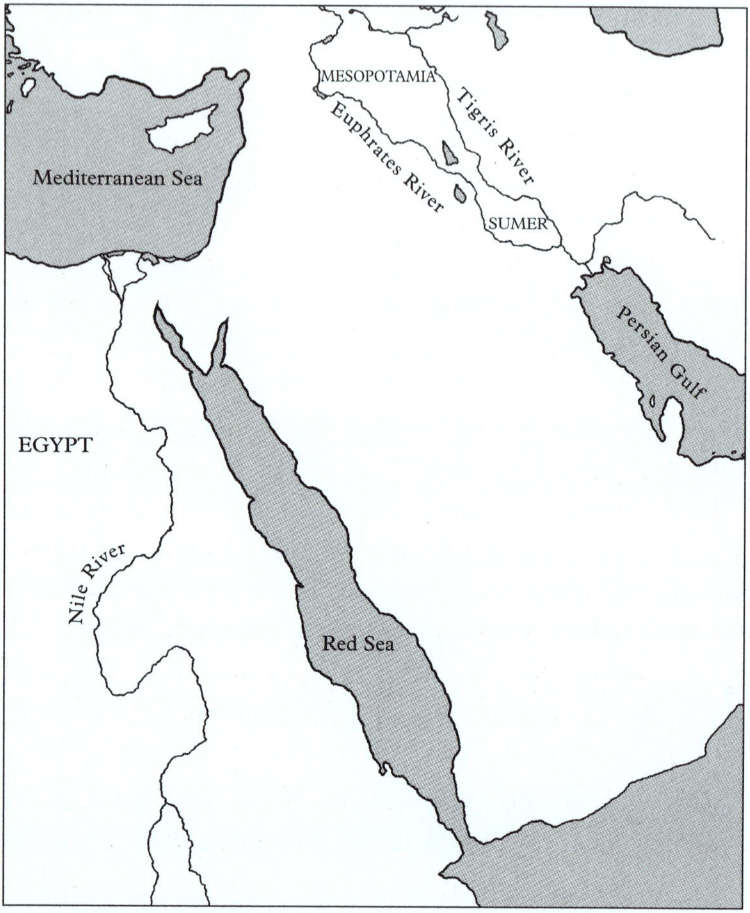

Mesopotamia and Egypt

After several hundred years, the Egyptians came up with an idea that was even better than clay. They learned how to make paper and ink.

Egyptian paper was made from reeds that grew along the banks of the Nile. The Egyptians learned how to soften the reeds, arrange them into crosswise layers, and then dry them into thin sheets. These sheets became reed-paper, which we now call *papyrus*.

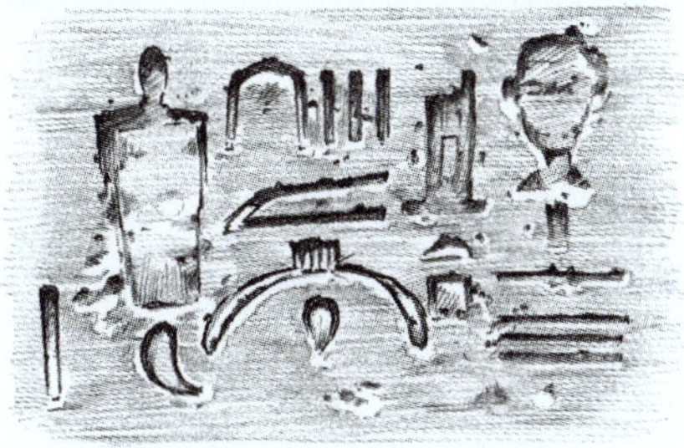

Egyptian Hieroglyphs

It was much easier to write on paper than on clay or stone. Paper was also easier to carry around; you could fold it up and put it into your pocket, or roll it up into a scroll. And paper took up less room. When they started using paper, the Egyptians thought they had found the best way to keep records.

But paper has a problem. When paper gets wet, the ink on it dissolves and the paper falls apart. And paper also starts to fall apart over time. The older paper gets, the more likely it is to crack up and turn into dust.

We know a lot about Egyptian history from the times that Egyptians wrote on stone, because those stone writings have lasted for centuries—from Egyptian days until now. We know a lot about Sumerian history too, because clay tablets last for a long time if they've been baked hard.

But we don't know a great deal about what happened in Egypt after the Egyptians started writing on paper, because in the thousands of years that have gone by, most of the paper writings of the Egyptians have crumbled and disappeared.

Note: The Sumerians and Egyptians used cuneiform from about 3200 BC/BCE, with Sumerian writing developing slightly earlier.

Chapter Four
The Old Kingdom of Egypt

Making Mummies

After King Narmer united Upper and Lower Egypt into one country, Egypt grew to be rich and powerful. We call this time in Egyptian history the Old Kingdom of Egypt. The Old Kingdom lasted for almost a thousand years—until about the year 2100.

Before we go on, let's look at that date a little more closely. Usually people write this date with a "BC" or "BCE" after it. "BC" means "Before Christ," and "BCE" means "Before the Common Era."

About fifteen hundred years ago, historians began to use the birth of Jesus as a way to count years. In this system, Jesus was born in "Year 1." Dates before Year 1 count down from highest to lowest (for example, 99, 98, 97 … and so on), and end at Year 1. The "Common Era" begins with Jesus's birth. The years after Jesus's birth are called "AD" or "CE." "AD" stands for Anno Domini, or "The Year of Our Lord" in Latin and usually precedes the date, grammatically. "CE" means "Common Era." In the Common Era, dates are counted forward (for example, 2006, 2007, 2008, 2009 … and so on). The timeline on the next page shows the BC/BCE years getting smaller as they approach Year 1, and the AD/CE years getting larger as they move away from it.

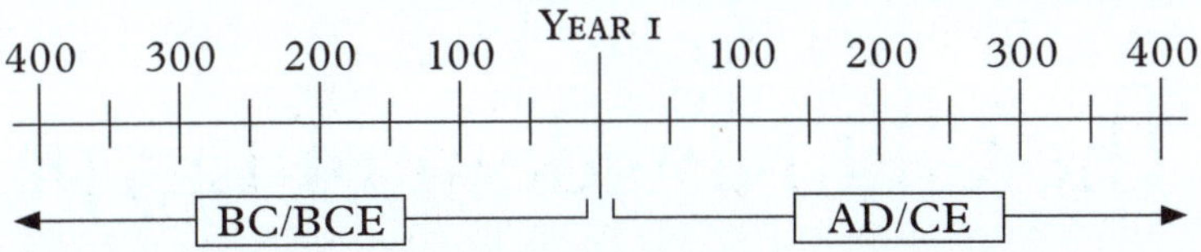

During the Old Kingdom of Egypt—from about 3000 BC or BCE through about 2100 BC or BCE, or about 900 years—the Egyptians began to make mummies for the first time. Mummies were the bodies of dead people, treated with spices and salts and wrapped in linen so that they wouldn't decay. The Egyptians believed that dead people went on to another life in the afterworld. But they also believed that the dead could only enter the afterworld if their bodies were preserved. This was called *embalming*.

Embalming was a very complicated process. Only *priests*—men who were in charge of worshipping the gods—were allowed to make mummies. And it took more than two months to make a mummy!

Let's imagine that we're back in the Old Kingdom of Egypt, at the time of the pharaoh Cheops. Cheops has been pharaoh for years. He has made Egypt's army strong, and he's kept Egypt safe from enemies. But in the middle of the night, word comes from the palace that Cheops is dead.

Instantly the priests start to make preparations. They collect all the things they'll need to make Cheops's body into a mummy—salt, spices, oil, and linen. Cheops is carried from the palace to the temple, where the priests are waiting for him.

The priests take the body to a holy place inside the temple. They wash it with wine and spices. Then they take all of Cheops's organs—his liver, his stomach, his lungs, and his intestines—out of his body. They cover the organs with special spices to preserve them.

Cheops's heart gets special treatment. The chief priest takes the heart out, washes it, wraps it in linen strips, and puts it back into Cheops's chest. The Egyptians believe that Cheops will need his heart in the afterlife. They think that when Cheops reaches the afterworld, the god Osiris will weigh his heart on a special scale. If his heart is good, it will be light and Cheops will spend the rest of the afterlife in happiness. But if his heart is full of sin, it will be heavy—and a monster will eat it!

After they finish with the heart, the priests cover the pharaoh's body with salt and more spices and leave it covered for forty days. During this time, Egyptians mourn the death of their king.

When forty days have passed, the priests come back and uncover the body and the organs. They wash the organs and the body again and cover them with oil and more spices. They put the liver, the stomach, the lungs, and the intestines into four special jars called *canopic jars*. Each jar has the head of a god on top of it. These gods are supposed to protect Cheops's organs.

Then the priests wrap Cheops's body in strips of linen. They put special pieces of jewelry between the linen strips. The jewelry is supposed to protect Cheops on his journey to the afterworld—just like magic. They make a gold mask that looks just like Cheops, and put it onto the mummy's face, so that the gods will recognize the mummy when Cheops arrives in the afterlife. Finally, the chief priest holds a special ceremony. He touches the mummy's mouth with a special tool. He thinks that this will allow Cheops's mummy to hear, see, and talk in the afterworld.

At last, the mummy is finished. But before Cheops is buried, he has to be put into three coffins. The first coffin is gold and has Cheops's face on the outside. This gold coffin is put into a wood coffin to protect it. Then Cheops's wooden coffin is carried through the streets in a huge funeral procession, all the way to his tomb—a pyramid!

Inside the pyramid is a special burial chamber. The chamber has a big stone coffin in it, called a *sarcophagus*. The wooden coffin is placed inside the sarcophagus. The stone lid of the sarcophagus is so heavy that four men have to push it into place. Now Cheops's mummy is safe inside all of its coffins. His spirit can begin the journey to the underworld.

Before the Egyptians leave the burial chamber, they make sure that Cheops has everything he'll need to be comfortable in the next life. They fill the chamber with furniture, jewelry, clothes, and food for him to use. They leave toys and games for Cheops to play with, and scrolls for him to read. They even bury a full-sized boat beside the pyramid, so that Cheops can sail through the afterworld.

Finally, they leave the burial chamber and seal up the door. Cheops's body will lie undisturbed for hundreds of years—until grave robbers discover that his tomb is full of treasure.

Egyptian Pyramids

All of the kings and important people buried in Egypt had gold and jewels in their graves. And everyone in Egypt knew that the graves were full of treasure.

What do you think happened?

At first, the Egyptians of the Old Kingdom dug underground rooms in the desert to bury their mummies. But thieves knew that the mummies had jewelry and treasures buried along with them. Grave robbers often broke into these underground rooms and stole all the treasure. So the Egyptians started to build stone tombs out of huge stone blocks with a hole, or shaft, cut into the middle. The mummy and all its clothes, furniture, and jewelry were lowered down the shaft into a treasure room. Then the shaft was filled with stones to keep anyone else from climbing in. We now call these *mastaba tombs*.

Mastaba tombs were better and safer than tombs dug into the earth, but even mastaba tombs weren't good enough for pharaohs. The pharaohs were buried in the biggest tombs of all—*pyramids*. Pyramids were giant fortresses, made to keep the pharaohs and their treasures safe. And pyramids were important for another reason. They pointed upwards to the sky. The Egyptians believed that the pharaoh was a god, and that he would rise up and join the other gods after his death. They thought that the dead pharaoh would climb up to heaven, using the sides of the pyramids like steps.

Cheops spent over twenty years building his pyramid before he died. He knew that he would be buried in this pyramid, and he wanted his pyramid to be the biggest of all. His pyramid still stands in the desert near Giza (which today is called Cairo, Egypt). It is called the Great Pyramid, because it is the largest of all the pyramids that the Egyptians built for their pharaohs.

The Great Pyramid was built around 2550 BC/BCE. It was the highest building in the world for four thousand years. It was built with over two million blocks of stone—and each block weighs almost three tons. That's as heavy as an elephant! And the Egyptians didn't have any cranes, bulldozers, or earthmovers.

Instead, they cut the stone blocks out by hand, with copper and stone tools. Then they built ramps out of rocks and earth up the sides of the pyramids, and dragged the stone blocks up the ramps with ropes. Hundreds of men pulled together to move the largest stones. Thousands of

Pyramids of Egypt

Egyptians worked on the Great Pyramid, year after year. Finally, the pyramid was finished. Then the Egyptians pulled the ramps down and covered it with sheets of white limestone. Archaeologists think that the pointed stone at the very top of the Great Pyramid even had a golden cap on it. The white stone and golden top are gone now, but when the Great Pyramid was first built, it shone in the sun.

Inside the Great Pyramid was a burial chamber, just for Cheops. But there were also empty chambers and unfinished rooms, and passages that led off into dead ends. Cheops hoped that any thief who broke into the pyramid would get lost in the maze of rooms before he could find the treasure. And after the pyramid was finished, workmen sealed off the door to the outside. They slid huge plugs of stone down the passage to block the way into the pyramid—and then went out through a small escape passage that had been dug down into the ground and came up in the desert outside.

The Great Pyramid even has its own watchdog. Near the Great Pyramid, the Egyptians built a mysterious monument shaped like a *sphinx*—an imaginary animal with a man's head and a lion's body. We now call this giant limestone animal the Great Sphinx. The Great Sphinx is as tall as eleven men standing on each other's shoulders. And it is almost as long as a football field. The Sphinx was made out of limestone, which is a kind of stone that is easily chipped and broken. Desert sand keeps burying it and wearing it away. Its nose is broken. But even though it is almost five thousand years old, you can still see that the Sphinx has the face of a man. Many people think that the Sphinx was built to protect the pyramids.

But thieves found Cheops's burial chamber anyway. They got past the Sphinx and through the maze of passages inside the Great Pyramid and stole Cheops's treasure—and his mummy. By the time archaeologists made their way into the pyramid, Cheops and his gold had disappeared forever.

Note: Cheops is also known as Khufu.

Chapter Five
The First Sumerian Dictator

Sargon and the Akkadians

Do you remember how the Egyptians used to be divided into two countries—Upper Egypt and Lower Egypt? They spent all their time and energy fighting each other. But once King Narmer conquered Lower Egypt and made the Egyptians into one country, the Egyptians could spend their time on farming and on building instead of on war. Egypt grew richer and stronger once all the quarreling Egyptians were united into one.

The same thing happened over in Mesopotamia, between the Tigris and Euphrates rivers.

People who were called the Sumerians lived in Mesopotamia. You've learned a little about the Sumerians; they wrote picture writing, called cuneiform, on clay tablets. The area where the Sumerians lived was called Sumer. But Sumer wasn't really one country. It was filled with villages of farmers. The villages grew larger and larger until they became cities. Each city built thick walls and high towers to protect itself. Each city had its own king and its own army. And the cities fought with each other all the time! We call them *city-states* because each city was like a separate country. The cities put all their energy into protecting themselves from their neighbors.

But one Sumerian wanted to make all the quarreling cities into one country—just like King Narmer made Egypt into one country. This man was named Sargon.

There are many stories about Sargon. Here is one of the oldest of those stories.

SARGON DIDN'T REMEMBER HIS FATHER OR HIS mother. He just floated down the Euphrates River in a basket when he was a baby! The basket got stuck in the reeds at the edge of the river near a city-state called Kish.

One of the servants of the king of Kish happened to be down at the river, getting water in a jug. He heard a strange sound. Where was that sound coming from? The servant saw a basket. He bent down to look inside and saw a crying baby—the baby Sargon.

The servant took the basket back to the palace of the king of Kish. The king gave him permission to keep the baby and raise it. So Sargon grew up inside the palace. He became strong, handsome, and popular with the other courtiers.

Of course Sargon must have had parents—but we don't know who they were. But we do know that Sargon became the cup-bearer to the king. At every meal, he would bring the king his wine in a golden cup. The king's cup-bearer was one of his most trusted servants, because it would have been very easy to poison the king's wine. But the king of Kish trusted Sargon.

He shouldn't have! Sargon made friends with the most powerful people at the palace—including the commanders of the army. He became so popular that he convinced the army to follow him instead of the king. And he even persuaded the army to kill the king, and make him, Sargon, the ruler instead. This happened around 2334 BC/BCE.

But that wasn't enough for Sargon. He didn't want to be king of just one city. He wanted to be king of the whole land of Mesopotamia. So he started to attack the cities all around him. He fought over fifty wars to conquer Mesopotamia. Eventually, Sargon ruled all the country between the Tigris and Euphrates rivers. He built a new capital city called Akkad, and named his new empire Akkadia.

Now, Sumer was united into one country under one ruler.

Sargon, king of Mesopotamia

But many of the cities Sargon conquered didn't like being part of the Akkadian Empire. They were used to making their own laws and running their own affairs. Sargon knew that to stay in charge, he would have to make the cities all obey *his* laws.

So he used his army to force all the Akkadian cities to follow him. He sent soldiers from the Akkadian army to live in each conquered city. They made sure that the people who lived in the city were following Sargon's laws instead of their own. If the conquered cities didn't obey, the soldiers punished them. This is called a *military dictatorship*. *Military* means "having to do with the army." A dictatorship is when people have to obey the government without asking any questions. In a military dictatorship, the army is in charge.

Sargon's empire lasted for years—but only because he used the power of his army to keep it together.

Chapter Six
The Jewish People

God Speaks to Abraham

Sargon the Great ruled over many cities in Mesopotamia. One of the cities in Sargon's empire was called Ur. And a man who would become very well known lived in the city of Ur. His name was Abram. The book of Genesis, in the Christian Bible and in the Jewish Torah, tells us this story about Abram.

Long ago, Abram lived with his father Terah in the city of Ur. He helped his father to run his business. Terah was a merchant; he bought and sold copper, gold, purple and scarlet cloth, cinnamon, and salt. He grew rich buying and selling in Ur.

Terah should have been happy. Ur was the perfect place for a merchant to live. The city was built right on the banks of the Euphrates River, so that traders could sail right up to the city with their goods. But Terah lived in difficult times. After Sargon's death, his empire had fallen apart. The kings of the cities around Ur were fighting with each other. Tribes of wild people called Gutians were invading the land between the rivers. If Ur was attacked, the city might be burned. Terah could lose all of his riches in the war.

Terah worried and worried. He asked the ancient Mesopotamian gods what he should do. He made extra sacrifices to the moon-god—the special god of the city of Ur. He even went to Ur's largest *ziggurat* and asked the moon-god to protect him from evil. (The ziggurats were special pyramids, built with steps up the sides so that priests could go up to the top and sacrifice to the gods.)

Finally, Terah decided that he would take his family and leave Ur. He took Abram and Abram's wife Sarai with him, and set off to find a better place to live. They traveled along the banks of the Euphrates River, looking for a city to settle in. When they arrived at the city of Haran, up in the north of Mesopotamia, Terah liked what he saw. Haran was a rich city where people came to trade. And the people of Haran also worshipped the moon-god, so Terah felt right at home.

Terah and Abram and Sarai settled into Haran. Terah started to work as a merchant again. Abram took care of the sheep, goats, and cows that Terah bought with all the money he earned. The whole family was doing well.

But Terah was an old man, and after several years in Haran, he died. Then Abram became the head of the family.

One night after Terah's funeral, Abram went out for a walk in the dark. He leaned his arms on the fence surrounding his flocks, and listened to the noise of the sheep and goats. He wondered whether he should keep on farming, or whether he should become a merchant like his father. Maybe he should go back to Ur, where the rest of his relatives were. He thought to himself, "Maybe I will ask the moon-god, or one of the other gods, to tell me what to do."

Suddenly he heard a voice say, "Abram!"

He looked around, but he didn't see anyone! "Who are you?" he said. "Are you one of the gods?"

"I am the one God," the voice said, "and there is no other God except for me!"

"What do you want me to do?" Abram asked.

"Leave Haran," God said, "and go to the land I will show you. I will give it to you and your children. I will make you into a great nation! I will bless your friends and curse your enemies. And everyone on earth will be blessed because of you."

God told Abram to go to Canaan. Abram had never thought about going to Canaan. After all, there were no large trading cities there. There were no rivers. It was far, far away from Mesopotamia—the only civilized place that he knew. Strange, wild tribes lived in Canaan. Why would he go there?

But Abram decided to do what God told him. He took Sarai, all his servants, and all of his sheep, goats, cows, and camels. And all of them left the safe city of Haran and started off into the wilderness.

Finally they arrived in Canaan. When they got there, God appeared to Abram again.

"I will make an agreement with you," God said to Abram. "Obey me and worship me. You will be the father of a whole new nation, and I will give the whole land of Canaan to you and your children and grandchildren. I am going to change your name from Abram to Abraham, because Abraham means 'father of many children.' And I am going to change Sarai's name to Sarah, because Sarah means 'princess.' Sarah will be the mother of a whole nation of people!"

Abraham thought this was very funny, because he was an old man—older than your grandparents. He laughed and laughed at God's promise. "How can Sarah and I have children?" he asked God.

"Nothing is impossible for God!" God said. And the next year, Sarah had a baby—when she was at least ninety years old! Abraham and Sarah named their son Isaac, which means "laughter," because they had laughed at God.

Isaac had a son named Jacob. And then Jacob had sons—twelve of them. These twelve sons all had families of their own. All of these families lived in Canaan.

Eventually, each one of Jacob's sons had a whole tribe of people named after him. The tribe of Judah was named after Jacob's son Judah. The tribe of Benjamin was named after his youngest son, Benjamin. These twelve tribes became known as the nation of Israel, or the Jewish people.

Note: For more on this story, please see *Appendix Four*, on page 404.

Joseph Goes to Egypt

The book of Genesis, in the Bible and the Torah, tells us a story about what happened next. Jacob's twelve sons didn't always get along with each other. They all wanted to be their father's favorite. But Genesis says that Jacob loved his son Joseph the best, more than his brothers. And this led to all sorts of trouble!

One day, Joseph was out in the fields with his brothers, watching his father's sheep. Suddenly he heard his father Jacob calling, "Joseph! Joseph!"

"Watch my sheep for me!" Joseph told his brothers. He ran quickly to his father's tent. "Yes, Father?" he asked.

"Joseph," Jacob said, "you are very special to me. So I've made you a beautiful coat to wear." He held out a beautiful coat—as colorful as a field full of flowers and as soft as a cloud, trimmed with a border of purple. Joseph could hardly believe his eyes. He was used to plain clothes, made from the skin of goats and the wool of his father's sheep. He took the coat and slipped it on.

"Thank you, Father!" he said. "I'll always wear it—even while I'm tending the sheep!" And he ran back to his flock of sheep. "Look, Judah!" he shouted. "Look, Benjamin! Look, all of you! Father made me a special coat!"

His brothers stared at the coat. "Why didn't I get one?" Judah asked. "I'm older than you are!

Why did Father make a coat for you, and not for any of the rest of us?" All the brothers grumbled and complained about Joseph's coat.

But Joseph wore the coat day and night. He boasted about his coat. He bragged about how much his father loved him. Finally, the other eleven brothers could stand it no more.

One morning, they were all out in a field a long way away from Jacob's tent when they heard Joseph coming. "Here comes our father's favorite!" they complained. "Let's get rid of him so that we never have to hear him brag about his colored coat again!" And when Joseph came, they grabbed him, took his coat away, and threw him into a pit in the ground. When they saw some desert traders coming along, they pulled Joseph out of the pit and sold him to the traders as a slave. Then they smeared some goat blood on Joseph's coat and took it back to their father.

"Look," they said. "We found this out in the desert. A lion must have killed Joseph!"

Jacob wept and wept, because he thought that Joseph was dead. But the desert traders took Joseph down to Egypt and sold him to the royal court of Egypt as a slave.

Down in Egypt, Joseph lived in the house of Potiphar, the captain of the pharaoh's guards. He missed his father. He cried at nights because his brothers had been so cruel to him. But he worked hard in Potiphar's house. Soon, Potiphar took notice of him. He trusted Joseph more and more and gave him more and more responsibility.

Soon, Joseph was running Potiphar's whole household!

But Potiphar's wife decided that Joseph had too much power in her husband's house. She told lies about Joseph to Potiphar. Potiphar believed his wife—and he had Joseph thrown in jail.

"What will happen to me?" Joseph thought. "Will I never be free? First my brothers sell me as a slave, and then I end up in the pharaoh's jail! What will I do?"

One morning, one of the other prisoners looked troubled. "What is the matter?" Joseph asked.

"I had a strange dream," the man said. "I dreamed that a vine grew up out of the ground, right in front of me. The vine grew branches, the branches grew grapes, and the grapes got ripe—right there in front of my eyes! Then I squeezed the grapes into a cup and gave the cup to Pharaoh."

"I know what your dream means!" Joseph exclaimed. "It means that Pharaoh is going to take you out of jail and forgive your crimes!"

"How do you know?" the dreamer asked.

"Only God knows what dreams mean," Joseph said, "and he showed me the answer to your dream."

Sure enough, three days later soldiers appeared at the jail's door and took the prisoner away. "You've been pardoned," they said. "You can return to Pharaoh's palace and work for him again."

As the dreamer was walking away, Joseph called after him, "Remember me! Tell Pharaoh that I am innocent, so that I can get out of jail!"

But the dreamer forgot all about Joseph, and Joseph stayed in prison for months and months and months.

One night, the pharaoh himself had a terrifying dream. When he woke up, he said, "Who can tell me what my dream means?"

Then the dreamer remembered Joseph. "Great Pharaoh," he said, "the Israelite in your prison knows what dreams mean. His god tells him!"

"Get him at once!" the pharaoh said.

So Joseph was brought from prison, right to the pharaoh's throne room. Pharaoh said to him, "I had a terrible dream. I dreamed that I was standing by the river Nile, and that seven big, fat cows walked up out of the water and started to graze on the riverbank. Then, seven ugly, thin cows came up from the water—and swallowed the fat cows right up! What does it mean? Can you tell me?"

"My god gives me the wisdom to understand dreams," Joseph replied. "He tells me that the seven fat cows stand for seven good years, when the Nile will overflow, the crops will grow, and the Egyptians will have plenty to eat. But the seven thin cows stand for seven years of famine. The Nile won't flood, and your crops will die. Pharaoh, you should choose a wise man and put him in charge of gathering grain during the seven good years. Store the grain, so that the Egyptians will have something to eat during the years of famine."

"A wise man?" the pharaoh said. "No one is wiser than you, Joseph. I will put you in charge of gathering the grain. You will be second in command to me."

The Pharaoh of Egypt

So Pharaoh took the ring off his finger and put it on Joseph's finger. And he gave Joseph white linen robes and a gold chain to wear around his neck. He gave Joseph a chariot to ride in, and men to run in front of him and shout, "Make way!"

Joseph went all around Egypt, collecting grain from the farmers and storing it. Sure enough, for seven years the Nile overflowed and crops were good. But then famine came. The Nile was low, and the ground became dry and cracked. The sun beat down on the fields, and the crops died. The Egyptians began to get hungry.

Then Joseph started to hand out the grain that he had saved, a little bit for each family. In the lands around Egypt, people were hungry because of the famine. But in Egypt, everyone had food to eat.

Up in Canaan, Jacob and his family were starving. There was no water; their sheep and goats were dying, and their crops had failed. Finally Jacob said to his sons, "I hear that they have grain in Egypt. Go and get us some!"

Joseph's brothers walked for days and days and days through the hot sand to reach Egypt. When they got to the pharaoh's palace, they were tired and thirsty and sweaty. They waited in a long, long line of hungry people before they could go into the room where Joseph sat, giving out grain.

When they got there, they didn't recognize Joseph at all. He had been in Egypt for years and years. He had grown up. And he was dressed like an Egyptian.

But Joseph recognized his brothers. They had sold him as a slave—and now they were here, asking him for food.

For weeks, Joseph didn't tell his brothers who he was. But finally, he could no longer bear to keep his secret. He invited them for a big dinner. And when dinner was over, he sent all his servants away.

"I am Joseph!" he said to his brothers. "Is my father still alive?"

The brothers could hardly believe their eyes. And they were terrified. "Now we are in his power!" they whispered to each other. "He will kill us!"

But Joseph said, "I forgive the evil thing you did to me. God sent me ahead of you so that you could come and get food from me during this famine. Go back to Canaan and get all your flocks and your families and your tents. Come and live in Egypt, where there is plenty of food!"

So Joseph's father and brothers and all their families—the Israelites—came down to Egypt and lived there, on the banks of the Nile. The Israelite nation grew larger and larger. They kept on worshipping their one god, even though the Egyptians believed in many different gods.

And as long as Joseph lived, Pharaoh was kind to the Israelites and let them have a part of Egypt for their very own.

Chapter Seven
Hammurabi and the Babylonians

Hammurabi's Code

You can probably tell that Mesopotamia was not a very peaceful place to live. City-states fought each other. Powerful leaders tried to build empires by conquering other city-states. Sometimes the empires lasted for a long time. Sometimes they collapsed in just a few years—and another powerful leader tried to take over. The people of Mesopotamia lived with war all the time. Sometimes they stayed inside their city walls and hoped that they would be safe. But sometimes they fled. They would travel to another place, hoping to avoid trouble.

Around 1792 BC/BCE, a king named Hammurabi inherited the throne of Babylon from his father. Babylon was a city near Kish (the home of Sargon). At first, Hammurabi only ruled a small area of the land around his own city. But soon he began to conquer some of the smaller cities around him. He convinced the kings of other cities to swear allegiance to him. Soon he ruled over the whole southern part of Mesopotamia. This area was called Babylonia, after the city of Babylon.

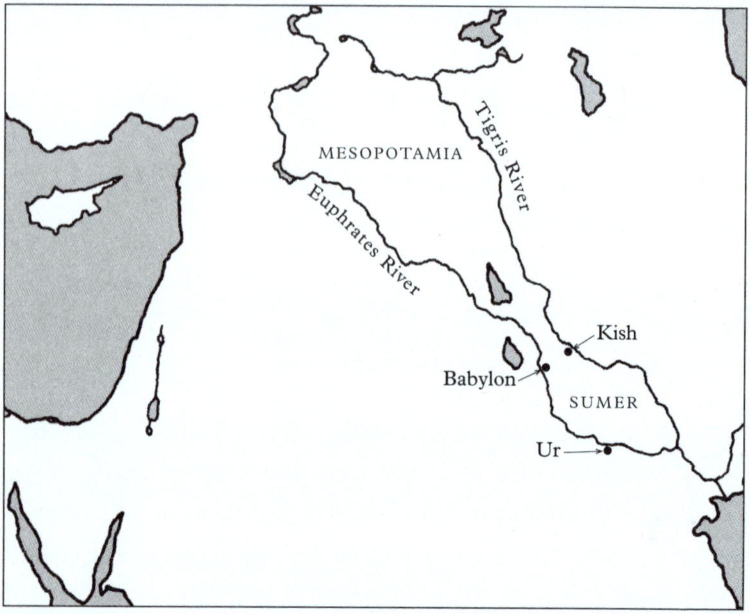

Babylonia

Hammurabi didn't want people to obey him just because his army was strong. He wanted his empire to be governed by just laws. He believed that the chief god of Babylon, Marduk, made him king so that he could treat people fairly. In one of his letters, Hammurabi calls himself "the reverent god-fearing prince." He says that his job as king is "to make justice appear in the land, to destroy the evil and the wicked so that the strong might not oppress the weak."

Hammurabi wanted people to follow his laws because they were right, not just because soldiers were making them obey. He also wanted his whole empire to follow the same laws and rules. So Hammurabi wrote down all of the laws that he thought were fair. He had them carved in stone, on a monument that showed him getting the laws from the sun god. These laws are called the Code of Hammurabi. They were unusual because everyone had to follow them—rich people, poor people, soldiers, farmers, merchants, and even kings.

Here are some of the laws in the Code of Hammurabi. Do you think these are fair? Why or why not?

- If someone cuts down a tree on someone else's land, he will pay for it.
- If someone is careless when watering his fields, and he floods someone else's field by accident, he will pay for the grain he has ruined.
- If a man wants to throw his son out of the house, he has to go before a judge and say, "I don't want my son to live in my house anymore." The judge will find out the reasons. If the reasons are not good, the man can't throw his son out.
- If the son has done some great evil to his father, his father must forgive him the first time. But if he has done something evil twice, his father can throw him out.
- If a thief steals a cow, a sheep, a donkey, a pig, or a goat, he will pay ten times what it is worth.
- If he doesn't have any money to pay with, he will be put to death.
- An eye for an eye, and a tooth for a tooth. If a man puts out the eye of another man, put his own eye out. If he knocks out another man's tooth, knock out his own tooth. If he breaks another man's bone, break his own bone.
- If a doctor operates on a patient and the patient dies, the doctor's hand will be cut off.

- If a builder builds a house, and that house collapses and kills the owner, the builder will be put to death.
- If a builder builds a house, and that house collapses and kills the son of the owner, the son of the builder will be put to death.

Hammurabi, king of Babylonia

Hammurabi was a very religious man. He believed that the gods themselves had given him the Code of Hammurabi. So he rebuilt many of the temples and ziggurats that had been destroyed in fights between city-states. He encouraged his people to sacrifice to the gods, and to learn more about them. At that time, people in Babylon believed that they could find out what the gods were doing by watching the movements of the planets and stars. So they spent a lot of time studying the sky. They knew where all the constellations were. They knew the difference between stars and planets.

From watching the sky, the Babylonians were able to figure out that the earth goes all the way around the sun. They called the time that it took the earth to go all the way around the sun one time one "year." Then they divided this year into twelve months. They were the first people to divide a year into twelve months, just like we do today.

The Babylonians were also the first to divide a day into twenty-four hours, and to divide an hour into sixty minutes. So whenever you look at a calendar to see what day of the month it is, or look at a clock to see what time it is, you're using methods that we inherited from the Babylonians.

Chapter Eight
The Assyrians

Shamshi-Adad, King of the Whole World

Hammurabi was the most powerful king in southern Mesopotamia. But up to the north, another king was building another empire. His name was Shamshi-Adad, and he didn't want to be a fair ruler who made good laws. He just wanted to rule the whole world.

Shamshi-Adad lived in a city called Assur. Babylon was in the south of Mesopotamia, next to the Euphrates River. But Assur was in the north part of Mesopotamia, beside the Tigris River. When Shamshi-Adad became king of Assur, he decided that Assur should be the center of a new empire. He started out by building a huge temple to the god he worshipped, the God of Winds and Storms. The temple was made out of cedar logs, covered with silver and gold. Shamshi-Adad even rubbed the foundation with oil, honey, and butter to make his god happy. He wanted the God of Winds and Storms to be on his side and to give him more power, so that he could win battles more easily.

On the day that the temple was finished, Shamshi-Adad announced, "The God of Winds and Storms loves the city of Assur more than any other city in the world! And he wants me to be the king of the whole world."

The people of Assur all shouted, "Shamshi-Adad will be king of the whole world!"

Then Shamshi-Adad gathered his army together and set off to conquer the cities of Mesopotamia. His two sons went with him to fight beside him. Every time Shamshi-Adad conquered a new city, he made his sons the new rulers of that city. Soon the Assyrian army had conquered all the cities nearby.

Shamshi-Adad wanted the people of Mesopotamia to be afraid of him. He was a dictator—he didn't allow any of the people in his new kingdom to ask questions about his laws and his commands. He just wanted them to obey him immediately.

How did he get them to obey? He killed anyone who wouldn't do exactly what he said. When he conquered a city, he chopped off the heads of all the leaders and put them up on stakes around the city. He burned buildings and told his soldiers to destroy everything they could find.

No wonder everyone in Mesopotamia was afraid of the Assyrians! Soon, Shamshi-Adad didn't even have to fight battles to conquer cities. As soon as he got near a city's walls, the leaders would come out and surrender. They would offer to pay him money and to call him their king, if he would just let them live. Shamshi-Adad would agree to spare their lives—but only if they would do exactly what he said and obey every single one of his decrees.

Now Shamshi-Adad's empire spread all over the northern part of Mesopotamia. He named his empire Assyria, after the city of Assur. And he called himself the King of the Whole World.

But this wasn't exactly true. Remember Babylon, down in the south of Mesopotamia? Babylon had an empire too. Shamshi-Adad never tried to conquer Babylon, or to take Babylon's cities away. He knew that Babylon was too strong for him.

When Shamshi-Adad died, he left one of his sons the job of ruling over the whole Assyrian Empire. He left the other son in charge of one of the biggest cities in Assyria, the city of Mari. He hoped that the two young men would work together to keep his empire strong.

But the brothers bickered with each other. They wrote each other nasty letters. They complained about each other. They didn't keep Assyria united and strong.

Soon, Hammurabi decided that he wanted to make Assyria part of the Babylonian Empire. He marched up into northern Mesopotamia with his army. He destroyed the city of Mari, and he took over the city of Assur. Now the Assyrians had to pay tribute to Hammurabi, and call Hammurabi "King of the Whole World."

But Hammurabi wasn't as cruel as Shamshi-Adad had been. He let some of the Assyrian leaders stay in charge of their cities, as long as they followed his Code of Laws. And he didn't chop off the heads of leaders, or burn their houses.

The Assyrians agreed to obey Hammurabi. But all the time, they were thinking, "One day we will be free again—and we will try to conquer the world one more time."

The Story of Gilgamesh

Both the Babylonians and the Assyrians told stories about a great, mythical king named Gilgamesh. The story of Gilgamesh is one of the oldest fairy tales in the world!

Once upon a time, a king named Gilgamesh ruled the city of Uruk. Gilgamesh was part god and part man. He was the strongest king on earth. He could lift huge stones with one hand and leap over high walls without even trying hard. He was young and healthy, and he had all the money and power any man could ever want.

But Gilgamesh was as cruel as he was strong. He made the people of Uruk serve him day and night. He took their money and their food. He took their children to be his slaves. He never thought of others—only of himself.

The people of Uruk were desperate to get rid of this wicked king. So they called out to the sky-god, Anu. "Help us!" they cried. "Our king is evil, and we cannot fight him, because he has the strength of a god!"

Anu looked down from the sky and was displeased with what he saw. "Look at this king, Gilgamesh!" he said. "He has all the strength and power in the world— and yet he is cruel to the weak and helpless. This is not right. I will send an enemy to teach him a lesson."

So Anu created a monster called Enkidu—a monster who was half man and half animal, with the strength of a dozen lions. "Go and fight Gilgamesh," he told Enkidu, and sent the beast-man down into the wild wastelands around the city of Uruk.

Meanwhile, Gilgamesh had a nightmare! He dreamed that a huge axe appeared at his door—an axe so big and sharp that he couldn't even lift it.

When he woke up, he asked his mother what the dream meant. "A man is coming who can destroy you!" his mother told him. "You will have to make friends with him—or die!"

Enkidu came closer and closer to the city of Uruk. But in the forest outside the city's walls, he met the son of a trapper, out checking his father's traps. When the boy saw the naked wild man, he was frightened. But he felt sorry for Enkidu, because the beast-man had no clothes or food, and could not even speak. So he took Enkidu home with him and introduced him to his friends, shepherds who tended their flocks outside the city walls.

Enkidu lived with the trapper's son and the shepherds for a long time. They taught him how to talk, how to eat, and how to wear clothes.

One day, Enkidu and his friends went into Uruk, to the wedding of a great man who was giving a feast for the whole city. But during the wedding feast, Gilgamesh decided that he wanted the bride. He marched into the hall, grabbed the beautiful girl, and started to drag her away.

Enkidu was furious. He leaped up in front of the door. "You may be the king," he shouted, "but you'll have to kill me before you take this woman away from her bridegroom!"

No one had ever told Gilgamesh what to do! He leaped at Enkidu and tried to wrestle him to the ground. They fought all up and down the wedding hall until the food was smashed underfoot and both of them were bleeding. Gilgamesh had never before met anyone so strong. Finally he won the match—he pinned Enkidu down and sat on him.

But he was so tired from fighting that he could barely move. He gasped out, "Let us be friends from now on!"

From then on, Enkidu and Gilgamesh were friends. Gilgamesh became kinder to the people in his city, and he and Enkidu had many adventures together.

One day, the bull of the gods escaped from the sky and came down to earth. It came charging through Gilgamesh's kingdom, killing hundreds of people. It was so powerful that whenever it breathed, huge holes and chasms opened up in the earth. The people called to Gilgamesh and Enkidu for help.

Slaying the bull of the gods

Enkidu killed the bull and delivered the whole country. But the gods were angry with Enkidu for killing their bull. They sent terrible illness upon him. He suffered in pain for twelve days, and then died.

Gilgamesh mourned his friend's death. He ordered the whole world to weep over Enkidu. He stopped taking baths; he even stopped eating. He could not bear the thought that death had taken Enkidu away.

Finally, he decided that he would have to find the secret of eternal life and conquer death itself. He planned out a journey to go and see Utnapishtim—the only immortal man on the whole earth.

He traveled for a year and a day, and finally reached Utnapishtim's home. "What is the secret of eternal life?" he asked Utnapishtim.

"If you can stay awake for six days and seven nights," Utnapishtim told him, "you too can become immortal."

Gilgamesh agreed—and instantly fell asleep. He woke up seven days later.

"Give me another chance!" he begged.

"Well," Utnapishtim said, "there is one more chance for you. If you can swim all the way down to the bottom of the ocean, you will find a magical plant that lives on the sea's bottom. Pick it and eat it, and you will become young again."

Gilgamesh leaped up, tied a stone to his feet, and jumped into the ocean. He sank all the way down to the bottom. There he found the magic plant. He picked it, swam back up to the top of the ocean, and began the long journey home.

"When I get home," he thought, "I will eat the plant, and then I will live forever."

But one night, while Gilgamesh slept, a snake slithered up to him and found the plant. It smelled

> good—so the snake ate it, and immediately became young again. That is why snakes shed their skins. When they begin to get old, they just climb out of their wrinkled, old skins and become young again.
>
> But Gilgamesh woke up to find his magic plant gone. He went home to Uruk, weeping and mourning. And like all men, he became old and died.

Gilgamesh was dead—but his story was told to all the children of Uruk, and has been told to all their children, and to their children's children, until this very day.

Note: The Gilgamesh Epic was composed between 3000–1200 BC/BCE. Shamshi-Adad ruled c. 1813-1781 BC/BCE.

Chapter Nine
The First Cities of India

The River-Road

The Egyptians lived on the Nile River. The Assyrians and the Babylonians lived on the Tigris and Euphrates rivers, in Mesopotamia. Why do you think that ancient people wanted to live near rivers?

People who lived near rivers had plenty of water to drink and to use on their crops. But there's another reason why ancient cities were built near rivers.

Imagine that you live in ancient Mesopotamia, down near Ur. Let's pretend that you're a merchant, like Terah was in our story about Abram. You've got a wonderful crop of wheat this year, and you've just heard that the wheat in Assyria all got washed away in a flood. The people in Assyria will pay twice as much for wheat as the people in Ur—because there's wheat all over Ur, but almost none in Assyria. So you decide that you'll travel north to Assyria with your wheat and sell it there. You can make a lot of money that way.

How will you get from Ur to Assyria? Remember, you don't have a car or truck. If you're going to go all the way to Assyria, you'll have to use a cart pulled by cows. You can't walk, because the wheat is too heavy to carry. And your cart has wheels made out of wood, because rubber hasn't been invented yet.

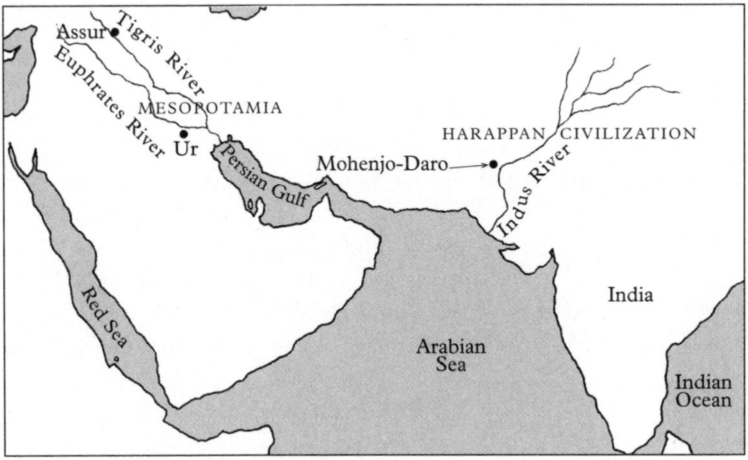

Mesopotamian and Harappan Cities

How long do you think the wheels last? Will you have to stop and fix them, between Ur and Assur? How fast do cows walk? How long do you think it will take you to walk at the pace of a cow all the way to Assyria? Let's think about the ground in Mesopotamia for a minute. In this area, the ground is either sandy or rocky. Remember—there are no bulldozers and paving machines to make nice smooth roads. So, for part of the way to Assyria, you'll have to walk on sand.

What's difficult about walking on sand? Think about being at the beach. Do your feet sink into the sand? What if you were pulling a very heavy cart with wooden wheels? Would the wheels sink into the sand? Let's also think about rocky ground. How will your cart go on rocky ground? Going to Assur with carts and cows doesn't sound like a very easy trip!

Can you think of another way to get from Ur to Assur?

You could put all your wheat on a boat. Then you could sail from Ur on the Euphrates River down to the Persian Gulf. And then you could sail back up the Tigris River. By sailing in your boat, you could get there in less time, and with a lot less work.

Cities grew up on rivers because it was easier to ship food, metals, wood, and other goods up and down the water—much easier than dragging heavy loads over land. The cities in Mesopotamia used the Tigris and the Euphrates rivers to trade with each other.

But they didn't just trade with each other. They also traded with countries to the east. And one of the countries they traded with was India.

The people of India also used a river as a road. Their river was called the Indus, and the land around the Indus River was called the Indus Valley. The people of India settled in this valley because they could drink the river's water, fish in it, and use it to water their fields. They also sailed up and down the Indus River, trading with each other.

Eventually, the people of India sailed out into the Arabian Sea. The Arabian Sea was the largest body of water they had ever seen! They must have thought that they were in a sea that had no shores and would never end. But they were brave; they kept exploring. Soon they learned that they could sail up to the cities of Mesopotamia and trade with them.

If the people of India had tried to go across the land to Mesopotamia, they would have had to cross a mountain range. But by boat, the trip wasn't difficult at all. So the people of India—like the Mesopotamians—built large cities near the Indus River, and made money by trading with other cities. Today we call their civilization the Harappan civilization. It was strongest between 2000 and 1750 BC/BCE.

The Mystery of Mohenjo-Daro

The people who lived in the Indus Valley built cities, just like the people in Mesopotamia. But there weren't any empires in the Indus Valley. No great warrior—like Sargon or Hammurabi or Shamshi-Adad—tried to unite all the Indus Valley cities (the Harappan cities) into one kingdom. The people of the Harappan cities stayed independent.

A farmer living in the Indus Valley had a different life from a farmer in Egypt or in Mesopotamia. He grew grain, but he also grew fruit, like melons, and cotton. And he used water buffalo and elephants to work his fields! A farmer in Babylonia would have been amazed to see an Indus Valley farmer, walking along beside his elephant as he harvested his cotton and melons.

The cities in the Indus Valley were built around huge circular mounds called *citadels*. Each citadel had a stronghold on it—a place to go in case enemies attacked. All around the citadel, people built their houses out of mud bricks that had been baked hard in ovens. The houses were very comfortable. They had courtyards, wells, and even toilets and drains. People living in the houses could haul water up out of their wells, rather than going all the way to the river for water. Large public baths, like big swimming pools, meant that everyone could stay clean and cool.

And the drains took waste out of the houses, down into deep gutters that ran along the streets. The citadel cities were some of the biggest in the world. Mohenjo-Daro had over forty thousand people living in it.

But something happened to the cities of the Indus Valley. Around 1750 BC/BCE, people began to leave their homes. Eventually, the cities were almost entirely deserted. The buildings, drains, wells, and citadels crumbled. Slowly, sand and dirt covered over the cities. For hundreds of years, no one knew that the citadel cities were even there.

Finally, archaeologists started to dig in the ground around the Indus River. They found the remains of the great citadel cities. They found ruined walls and citadels.

But they couldn't find any clues about why people stopped living there. They found some writing that the Indus Valley people left—but we can't read the writing, so we don't know what it says. In Mohenjo-Daro, archaeologists found skeletons lying in the street, as though people died right there in the road and weren't even buried.

An ancient statue from the Indus Valley

What happened to the citadel cities?

We'll probably never know for sure. But the people of India still tell ancient stories, passed down over thousands of years. These stories come from long ago, from the time when the citadel cities were still flourishing. Maybe these stories are clues. One is called "The Hunter and the Quail."

ONCE, A flOCK OF QUAIL LIVED ON THE BANKS of a river. They had plenty to eat and drink, but they were afraid of the hunter who came every evening to catch them. He would creep up to the edge of the flock with his net and then leap out of the bushes. When the quail scattered, he would catch the nearest bird in his net, carry it back to his house—and eat it for dinner!

One day the oldest of the quail said, "It is easy for the hunter to catch just one of us. But what if he threw his net over all of us? We would be strong enough to escape!"

So the next evening, when the hunter leaped out the bushes, the quail all stayed in one flock. The hunter flung his net over the quail, but they rose up from the ground together, pulled the net out of his hands, and flew away, still side by side. All together, the quail were too strong for the hunter.

The quail were very pleased! Now they didn't have to be afraid. Night after night, they stayed together, pulled the hunter's net out of his hands, and flew away.

But soon the quail began to push and jostle at each other, as they crowded together in their safe, strong group. "You're stepping on my claw!" cried one. "You're rumpling my feathers!" cried another. "You're squeezing me until I can't breathe!" complained a third.

> Finally they scattered—and the hunter, who had been waiting in the bushes, leaped out and netted them, one by one. As he headed back to his house, he said, "Together, they are free. But apart, they are supper!"

What does this story mean? Perhaps it means that the citadel cities, staying independent and separate from each other, were defeated by invaders. Maybe that's what happened to Mohenjo-Daro. Maybe, if they had united together into one kingdom, the citadel cities would have survived.

But we will never know for sure.

Chapter Ten
The Far East: Ancient China

Lei Zu and the Silkworm

The people who lived in Mesopotamia, between the Tigris and the Euphrates rivers, thought they lived at the very center of the world. They called India the East, because they had to sail east to reach it. They thought of India as a strange and distant place.

But there was a country that seemed even stranger and was more distant than India: China. To the Assyrians and the Babylonians, China was the "Far East." It was all the way on the edge of the world!

The people of China and the people of the Fertile Crescent didn't know very much about each other. But even though they lived far away, the Chinese people chose to live near a river, just like the Egyptians and Babylonians and Assyrians did. Ancient people needed rivers to survive.

The people of China first lived between two rivers called the Yellow River and the Yangtze River. The area between the rivers was called the Yellow River Valley. The earliest people of China settled between these rivers, in the Yellow River Valley, and grew crops—especially rice, because it grows well in wet ground.

At first, the Chinese lived in separate villages, just like the people of Mesopotamia. But eventually a great leader

Huang Di united the villages of the Yellow River Valley

united the different villages of the Yellow River Valley into one kingdom.

The leader who united the Chinese villages was named Huang Di. He lived so long ago that we really don't know very much about him—but there are plenty of stories about his rule. Legends say that Huang Di first discovered medicine, and taught Chinese physicians how to cure illnesses. And his wife, the Empress Lei Zu, discovered that silkworms make their cocoons out of silk threads.

Here is a very old story about Lei Zu and the silkworms.

ONE DAY THE EMPRESS LEI ZU SAT IN HER garden beneath the mulberry trees. Outside the palace walls, she could hear the noises of trading caravans, the sound of camel hooves on stone, and the cries of street merchants selling candy, jewelry, and tea. But Lei Zu's walled garden was quiet and peaceful. The breeze moved the leaves of the mulberry tree above her.

"Min Lai!" she called to her maid. "Bring my lunch out here. I will eat in the garden today!"

Soon Min Lai brought out the empress's favorite meal—turtle meat with garlic and ginger, candied fruit, rice, and a pot of steaming, fragrant tea. Lei

Zu breathed in the rich smell of tea as she poured it into her cup. She lifted the cup to her mouth.

Something splashed into it, right in front of her nose!

She looked down into her cup. There, floating in the hot water, was something small and round and white. She glanced up into the branches of the mulberry tree. Hundreds of little white cocoons were dangling just over her head—the cocoons of the silkworm. Inside the cocoons, the silkworms were changing into moths. Soon they would chew through the cocoons and fly away.

"Look, Min Lai," she said. "A silkworm cocoon fell right into my tea!"

"Let me get you a fresh cup, Empress Lei Zu," the maid offered.

"Wait," Lei Zu said. She carefully lifted the cocoon out of her cup. It seemed to be made from a thin, bright thread, wrapped a hundred thousand times around the silkworm within. The hot water had begun to unravel it. Lei Zu pulled gently at the end of the thread and drew it out, longer and longer and longer. She rose from her seat and walked through the garden, trailing the thread behind her. It was so long that she circled the garden with it a dozen times. The thread was so light that it floated on the wind, and it shone in the sun like melting silver.

"If only I could weave this into cloth!" Lei Zu marveled. "What a robe I could make for my husband, the emperor!"

"But it is too thin to weave!" Min Lai said.

"Pick me another cocoon, Min Lai," the Empress said. "We will unravel another thread."

All afternoon, the Empress and her maid unraveled the fine, shining threads from the silkworm cocoons. They twisted the threads together until they were as thick as a thread of cotton. And then the Empress called her dressmaker.

"Can you weave a cloth from these threads?" she asked.

"I have never seen threads like these!" the dressmaker exclaimed. "They are as fine as hairs, but as soft as the petal of a flower."

She took the threads away and wove them into a cloth that shone like water in the sunshine, and from that cloth Lei Zu made a robe for her husband, the emperor. When he saw it, he gasped with wonder.

"From now on," he said, "we will call this silk. The secret of making this wonderful cloth must never leave the palace. Only the royal family can know this treasure was yielded by the silkworm cocoons!"

So from then on, Lei Zu and her court made the wonderful cloth called silk. They fed the silkworms on trays of mulberry leaves, waited until the worms wove their cocoons, and then carefully unraveled the cocoons for their precious threads of silk.

Was this how the royal family of China discovered silk? We'll never know for sure. But we do know that very soon, China became famous for its silk—the cloth that no one else in the world knew how to make.

The Pictograms of Ancient China

Huang Di and the rulers who followed him didn't leave any written records about their empires. So almost everything that we know about these very ancient Chinese rulers has been passed down in stories and legends, from person to person, over thousands of years. We don't know what parts of the stories are true, and what parts were added to make them more interesting and more exciting.

We do know that the Chinese went on living in the Yellow River Valley and that they grew rice, raised silkworms, and tried to defend themselves against invaders.

And we know that a new leader came to power, hundreds of years after Huang Di. His name was T'ang, and his family was called the Shang family.

T'ang became king around 1766 BC/BCE. His family would rule the Yellow River Valley for the next five hundred years. In China, this was called a *dynasty*—one family keeping control of a country for many, many years, passing the crown along from father to son, from brother to brother, or from uncle to nephew.

We know much more about the Shang dynasty than we do about the rulers who came before it, because during the rule of the Shang family, the Chinese began to use bronze. They made weapons, wheels, and farming tools out of bronze. These tools and weapons made of bronze didn't rot away like wooden tools. Thousands of years later, archaeologists discovered the bronze tools and weapons, buried beneath the ruins of Shang buildings. The bronze weapons tell us that the Chinese who lived during the rule of the Shang dynasty knew how to fight with bows and arrows. They used chariots when they attacked their enemies, and they wore shields and armor to protect themselves. The farming tools tell us that they grew wheat and mulberries, as well as rice, and that they used plows pulled by horses to farm their fields.

But that's not all the Shang dynasty left us. During the rule of the Shang, the Chinese began to use writing for the very first time. And we can still read this writing, because it was often engraved on bones and on bronze plaques that have lasted for thousands of years.

At first, this early Chinese writing was made up of pictures. These special pictures are called *pictograms*. *Picto* means "picture" and *gram* means "writing." Pictograms are words that look like pictures. For example, here's a pictogram for "sun":

It's a picture of the sun, with the sun's rays shining out at both sides.

The pictogram for "water" looks like this:

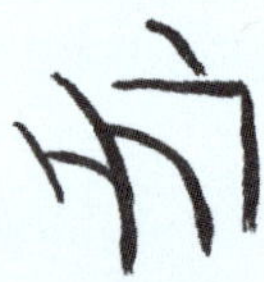

Can you see the waves in the water?

Here's a Shang dynasty pictogram that means "house":

Here is a Shang pictogram that means "bow and arrow":

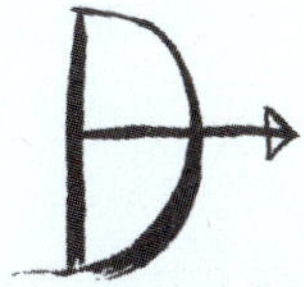

And here's a more complicated pictogram that means "soldier":

This soldier is carrying a *halberd*, a weapon that has an axe on one side and a dagger on the other.

The Chinese people used these pictograms to write simple messages. The pictograms look almost exactly like the words they represent.

Farming in Ancient China

Most people who lived in ancient China were farmers. They raised animals like pigs, chickens, and cows. They grew grain, just like people in Egypt and in Mesopotamia.

But the people of China grew a kind of grain that the Egyptians and Mesopotamians couldn't grow—rice.

Rice will only grow where the ground is very wet for most of the year. The ground in Egypt and Mesopotamia was too dry for rice. But near the Yellow River in China, whole fields stayed wet for months and months. Rice could grow there.

Here is a story about how life might have been for a farming family in ancient China.

CHIN WAS SEVEN YEARS OLD. HE LIVED WITH his father, a rice farmer, and his mother, his grandfather, and his little sister.

One spring morning, Chin woke up before sunrise. The room where he slept with the rest of his family was still dark. But Chin was too excited to go back to sleep. This morning, he would go with his father to work in the rice fields for the very first time! He hoped that it wouldn't rain. But he couldn't see out past the stiff paper that covered the windows.

Chin got up and tiptoed out of the room, past where his parents, his grandfather, and his little sister lay sleeping on their pallets on the floor. He opened the door as quietly as he could. From his front steps, he could hear the roar of the Yellow River. The river was fuller than usual because of the spring rains, and it was so noisy that the people in Chin's little village could hear it a mile away.

Chin looked up. The sky was just beginning to turn a beautiful clear pink. A spring breeze was blowing. It was going to be a wonderful day! He could hear the pigs rooting and grunting behind the house, and the chickens scratching around the edges of their pen. Chin fed the three pigs and the four chickens every morning. He decided that he would feed them right away, before his father got up. Then all his chores would be finished.

After he fed the animals, Chin washed his hands, combed his hair, and dressed. He picked up his sleeping mat and put it outside to air. Then he knelt down beside his father's pallet and whispered, "Father? Are you awake? Are you well this morning? Can I bring you water or food?" Chin did this every morning; it was his duty, as the oldest son, to make sure that his father had everything that he needed.

Chin's father opened his eyes and laughed. "Are you ready to go to work already?" he said.

"Can we go right now?" Chin asked eagerly.

"Wait until I've had my rice and tea!" Chin's father said, getting up.

Chin waited impatiently by the door. His mother was grinding rice into flour; she would make the flour into little sweet cakes for dinner. Chin's baby sister played on the floor with her favorite rag doll. Finally, Chin's father finished his breakfast. He led Chin down the hill towards the river, where the rice fields stood.

Weeks before, the Yellow River had flooded out over the rice fields. It spread water all over the flat land, deeper than Chin was tall. Then the water began to flow away back into the river, leaving soft, fertile mud from the river's bottom all over the ground. But water still stood ankle-deep all over the rice fields.

"Do you see these tiny rice plants, here in this special bed?" Chin's father asked. "Today I'll be moving them out into the field so that they can grow larger. Your job will be to pull weeds out of the field while I plant."

Chin rolled up the legs of his pants and waded out into the water. The water was ice-cold. At first his feet hurt from the cold. Then they started to go numb. He had to put his hands down into the water to pull weeds. His fingers were stiff with cold. But he kept working. He could see his father, planting rice seedlings up ahead of him. His father never stopped working! Chin was determined to work as hard as his father. The sun rose up higher and higher, and Chin's back and head grew warm in the sunshine. But his fingers and feet ached with cold.

Finally his father called him back to dry land. "You've worked like a man this morning!" he said. "Let's go back to the house for our midday meal."

Chin followed his father back up to the house. His back hurt from bending over. His feet were wet and chilly. His hands were covered with cold mud. But he was proud of the work he had done.

Back at the house, his mother had fixed him a special treat— meat to go along with his rice. And his father poured him a cup of hot steaming tea to warm him.

Chin huddled beside the clay stove, listening to his grandfather tell about the great floods of long ago. "When I was a boy," his grandfather said, "the spring rains came down and down and down, day after day, until the Yellow River rose up and overflowed its banks. But it didn't just flood our fields. Great rushing floods swirled down on our village and swept our houses away. We were left homeless!"

Chin shivered. He hoped that the Yellow River would never flood his home!

Note: According to legend, Huang Di ruled around 2690 BC/BCE. Lei Zu is also known as Xi Ling-shi. The Shang dynasty ruled 1766–1046 BC/BCE.

Chapter Eleven
Ancient Africa

The Peoples of West Africa

When you first started to learn about ancient times, you read about the nomads who settled in the Fertile Crescent, between the Tigris and the Euphrates rivers. If you were to put your finger on a map between those two rivers and then move your finger *right* (or *east*), you would cross over the land of the Sumerians and of the Babylonians and the Assyrians. You would cross the top part of India, where Mohenjo-Daro used to be. If you kept on going right, you would end up in China, where Chin and his family grew their crops beside the Yellow River.

If you put your finger on the Fertile Crescent and then moved it *left* (or *west*), you would come to Egypt and the Nile River, where the pharaohs lived. We know a great deal about the history of Egypt, because the Egyptians left thousands and thousands of *artifacts* (treasures and everyday objects) behind them. Archaeologists dug up the artifacts and used them to learn more about ancient Egypt. And the Egyptians also left us writing on stone tablets. Historians read these tablets and wrote down the history of the ancient Egyptian Empire.

But if you keep moving your finger on down the Nile River, you will see that Egypt is only one small part of a

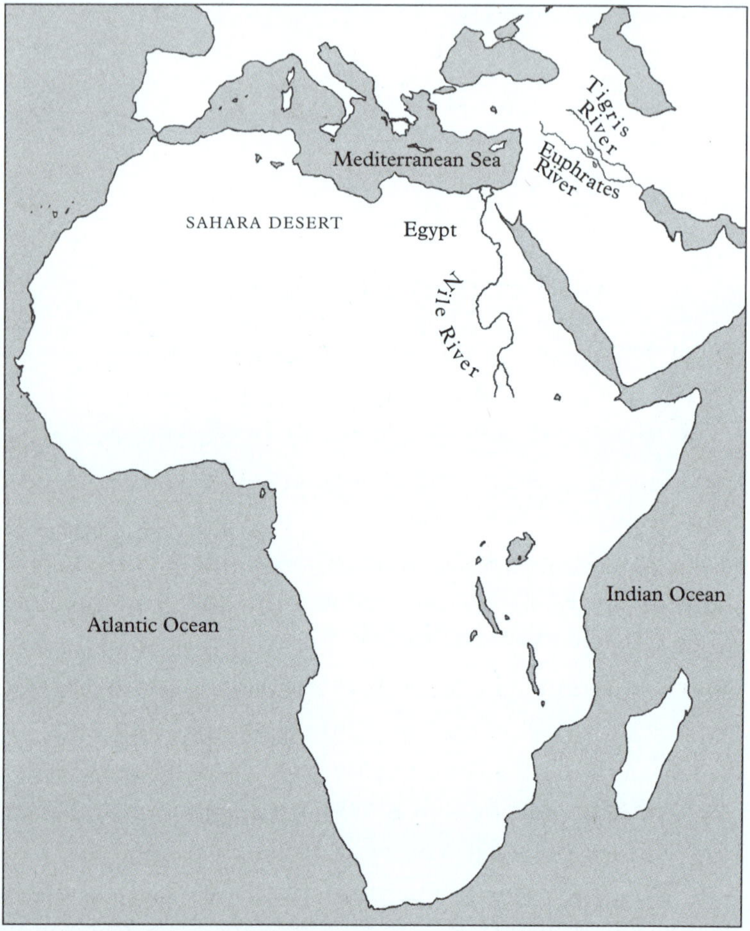

Ancient Africa

whole huge continent (a large piece of land with many countries on it). This continent is called Africa.

The people of ancient Africa did not leave written records or thousands of artifacts behind them. So we don't know as much about long-ago Africa as we do about ancient Egypt. But we do know that people have lived in Africa from the very earliest times.

If you were to move your finger left from the Nile River, you would come to a huge, sandy desert—the Sahara Desert. Today, the Sahara Desert is as hot and dry as an oven. The ground is cracked and parched. Sand drifts over the iron-hard ground and piles up in huge drifts called dunes. The only water lies in *oases*—little patches of land where water collects and a few scrubby palm trees can grow. Tiny villages sometimes settle in these oases. The people raise desert animals that don't need much water—sheep, camels, and goats. They eat the dates that grow on the palm trees. Sometimes, one tree is owned by several families, who share it!

Life in the Sahara Desert is difficult and dangerous. But long ago, this part of Africa wasn't a desert. It was a green, fertile place full of water and trees. Rivers and streams used to run where rocky, barren valleys now lie. Grassy meadows once grew where shifting sands now blow. Herds of gazelles and antelopes roamed through the green plains. Fish, crocodiles, and hippopotami swam in the rivers. Wild cows and sheep lived in the forests. The people of the Sahara were farmers, just like those who lived in the Fertile Crescent. They hunted wild animals and raised their own plants and animals for food.

How do we know this? Archaeologists who dug down through the hard dirt of the Sahara Desert found ancient pollen from trees and seeds from grasses and flowers. None of these trees or flowers grow in the Sahara today, but they left their seeds in the ground long, long ago. The archaeologists also found bones of animals that used to live in the Sahara, back when there was enough water for them. In one place, the people who lived in a Saharan village had eaten a feast of turtles. There were hundreds of shells that had been cracked open for their meat. In another place, the villagers had eaten an entire giraffe—except for its head.

The ancient people of Africa also left paintings behind them. They drew pictures of their way of life on the stone walls of caves. In these paintings, we see men growing crops and taking care of herds of animals. We see women in beautiful clothes, riding tame cows. These pictures tell us about the way the Sahara used to be.

But then something happened in the Sahara. The rains got scarcer and scarcer. Trees began to wither and die. The grass died too, and the ground dried up until it was nothing more than dust and sand. The rivers stopped flowing and the streams disappeared. The animals went farther and farther south, down to the parts of Africa where there was still water and food. And the people of the Sahara went south too. They traveled for weeks and weeks. They settled around the lakes and rivers in central Africa and began a new life.

And above them, the Sahara turned into desert.

From now on, Africa would be divided by the huge dangerous desert. Up along the coast of the Mediterranean Sea, people from Mesopotamia and Egypt would settle down and live in the northern part of Africa. And down below the Sahara Desert, the people of Africa would live for centuries in peace, cut off from the rest of the ancient world by the massive sands between them.

Anansi and Turtle

The ancient people of Africa didn't leave mummies or clay tablets behind them. But they did leave stories, passed down from person to person.

Anansi the Spider is a favorite character of African storytellers. Anansi is a tricky spider who often gets his way. But sometimes he is outwitted. Here is a story about Anansi and his friend Turtle. It comes from the Yoruba people of Nigeria, a West African country that is just south of the Sahara Desert. In this story, Anansi is hungry, and he's looking forward to eating a good supper of yams. (Yams are a little bit like potatoes, only sweeter, and rough on the outside like a coconut. The people of Africa have grown them in the ground for thousands of years.)

ANANSI THE SPIDER WAS HUNGRY! HE HAD dug some of the fattest yams ever out of his garden, and had baked them carefully in his clay oven. Now they were ready to come out. The yams smelled wonderful, and he couldn't wait to dig in.

But just as he was sitting down to his meal, along wandered Turtle. Now, Anansi and Turtle were friends. But when Anansi looked at his yams and then looked at Turtle, he thought, "There are just enough yams for me! If Turtle eats half of them, I'll still be hungry!"

"Oh, Anansi!" Turtle said. "How wonderful those yams smell! It has taken me all day to crawl over to your house for a visit, and I haven't eaten my lunch or my supper. Please, share your yams with me."

Now, in Africa it is the custom to share your meal with any visitor who asks. So Anansi couldn't say no. He said grumpily, "I would be happy to share my yams with you, Turtle. Have a seat. Help yourself."

Turtle sat down and reached for the fattest yam. But just as he was about to touch it, Anansi shouted, “Stop! Are you going to eat with those filthy flippers? Really, Turtle, don’t you think you should wash off first?”

Now, Turtle had been crawling all day. He was dirty and sandy and hadn’t come across any water. But he looked at his flippers. They certainly were dirty.

“Where should I wash?” he said.

“Go wash in the river,” Anansi said. “It’s only half a mile away.”

Poor Turtle! He got up and crawled off to the river to wash his flippers. By the time he came back, the yams were half gone. Anansi said with his mouth full, “Sorry, Turtle, you were so long that I had to start eating. But go ahead and have some yams.”

Turtle reached for the yams. But his flippers had gotten dirty again from his journey back up from the river. “Turtle!” Anansi yelled. “Didn’t I say that you should wash yourself off? Don’t come to the table dirty!”

Anansi the Spider and Turtle

Turtle crawled wearily away to wash himself again. When he climbed slowly back up from the river, he was very careful to stay on the grass. But when he got to the table and reached out his clean flipper for a yam, the last crumbs were gone.

Turtle looked sadly at the empty platter. "Well," he said, after a little while, "thank you for inviting me to supper, Anansi. The next time you come by my house, be sure to share my dinner with me."

And he got down and crawled away, still hungry.

A few days later, Anansi was going by Turtle's house on the riverbank. "Turtle told me that he would share his food with me," he thought. "I'll stop and eat with him." So he bounced up and knocked on Turtle's door.

"Turtle, Turtle!" he cried. "I'm ready for supper!"

Turtle opened the door and blinked at Anansi. "Supper is all ready," he said. "Come along with me. It's right down here."

Turtle led Anansi to the river's edge. "I've set the table right down there at the bottom of the water," he said. "Dive on down and eat with me!" And with that he slipped into the water, swam down to the river's bottom, and started to eat.

Anansi ran back and forth on the bank. First he tried jumping into the water. But he was so light that he floated on the top. He tried to swim down. He tried to make himself sink. But nothing worked. Down below, he could see Turtle polishing off all the food.

Finally Anansi stuffed the pockets of his tiny jacket full of pebbles and jumped back into the water. He sank like a stone right down to the bottom, where Turtle was eating his way through a whole platter full of delicious food.

Turtle pushed the platter over. "Here," he said. "Have some. But first, Anansi, take off your jacket. It's so rude to wear a coat at the table."

Anansi started to unbutton his jacket. But as soon as it was off his shoulders, he popped right back up to the surface of the water. When he stuck his head underwater, he could just see Turtle finishing off the very last morsel of food.

"Thank you for supper, Turtle," he said gloomily. And he swam back to the riverbank, wet and hungry.

Moral: If you try to be too smart, you might find that someone else outsmarts you instead.

Anansi and the Make-Believe Food

Another story about Anansi tells us about a time when food was very scarce and the rivers and streams were drying up. It may even come from the days when the people of Africa were leaving the Sahara for greener places. Here is the story:

THERE HAD BEEN NO RAIN FOR MANY, many days.

The crops had all withered away. The animals were starving. Anansi and his whole village were hungry too. And day after day, the sun shone down and the blue sky stayed empty of clouds.

Finally, Anansi said, "If someone doesn't go find some food, we will all die of hunger! I am going to walk until I find a village where there is food, and bring some back for all of us."

So Anansi started out. He walked and he walked and he walked until the sun went down. He walked all night. When the sky began to get light the next morning, he saw smoke from the chimneys of a village, far in the distance.

He walked until he reached the village. And then he stood with his mouth open. The village was full of—yams!

Anansi adored roasted yams. And in this village, there were no people, just yams—walking around in the streets, sweeping the steps of their huts, and sitting under the palm trees, talking to each other. When the yams saw him, they all jumped up.

"A visitor! A visitor!" they said. "Would you like to eat us roasted, boiled, or fried?"

"I—I don't care," Anansi stammered. "Maybe—roasted?"

"Roasted!" all the yams cried. They jumped into the fire one by one until they were nicely roasted, and then lined up for Anansi to eat them. He was just getting ready to take a bite out of the first one when he saw another spire of smoke, far away.

"What is that?" he asked.

"Oh, that's just the plantain village," the yams said. "Aren't you going to eat us?"

Now, a plantain is like a banana. And Anansi liked fried plantain even more than he liked roasted yams. So even though the yams begged him to stay and eat them, Anansi jumped up and ran towards the plantain village.

It took him hours to get there, and by the time he arrived he was hot and thirsty and even hungrier. But all the plantains ran out to meet him. The little baby plantains danced around his feet, and the big plantains jumped up and down for joy.

"How would you like to eat us?" they asked. "Roasted, boiled, or fried?"

"Any way you want!" Anansi cried.

"Fried!" the plantains shouted. So they jumped into a big pot of oil, one by one, and lined up to be eaten. But just as Anansi was getting ready to sink his teeth into the first crispy, savory plantain, he saw another spire of smoke, far off in the distance.

"What's that?" he asked.

"Oh, that's just the rice village," the plantains said. "Aren't you going to eat us?"

Now, if there was one thing that Anansi liked even more than a fried plantain, it was a big bowl of boiled rice. So even though the plantains begged him to stay and eat them, Anansi got up and began to walk towards the rice village.

By the time he reached it, the sun was setting. He was so hungry that he grabbed the first little pieces of rice who ran out to meet him and started to eat them raw. But the other rice grains squeaked, "No, no! We will cook ourselves! How would you like to eat us—roasted, boiled, or fried?"

"Any way you like!" Anansi moaned. "Just feed me!"

"Boiled!" the rice shouted. So the rice grains threw themselves into a big pot of boiling water and climbed out into a big bowl. Just as Anansi was getting ready to plunge his hand into the hot, delicious bowl of rice, he saw one more spire of smoke.

"What's that?" he asked.

"We don't know!" the rice grains shrilled at him. "Just eat us!"

But Anansi thought, "Each village has been better than the one before! If I can get to that village, I'll get to eat something even better than rice!" So he left the bowl of rice and ran towards the strange village.

It was night-time when he got there. He ran eagerly into the center of the town—and stopped. It was his own village, and there was no food anywhere to be seen.

Anansi fainted. When he woke up, the people of his village were all gathered around him.

"Here," they said. "We boiled a fish bone and made you some fishbone-and-water soup. It's all we have. Where have you been?"

Anansi told them all about the yam village, the plantain village, and the rice village. But no one could ever find those villages again.

What do you think the moral of this story is? Maybe it is "Don't be greedy—eat whatever you're given."

Note: The climate changed in the Sahara around 3500 BC/BCE. We know little about the cultures that flourished in southern Africa before medieval times; the second volume of *The Story of the World* deals much more extensively with African history.

Chapter Twelve
Life in Early Crete

Bull-Jumpers and Sailors

We've been learning about people who lived near rivers: the Egyptians, the people of the Indus Valley, the Chinese of the Yellow River Valley, and the Assyrians and Babylonians who lived near the Tigris and Euphrates rivers in Mesopotamia.

But if we look over in the Mediterranean Sea, we'll find something different—people who lived completely surrounded by water. These people built their homes on an island called Crete.

Crete is a long, skinny island in the Mediterranean Sea, which is shaped a little bit like a duck flying. Long, long ago, a tribe called the Minoans settled down on the island of Crete. The Minoans entertained themselves in an unusual way—by leaping over bulls.

Imagine that you're standing on a hard dirt floor, in the middle of a huge arena…

All around you, crowds are shouting your name and cheering. You glance around you and see two other people in the arena with you, a boy and a girl. None of you have any weapons. Your hands are empty, and all you're wearing is a simple loose garment that allows your arms and legs to move freely.

> Suddenly a wooden door swings open in the arena wall. A huge black bull charges out into the arena!
>
> The shouts of the crowd get louder and louder. The bull paws the earth and shakes his head back and forth. His horns are sharp and tipped with gold. He swings his head towards you and sees you. He snorts and charges straight at you.
>
> But you don't run away. You wait until he's only inches away from you—and then you grab his horns and push yourself upwards. You somersault through the air, do a handstand on the bull's back, and land on your feet behind him. The girl in the arena with you is there to catch you. The crowd roars!
>
> You turn and see your other teammate vault onto the bull. As he lands on his feet, you grab his arm to help him stay standing. The bull comes to a halt, confused. The three of you bow to the crowd and then turn to do it all over again.

If you were a boy or girl in ancient Crete, you might find yourself part of a bull-jumping team like this one. The Minoans, who lived on the island of Crete, trained athletic children to become bull-jumpers. The children learned the kind of gymnastics that children still learn today—somersaulting, balance exercises, tumbling, and vaulting. But instead of doing their vaulting over a piece of equipment, the students learned how to vault over the backs of small animals such as goats—and then finally were taught how to leap over the backs of bulls.

Bull-jumping festivals were held to honor the Minoan gods, who were thought to take the form of bulls. At the end of every bull-jumping festival, the bulls were sacrificed to the gods.

During festivals, people came from all over Crete to cheer for the bull-jumpers. Bull-jumpers were treated like royalty. They were given the best food and the nicest places to live. They were showered with presents of gold, jewelry, and beautiful clothes. But bull-jumping was a dangerous sport, because bull-jumpers were often killed by the bulls they were supposed to leap over. Few bull-jumpers lived past the age of twenty.

The Minoans were known both for bull-jumping and for shipbuilding. In ancient times, the Mediterranean Sea was full of pirates. No one ruled the sea; it was controlled by bandits who sailed their small boats near the shore. These bandits attacked and robbed anyone who ventured out onto the water. Kings of the ancient world had learned how to build strong armies that fought on land. But none of them knew how to build big ships to carry their soldiers out onto the water. So the pirates roamed free on the Mediterranean Sea.

But the king of the Minoans was different. He knew that the Minoans had to be able to sail safely across the Mediterranean Sea to land, so that they could trade with other countries. So he ordered his craftsmen to build great ships that he could use to wipe out pirates and patrol the Mediterranean Sea.

The Minoan craftsmen learned how to build the ships. They were the greatest shipbuilders of the ancient world. And the king of the Minoans became the first king to have a navy—an army that knew how to fight on the water.

This navy drove the pirates out of the Mediterranean Sea and carried Minoan traders to other ancient countries so that they could buy and sell goods. The Minoan navy became the strongest in the world. It was so strong that the greatest palace of Crete didn't even have walls. No invaders could land on Crete's shores, because the navy kept them away.

King Minos and the Minotaur

The Minoans who lived on Crete were named after a legendary king named Minos. The Minoans told this story about Minos:

Minos was a son of the god Zeus, the chief of all the gods. But because he was half human, Minos couldn't live with the other gods. Instead, he lived on Crete, in a great and beautiful palace.

But this shining palace concealed a dark secret. Below the foundation of the palace, in a maze so twisty and complicated that no one could find the way in or out, lived a horrible monster—the Minotaur. The Minotaur lived in the dark, but people whispered that he was half man and half bull—and that he ate human beings.

King Minos didn't want to feed his own people to the Minotaur, so he ordered the nearby city of Athens to send him victims for the Minotaur's dinner. Every year, Athens had to send seven girls and seven boys to King Minos, or else (he threatened) he would destroy their city. Year after year, the Athenians sent this dreadful tribute to

Minos. They put the names of all the boys and girls of Athens into a bowl, picked out fourteen unlucky victims, and then put them on a ship and took them to Crete.

And year after year, the seven girls and seven boys disappeared and were never seen again.

On his eighteenth birthday, Theseus, the son of the king of Athens, decided to walk down to the seaside. The sea was blue, the sky was clear, and the sun shone. But the beach was full of weeping fathers and mothers, and the ship drawn up to the shore had black sails.

"Why does the ship have black sails?" Theseus asked. "Why are you all crying?"

"Because our sons and daughters are going to Crete," one mother answered him. "They'll be eaten by the Minotaur, and we'll never see them again."

Theseus was horrified! "Why didn't I know about this?" he demanded.

"Because you are the prince," another father told him. "Your name is never put into the bowl with the names of all the other young people of Athens! You'll never have to go to Crete and face the Minotaur."

"But that's not right!" Theseus said. "Let me go to Crete in the place of one of the young men. I'll face the Minotaur, and try to kill him. If I succeed, we'll put a white sail on this ship instead of the black one, and sail home to Athens. And no one will ever have to be sacrificed as tribute to King Minos again."

Theseus's father, King Aegeus, begged him not to go. But Theseus was determined, and in the end he had his way. He sailed to Crete with the other victims.

On the shore of Crete, they were greeted by the cruel King Minos himself, with his beautiful daughter Ariadne walking meekly behind him. "More food for the Minotaur!" King Minos said, with a great laugh. "Tonight, you'll visit the bull-man in the Labyrinth, his maze beneath my palace!"

He sent the fourteen victims to the prisons of Knossos to wait for nightfall. But Ariadne had fallen in love with Theseus at first sight. Just before dark, she found a torch, a sword, and a ball of wool, and crept secretly out of King Minos's palace, down to Theseus's prison cell.

"Theseus!" she whispered. "Do you want to kill the Minotaur?"

"Yes!" Theseus answered. "But how can I? He lives at the center of the Labyrinth, and no one who gets into that maze can ever get out again."

"I've brought you a torch to light your way," Ariadne said, "and a sword to kill the monster. Take this ball of wool and tie it to the doorframe of the Labyrinth. Then drop the ball and let it roll forward. It will lead you to the center of the maze, because the center is the lowest part of the whole Labyrinth. You'll find the Minotaur sleeping there. Kill it, and then follow the string back out to the doorway."

She unlocked the door of the cell and let Theseus out. He did as she told him, making his way through the dark passages of the Labyrinth with his torch throwing strange shadows all around him and the ball of wool rolling steadily forward in front of him. Suddenly the ball came to a stop. Theseus held up his torch. He was in the center of a huge underground room. It stank of some wild animal, and bones littered the floor. In the middle of the room, a monster—half man and half bull—lay asleep on a golden sofa.

The Minotaur

Theseus started forward, but the monster woke and leaped from his sofa with a roar. They fought together for hours, until finally Theseus struck the Minotaur dead with his sword. Then he made his way back up to the entrance of the Labyrinth, following the wool string until he saw the door to the outside up ahead of him.

Ariadne had already released his thirteen friends. Together, they slipped away to the harbor, boarded their ship, and set sail for Athens. They sailed into the harbor of Athens just as the sun rose over the city.

But in their haste, they had forgotten to put a white sail on their ship! The people of Athens came forward to meet them, but although some were rejoicing, others were weeping.

"Your Highness," one of them said to Theseus, "your father, the king, was waiting for you, on top of that far distant cliff. When the sun struck the sails of your ship, and he saw that the sails were black, he thought that you were dead. So he threw himself off the cliff and into the water. You are now the king of Athens."

Theseus was crowned king of Athens, but it was a bitter celebration for him. He built a monument to his father in the harbor of Athens. And he named the water around Athens the Aegean Sea, in memory of his father Aegeus.

It is still called the Aegean Sea today.

The Mysterious End of the Minoans

What happened to the Minoans?

The Minoans of Crete disappeared, mysteriously, more than two thousand years ago. Their civilization came to a sudden end. All the Minoans left Crete. Why did they do this?

Although no one knows for sure, many historians think that the Minoans left when a volcano erupted on a nearby island called Thera. Thera looked like a small island, and people lived on it, grew crops, and raised animals in its fields. But Thera was actually the top of an active volcano that poked up from the Mediterranean Sea.

One day, the small island began to shake underfoot. The people of Thera could feel constant small earthquakes. Many left the island at once, taking all their possessions with them. They thought that the gods of the sea were angry with them.

But not everyone left. The earthquakes eventually died away. The people who were still on Thera decided to stay. They started to rebuild the walls that had fallen down.

But the volcano wasn't finished. The volcano's funnel began to spit out bits of rock called *pumice*. Pumice and ash covered the whole countryside. Smoke began to come out of the ground.

Then the rest of the people of Thera fled in terror—and just in time! The volcano exploded, spraying lava and rock all over the island. Huge boulders were thrown up from the inside of the volcano and fell like rock bombs on top of the villages of Thera.

Suddenly, the volcano collapsed inward. The sea rushed in to fill the hole. Thera was no longer a round island—instead, Thera had become a ring of land surrounding a huge, water-filled *caldera* (a gigantic sinkhole caused by a volcanic eruption).

The island of Crete was still there. But a tidal wave thrown up by the volcano swept its shores. Huge clouds of ash, dust, and smoke floated down on the wind to cover it. Ash covered the crops. Food supplies were wiped out. People could hardly breathe because of all the dust and smoke in the air.

Historians think that many of the Minoans left the island of Crete because the volcano ruined the air and land. Others stayed, but they struggled against starvation. Finally they were forced to battle their neighbors for food. The Minoan cities were never strong and powerful again. Ash and dust had helped to bring the first great civilization of Crete to its end.

Note: The Minoan civilization reached its peak between 2200–1450 BC/BCE. The eruption on Thera cannot be dated with certainty, but probably occurred in either 1628 or 1520 BC/BCE. The remnants of Thera were eventually resettled; today, the island is known as Santorini.

Chapter Thirteen
The Middle Kingdom of Egypt

Egypt Invades Nubia

Do you remember reading about the Old Kingdom of Egypt? The Egyptians of the Old Kingdom built pyramids and temples. They traded with the Babylonians and the Assyrians. They worshipped their gods, made mummies, and buried treasure along with them. Egypt had capable pharaohs and a strong army. Life in Egypt was good.

But these peaceful times didn't last.

The pharaohs of Egypt became weaker and weaker. They lost control of their armies. They even lost control of their own courts and temples. Priests and palace officials and generals fought over who would be in charge. Egypt's power started to vanish. For a little while, it seemed that Egypt might fall apart, just like the kingdom of Sargon did.

But then, around 1991 BC/BCE, a new ruler came to the throne of Egypt. His name was Amenemhet.

Amenemhet wasn't born to be a pharaoh. He just worked for the government. But he was determined to bring Egypt back to its former glory. He seized the throne and became the new pharaoh of Egypt.

Amenemhet ruled during a new time in the country's history—the Middle Kingdom of Egypt. During the

Middle Kingdom, Egypt became a powerful country once more.

Amenemhet decided that his first job was to make Egypt bigger. He planned to conquer the countries that surrounded Egypt. And his first target was the kingdom of Nubia.

Nubia was south of Egypt, in Africa. Unlike the people of ancient West Africa, the Nubians didn't go down into the central part of Africa when the Sahara began to dry up. After all, they had the Nile River for water, and the rich mud of the Nile overflow for their crops. So the Nubian people stayed in their own country.

The Nubians traveled along the Nile River to sell many beautiful things to the Egyptians. They sold ivory, animal furs, ostrich feathers, and gems. And they brought gold into Egypt. Amenemhet knew that the Nubians dug gold out of the hills and ground of their kingdom. He thought that if he could become the ruler of Nubia, he would have plenty of treasure to make him rich.

So Amenemhet set off to conquer Nubia. He fought dozens of battles against the Nubians. They resisted him and killed many of his soldiers—but finally, Amenemhet was victorious. The Egyptians renamed Nubia "Kush." They painted pictures of their new African subjects on the walls of their tombs. The pictures show Nubians carrying gold, ebony, incense, furs, and monkeys as presents to the Egyptians.

For the next seven hundred years, the Nubians were ruled by the Egyptians. Slowly, they began to think of themselves as Egyptians. They learned the Egyptian language, followed the Egyptian religion, and obeyed the Egyptian pharaohs. The Egyptians began to respect them. And the Nubians gained power of their own in Egypt. One Nubian woman even became the queen of Egypt, when she married the pharaoh Amenhotep III! Her name was Queen Tiye.

Queen Tiye wasn't the only Nubian who moved into the palaces of Egypt. Eventually, the Nubians who lived in Kush founded their own dynasty—and became pharaohs of Egypt themselves. So the Egyptians were also Africans. And the people of Africa brought their own stories, traditions, and skills into the Egyptian Empire.

When we read about the greatness of the Egyptians, we are also reading about the greatness of Africa.

The Hyksos Invade Egypt

Back up in northern Africa, Amenemhet's sons and grandsons were still ruling the Middle Kingdom of Egypt. They were strong pharaohs who kept all of Egypt united. They didn't allow conquered people, like the Nubians, to rebel. They made money by selling iron and gold to other countries. Egypt had become rich and prosperous once more.

Amenemhet's family was a powerful dynasty. (Do you remember what a dynasty is? It's when one family rules a country for many years.) But after the dynasty of Amenemhet, other families ruled Egypt. The kings in these families were not good pharaohs. They couldn't keep control over all of Egypt's land. Once again, the priests and government workers started to quarrel with each other about who had the most power. The leaders of the army started to bicker with each other as well, so that the army became too confused to fight off invaders. No one was really in charge.

But this was a bad time for Egypt to become weak. Fierce enemies were getting ready to attack the pharaoh and take away his throne.

These enemies were from Canaan. Do you remember reading about Canaan? In your story about Abraham, Abraham heard the voice of God, telling him to go to Canaan. And do you remember what Abraham thought? He thought, "Why would I go to a wilderness filled with strange, wild tribes?"

Well, one of the strange wild tribes that lived in Canaan was called the Hyksos. They were warlike nomads who moved from place to place, looking for new land to conquer and new wealth to steal. They had been wandering around Canaan for years. A few at a time, the Hyksos had moved down into Egypt and settled. Eventually, a huge number of Hyksos lived in the Nile Delta. There were so many Hyksos that they had an entire city all their own.

Now they were ready to rule their new home. They picked up weapons and charged to Egypt's capital city to attack the pharaoh and his army.

Egypt's weak army wasn't ready for such a vicious attack. And the Hyksos had weapons that the Egyptians had never used before. They used new bows that could shoot arrows much farther than the Egyptian bows. They used war chariots pulled by horses. The Egyptians had no such chariots! The Egyptian army didn't know how to fight off these invaders with their strange new weapons.

So the Hyksos defeated the Egyptian soldiers and captured the largest cities of Egypt. They even took over the pharaoh's palace. From now on, the Hyksos were the rulers of Egypt.

This was the end of the Middle Kingdom of Egypt.

The Egyptians hated their Hyksos kings. They called them the "shepherd kings." They thought that the Hyksos were rude, unclean, and uncivilized.

But the Hyksos stayed in Egypt for over a hundred years.

Finally, a group of Egyptian princes got together and organized a rebellion. They armed themselves with strong bows, like the Hyksos bows. They got themselves war chariots pulled by horses, just like the Hyksos war chariots. They made bronze sickle-shaped swords, just like the Hyksos swords. And they drove the Hyksos out of Egypt—using fighting methods that they had learned from the Hyksos themselves.

The leader of the rebellious Egyptian princes, Ahmose, became the new pharaoh of Egypt. Under Ahmose and his descendants, Egypt became stronger than ever. Egypt got back the land it had lost to the Hyksos. And the Egyptian pharaohs used their new bows, chariots, and swords to conquer even more territory. Egypt became one of the most powerful kingdoms in the whole world.

This time in Egyptian history is called the New Kingdom of Egypt.

Note: The rule of Amenemhet is approximately 1980–1926 BC/BCE (the first portion of his reign was probably a coregency with his father). The Middle Kingdom of Egypt dates from 2040 to approximately 1720 BC/BCE. The Hyksos were expelled by Ahmose in approximately 1567 BC/BCE.

Chapter Fourteen
The New Kingdom of Egypt

The General and the Woman Pharaoh

After the Egyptians learned how to fight from the Hyksos, the New Kingdom of Egypt got more and more powerful. This is sometimes called the "Golden Age of Egypt," because Egypt was richer than ever before. Pharaoh after pharaoh came to the throne, ruled well, and kept the New Kingdom of Egypt strong.

We could never learn about all of these pharaohs! But we are going to read about two of the most interesting pharaohs: Thutmose I and his daughter, Hatshepsut.

Thutmose I: The General

Before he became pharaoh, Thutmose I was a general in the Egyptian army. Leading the army into wars was what he did best. Thutmose liked to fight!

Thutmose helped the Egyptian princes drive the Hyksos out of Egypt. When the leader of the Egyptian princes became pharaoh, Thutmose was his right-hand man. Then Thutmose married the pharaoh's daughter! And when that pharaoh died, Thutmose became the new pharaoh of Egypt. His rule began around 1524 BC/BCE.

Thutmose decided that his job as pharaoh was to make Egypt's empire even bigger—by conquering other countries. Thutmose's first battles were against the Nubians, who were trying to break away from Egypt. He went down and conquered the Nubian chiefs and reminded them that they were still part of Egypt.

But that wasn't enough for Thutmose. Next, he took his army and followed the Hyksos all the way up to Canaan. He defeated the tribes living in the south part of Canaan and made that land part of Egypt.

Thutmose I

Thutmose was very pleased with himself. The Hyksos had come down and taken over Egypt. Now he had gone up and taken over the land of the Hyksos. The victory made him so happy that he wanted to keep on fighting. He turned his army east, and he started to march. He conquered land all the way to the Euphrates River.

But he didn't cross the river—because Babylon was ruling between the Tigris and the Euphrates. Thutmose knew better than to start a fight with Babylon.

So he turned and went back home. But he had finished what he set out to do: He made Egypt bigger. By the time Thutmose died, Egypt was twice as big as it had been when he became pharaoh!

Hatshepsut: The Woman Who Pretended to Be a Man

Hatshepsut was a princess of Egypt—the daughter of a pharaoh. Her father, Thutmose, was one of Egypt's greatest pharaohs.

Thutmose had three children, but his favorite child was his daughter, Hatshepsut. Hatshepsut loved to listen to her father's stories of battles and conquest. She wanted to grow up to be pharaoh too. But back in ancient times, most people thought that women were too weak to rule countries. In ancient Egypt, royal women were allowed to get married and have children who could become kings or the wives of kings. If they didn't want to get married, they could work at the temple, serving the gods. But they could not become rulers themselves.

So when the pharaoh Thutmose died, Hatshepsut's brother became the next pharaoh. Hatshepsut didn't think this was fair. Her brother was sick most of the time, and he didn't pay much attention to his job ruling Egypt.

"I would be a better pharaoh than my brother!" she told herself. "But he is a man, and I am a woman. Will I ever get the chance to show what a good ruler I can be?"

Hatshepsut's brother got sicker and sicker, and one day he died. He had only been pharaoh for four years. Before he died, he told Hatshepsut that he wanted his son to be the next pharaoh. But his son was just a baby. So Hatshepsut said to the Egyptians, "I will help my brother's son rule Egypt until he is old enough to be pharaoh on his own." The Egyptian people agreed, and Hatshepsut was finally able to rule Egypt.

She wasn't the real pharaoh; everyone knew that her nephew would soon be old enough to rule. But when that day came, Hatshepsut announced that she would not give up the throne. "My father always meant me to be the crown prince," she told her people. "He wanted me to become pharaoh, rather than my brother."

"You can't do that!" the people in the palace said. "Only men can be pharaohs!"

Hatshepsut answered, "But the god Amun-Ra told me that I would rule Egypt. He said, 'Welcome, my sweet daughter, my favorite, the ruler of Upper and Lower Egypt. Hatshepsut, you are the pharaoh!' So the gods themselves want me to rule Egypt!"

"But no woman has ever been a pharaoh!" the people complained.

"Then pretend I am a man," Hatshepsut said. And she started to wear men's clothing. Whenever she sat on the throne, she even put on a false beard. Hatshepsut was so determined to be pharaoh that the Egyptians finally agreed to have her as their ruler. For over twenty years, Hatshepsut ruled Egypt—a queen, insisting that she was a king.

She didn't fight any wars, but she did lead expeditions into Africa. There, she bought gold, incense, monkeys, elephants, and other things that the Egyptian people loved. She built more monuments than any other Egyptian queen. Hatshepsut ruled over the Egyptians until her death.

Amenhotep and King Tut

Thutmose I and Hatshepsut were powerful rulers. But we remember two other pharaohs of Egypt for different reasons. The pharaoh Amenhotep tried to change the way that the Egyptians worshipped their gods. And we remember the pharaoh Tutankhamen because of the way he was buried.

Amenhotep: Many Gods or One God?

Amenhotep's father was pharaoh, so when he died Amenhotep inherited his throne. He became pharaoh around 1350 BC/BCE. He was the fourth pharaoh named Amenhotep, so he was known as Amenhotep IV.

At first, Amenhotep acted like any other pharaoh. He made laws. He sent the army out to stop rebellions. He married a princess from Nubia and had a daughter. He worshipped all of Egypt's many gods. As a matter of fact, he was named after one of Egypt's most important gods—Amun, a god of the sun who was sometimes called "the King of the Gods." Amenhotep sacrificed to Amun, gave money to his priests, and held big celebrations to honor this powerful god.

But then something happened to Amenhotep. He decided that Amun didn't exist. As a matter of fact, he decided that none of Egypt's gods were real.

The Egyptian people were horrified. After all, they worshipped dozens of gods. They were *polytheists*. *Polytheism* means "the worship of many gods." The Egyptians thought that there were many, many gods who controlled every part of life. The gods made the Nile flood; they made rain fall; they made women have babies; they provided food; they decided whether you would live or die. How could this pharaoh suddenly stop worshipping the gods?

Amenhotep didn't pay any attention to what his people thought. His mind was made up. Instead of many gods, he believed, there was only one god. He called this god Aten.

The old gods of Egypt had looked like human beings, but Aten didn't look like a man. He had to be drawn by a symbol. Amenhotep did his best to drive all worship of the old gods—polytheism—out of Egypt. He closed temples and made priests stop performing rituals. He told people not to sacrifice to the old gods. He even changed his name, so that he wouldn't be named after Amun, the King of the Gods, anymore. Now, instead of Amenhotep, he wanted to be called Akhenaten. This name means "worshipper of Aten."

Amenhotep was the first Egyptian *monotheist. Monotheism* means "worship of only one god." He spent much of his reign worshipping Aten. He built a whole new city with a huge, new temple in it for Aten. He wrote poetry to his god. One of his poems says:

> *Earth brightens when you dawn in lightland,*
> *When you shine as Aten of daytime …*
> *The entire land sets out to work,*
> *All beasts browse on their herbs.*
> *Trees, herbs are sprouting,*
> *Birds fly from their nests …*
> *Ships fare north, fare south as well,*
> *Roads lie open when you rise;*
> *The fish in the river dart before you.*
> *Your rays are in the midst of the sea.*[1]

1. "The Great Hymn to the Aten," translated by Miriam Lichtheim in *Ancient Egyptian Literature* (University of California Press, 2019).

As long as Amenhotep lived, he kept the Egyptians from worshipping all their gods. But as soon as Amenhotep died, the Egyptians rebelled! They closed the temple to Aten. They reopened all their other temples. They went back to worshipping all the old gods of Egypt. And they erased Amenhotep's name from all the monuments he had built. They took him out of all their records. They moved out of his new city and let it crumble away into ruins. They were so angry at Amenhotep for trying to make them worship just one god that they tried to forget he had ever been pharaoh.

Monotheism in Egypt had failed. Polytheism—the worship of many gods—had won, after all.

The Boy Buried With Treasure: King Tut

Tut became king of Egypt when he was only seven.

He grew up in the house of Amenhotep, the pharaoh who changed his name to Akhenaten. There, Tut was originally named Tutankhaten, a name honoring the god Aten. But when he became king, Tut changed his name to Tutankhamen, a name honoring Amun, the old "King of the Gods." King Tut helped to wipe out the worship of Aten. He encouraged the people to start worshipping the old gods again. He helped to erase Akhenaten's name from all Egyptian records.

But King Tut did not have much time to rule. He died when he was eighteen.

Tut wasn't buried in a pyramid. You see, robbers knew that the pyramids of Egypt were full of treasure. They broke into the pyramids and robbed them of all their gold and jewels.

Sometimes they even dumped the mummies of pharaohs out onto the floor and stole the golden coffins. So the Egyptians began to hide their tombs in the hills and mountains. They carved caves into the cliffs, put their pharaohs and treasures inside, and then blocked up the doors with stone to hide them. Their favorite place to bury pharaohs was a long, rocky valley catacombed with caves and passageways. This valley, now called the Valley of the Kings, has over sixty tombs in it. And the tombs are well hidden. Robbers never found King Tut's mummy. As a matter of fact, the tomb of King Tut was lost for thousands and thousands of years.

Over three thousand years later, a man named Howard Carter was working in the Valley of the Kings. He had spent years looking for the tombs of the pharaohs. He found Hatshepsut's tomb. He was convinced that another royal grave was hidden in the Valley of the Kings. But he was simply unable to find it.

One day, Howard Carter was moving a stack of stones when he found something unexpected—a step! He ran for help. His men, digging all through the day, uncovered more steps, leading down to a door in the stone. On the door, Carter found a name in hieroglyphs: Tutankhamen.

Carefully, Carter cut a hole in the door. He held up a light to the door. At first, all he could see was darkness. He moved his light from side to side. Suddenly, a beautiful golden gleam sprang out from the blackness. The room was full of gold.

Carter's friends were pressing in behind him. "What do you see?" one of them asked. "Can you see anything?"

"Yes!" Howard Carter said. "Wonderful things!"

The workmen slowly pried the door open. In front of them was a room filled with treasures. King Tut's throne, golden statues of the young king, game boards inlaid with ivory and jewels, rings, necklaces, jars, jewel-encrusted chests, figures of the gods and goddesses—all of these were crowded into King Tut's tomb.

Howard Carter and his friends kept on exploring. They found a whole series of rooms, linked together by hallways. Each room held more treasures. Finally, they came to the last locked door.

Carter opened it carefully. Inside, he saw a huge golden box. Then he realized that the box opened at the top. Inside this golden box, he found a heavy stone chest. Inside the stone chest, he found a golden statue of the king, lying on its back.

As soon as he touched the statue, he knew that it was actually a wooden coffin, carved to look like the king and then coated with gold. He pried the coffin open, expecting to see Tut's body. Instead, he found another wooden coffin, covered with gold. And when he opened this coffin, he found yet another coffin—this one solid gold, through and through. Carefully, he opened this final coffin.

And there at last was Tutankhamen's mummified body, wrapped in linen and soaked with spices. It was so well preserved that Howard Carter could even see the dead king's face!

Soon, people began to say that there was a curse on Tut's tomb. The man who helped Howard Carter open Tut's tomb, Lord Carnarvon, died only seven weeks after the burial chamber was first opened. Was this a result of the inscription found on the statue of Anubis, the god of death, inside Tut's treasure? The inscription reads, "It is I who hinder the sand from choking the secret chamber. I am for the protection of the deceased." Five months after Lord Carnarvon's death, his younger brother also died unexpectedly. And that's not all—Howard Carter's pet canary was swallowed by a cobra on the very day that the tomb was first opened! A cobra was also carved on Tut's mask—so that it would spit fire at all enemies of the king.

There were twenty-six people present when the tomb was opened. Within ten years, six had died. But the others lived into old age.

So you decide: Was there a curse in Tut's tomb?

Note: Thutmose I was a pharaoh of the eighteenth dynasty and ruled 1524–1518 BC/BCE. Hatshepsut was also a pharaoh of the eighteenth dynasty and ruled 1498–1483 BC/BCE. There are several pharaohs named Amenhotep; this is Amenhotep IV (ruled 1350–1334 BC/BCE), who married Nefertiti and changed his name to Akhenaten. Tutankhamen was born around 1343 BC/BCE and died around 1325, when he was probably eighteen. Carter found his tomb in AD/CE 1922.

Chapter Fifteen
The Israelites Leave Egypt

The Baby Moses

Do you remember reading about Abraham? The story of Abraham, in the book of Genesis, tells us that when Abraham lived in Ur, he was a polytheist—he believed in the moon-god and many other gods. But after Abraham heard a voice telling him to go to Canaan, he became a monotheist. He believed there was only one god, and that the voice that spoke to him was the voice of that one god.

Genesis also tells us that Abraham had a son named Isaac, and Isaac had a son named Jacob. Jacob didn't have just one son. He had twelve! Each one of those sons had a big family too. All together, Jacob's sons and their families made up a whole new nation. This nation was called "Israel." The Israelites—the people of Israel—were unusual in the ancient world, because they were monotheists. They only worshipped one god, and they tried to obey his commands.

Because God had told them to live in Canaan, the Israelites tried to stay there, even though it was a dry and rocky place. But then a famine came. It stopped raining. Plants wouldn't grow. Animals died. The Israelites had no food for their flocks, or for themselves. They were afraid that they would die, too.

Do you remember the story of Joseph? Joseph's brothers sold him to be a slave in Egypt. But Joseph became a very important man in Egypt. And he had plenty of grain and water. So he invited the Israelites down into Egypt. They packed up their tents, their animals, their families, and all their belongings and traveled down to Egypt. They started to keep their flocks and grow their crops on the banks of the Nile.

At first the Egyptians didn't mind having the Israelites in their country. But then they saw the Israelite nation growing larger and larger. Soon, the Egyptians started saying to each other, "What if these people decide to attack us? They might even take our kingdom away!" After all, that was exactly what the Hyksos had done, years before.

So the Egyptians made the Israelites into slaves. They forced the Israelites to make the mud bricks that they used to build their houses and temples. The Israelites were not allowed to carry any kind of weapons. They had to work hard for no pay.

But the Israelite nation kept growing bigger and bigger, and the Egyptians were still afraid. The book of Exodus, in the Christian Bible and the Jewish Torah, tells us a story about what happened next.

THE PHARAOH OF EGYPT SAT ON HIS THRONE, a frown on his face. "What will I do about all those Israelites in my country?" he thought to himself. "There are more and more of them all the time! Soon they will take over Egypt. If only they didn't have so many children."

And then he had an idea—a terrible, cruel idea. He called his soldiers to him. "Men," he said, "go out into the land of Egypt, to every Israelite home. Find out when the Israelite mothers are about to have their babies. Then kill every baby boy as soon as it is born!"

When the Israelites heard about this dreadful command, they wept and mourned. "God, save us!" they cried out. "Send us someone to deliver us from this wicked pharaoh of Egypt!"

An Israelite woman who lived near the banks of the Nile was just getting ready to have her baby when she heard the order. "Quickly!" she said to her daughter Miriam. "Help me hide! I don't want the soldiers to see me!"

So Miriam helped her mother hide in a back room of their house. When the baby was born, it was a boy—a fine, strong boy with a very loud cry.

"Quiet!" the mother whispered to her baby. "Don't cry so loud, or the soldiers will hear you!" For three months, the mother and baby hid from the soldiers of the pharaoh. But the baby got older and louder. He started to giggle and coo. The mother knew she could not hide him forever.

So she wove a basket out of reeds and coated the outside with tar so that it would float. She wrapped the baby in a warm, soft blanket, put him into the basket, and pushed it out onto the Nile River. And she sent her daughter Miriam to stand by the riverbank and watch to see what would happen next.

The baby floated down the river. He smiled at the sunshine and at the bird that landed on the edge of the basket to see what was inside. Finally, the gentle rocking of the basket lulled him to sleep. The basket drifted closer and closer to the side of the Nile, until it caught in the weeds at the water's edge.

Now, the daughter of the pharaoh liked to walk down to the Nile at the hottest part of the day, so that she could swim. She came to the edge of the water and saw the basket.

"What's in that basket?" she demanded. "Get it for me!"

One of her maids ran to fetch the basket. When the daughter of the pharaoh looked inside, she saw the baby boy. He opened his eyes and began to cry.

"Don't cry, beautiful boy!" she said to him. "You are mine now. I will keep you and raise you as my own!"

When Miriam heard this, she ran forward. "Lady," she said, "would you like me to find you a nurse to take care of the baby?"

"Yes," the daughter of the pharaoh said. "Bring me this woman and she can take care of my baby for me."

So Miriam hurried home and got her mother. And the baby and his mother were together again. She took care of him until he was old enough to live in the pharaoh's palace alone. The daughter of the pharaoh named him Moses.

The Exodus from Egypt

Here is more of the story of Moses, from the book of Exodus.

MOSES GREW UP IN THE PALACE OF THE pharaoh. But when he got older, he discovered that he wasn't an Egyptian. He was an Israelite. And he saw that his people were being beaten and mistreated.

So he went to see the pharaoh. "I am an Israelite," he said, "and I worship the one God of the Israelites. God says: Let the Israelites go!"

But the pharaoh didn't want to lose all his slaves. So he refused to let the people of Israel go.

When Moses saw that the pharaoh would not free the slaves, he told the pharaoh that God would send ten plagues on Egypt. Each one of these plagues showed that the God of the Israelites was more powerful than all the gods of the Egyptians. The Egyptians thought that the Nile was the bloodstream of their god Osiris—but the God of Moses turned the river to real blood and killed all the fish. Frogs were sacred to the Egyptians, because they belonged to the goddess Heket—but God sent so many frogs that the Egyptians found frogs in their beds, their clothes, their bathtubs, and even in their food. The Egyptians thought that Ra was the god of the sun, and was stronger than any other god—but the God of Moses covered up the sun and made darkness last all day long.

Finally the pharaoh told Moses that the Israelites could leave Egypt. They packed up all their belongings and left that very night.

But then the pharaoh changed his mind and sent his army after them.

The Israelites were running as fast as they could go. But when they looked behind them, they saw dust rising up from the hooves of the Egyptian army.

"Faster!" they cried. "Faster! Or the Egyptians will take us back to Egypt, and we will be slaves again!"

Then they looked up. Ahead of them they saw the shore of a sea—the Red Sea. Water lay in front of them, as far as they could see. And the Egyptians were behind them. They couldn't go forward, and they couldn't go backward.

"We are trapped!" they said. "Moses, have you led us out of Egypt only to kill us here on the shores of the Red Sea?"

Moses

> Then Moses raised his staff. God parted the waters so that the Israelites could walk through. Huge walls of water rose up on either side of them. They could see fish, swimming in the walls. But the ground beneath them was dry.
>
> They walked all the way through the Red Sea, to the other side. But behind them the Egyptians were still coming. The Egyptians drove their war chariots down into the sea as well.
>
> Then Moses lifted his staff again. The water flooded back over the Egyptians and drowned them all! The Israelites were finally free.

This part of Israel's history is now called the Exodus. The story of the Exodus shows monotheism winning out over polytheism, because the one god of Israel was able to conquer the many gods of Egypt.

The Israelites walked from Egypt all the way back up to Canaan, where Abraham had once lived. They lived in Canaan for many years and became a powerful kingdom in their own right.

The story tells us something else, too. Egypt, which had been powerful for a long time, was once again growing weak. The New Kingdom of Egypt had come close to ruling the world. But now, even a band of slaves without weapons could escape from the clutches of the Egyptian army.

Egypt was losing its strength once again.

Chapter Sixteen
The Early Greeks

The Mycenaeans

Do you remember the gigantic eruption of the volcano on Thera? That explosion brought an end to the power of the Minoans who lived on Crete. For many years, Crete was covered with dust and ash. Crops failed. Cows and sheep died.

The Minoans had been a great nation—but after Thera erupted, they were just ragged people trying to find enough food to stay alive.

Slowly, the ash and rock began to wash away from the fields and streams. Crops began to grow again. It was too late for the Minoans, though. The volcano had already destroyed their country and their way of life.

Soon, strangers landed on the shores of Crete. They were the Mycenaeans, and they came from the city of Mycenae, in Greece. Greece is the land just north of Crete. It juts out into the Mediterranean Sea like a set of many fingers, surrounded by small islands.

The Mycenaeans knew that Crete was now weak. They knew that they could conquer the island easily. And they wanted to own Crete for themselves. So they took over the whole island of Crete and settled there.

Now the Mycenaeans owned both their own city and the island of Crete. They learned how to build ships from the Minoans who stayed in Crete. They used these ships to sail to other islands. On each island, the Mycenaeans built a city called a *colony*. All of these cities were controlled by the Mycenaean king and his army.

Soon the Mycenaeans had colonies all around the Aegean Sea.

The Mycenaeans weren't the only people who lived in Greece. Other Greeks lived in the cities of Thebes and Athens. But the Mycenaeans had stronger weapons than the other Greeks. They made spear tips and sword blades from bronze. They learned how to use shields to protect themselves during battles. And they hammered out helmets from bronze, and lined them with fur and cloth to protect their heads from enemy swords.

The Mycenaeans were also the first Greeks to use horses in battle. Before this, soldiers had always fought on foot. But the Mycenaeans began to hitch horses to war chariots. They drove these chariots into battle. Enemy soldiers ran when they saw the warhorses and chariots charging straight at them!

With their armor, bronze weapons, and chariots, the Mycenaeans dominated the Aegean Sea and the islands in it. They were the first great Greek civilization.

The Greek Dark Ages

The Mycenaean Greeks were great fighters because they had bronze weapons and armor, and chariots that they could drive into battle. They spread their power all around the Aegean Sea because they were good at shipbuilding and sailing.

Greek Cities

They ruled their city and their colonies for several hundred years.

But the Mycenaean Greeks were facing disaster—although they didn't know it yet.

All around them, tribes of barbarians were also learning how to use bronze weapons and chariots. "Barbarian" wasn't a nice name! It was an insult. You see, the early Greeks thought of themselves as very civilized people. They lived in nice houses, made of stone or wood. They had their own kitchens and bathrooms. Greek women stayed home most of the day, supervising the household slaves who did most of the housework and cooking. Some Greek men worked as storekeepers, farmers, or fishermen. Others were craftsmen—they spent their time weaving cloth, creating pottery, or making other things for use in everyday life. Greek children went to school, or had tutors. They lived settled, ordinary lives.

But barbarians didn't have houses of their own or regular jobs. They couldn't read or write. They spoke strange, unfamiliar languages; the Greeks thought that these languages sounded like nonsense. (That's where we get the word *barbarian*—the Greeks thought that the newcomers sounded as if they were saying *bar-bar-bar-bar-bar!*)

These barbarians spent their time wandering around from country to country, attacking the people who lived there and trying to take over. The Mycenaean Greeks thought that the barbarians were ignorant, smelly, and uncivilized. They knew that Greek weapons and chariots were the strongest around. They figured that they could protect themselves from any barbarian attack.

But they were wrong.

The barbarian tribes who lived around the Aegean Sea discovered how to make weapons out of iron. These iron weapons were even stronger than the bronze weapons of the Greeks. The tribes learned how to use bows and arrows, and how to throw javelins. Now, the barbarians could kill the drivers of Greek chariots from a long distance away—before the Greeks could even get close enough to fight them. Some barbarians even learned how to build warships, so that they could attack the Mycenaean Greeks from the sea. These seafaring barbarians were called the Sea People. (Some of them settled in Canaan, and became known as the Philistines.)

The Greeks tried to fight off the barbarians. They built stronger and stronger walls around their cities. These walls were so strong and so big that we can still see them today.

But no matter how many walls the Mycenaean Greeks built, they couldn't keep the barbarians out.

The Sea People invaded them from the water. Other barbarians called Dorians came streaming down from the north. Greek cities were burned and destroyed. Greek armies were defeated. The Greeks fled away from these savage tribes. And soon the only people living in Greece were the barbarians.

For hundreds of years, the barbarians lived in Greece. But these tribes were a little bit like a bully who spends so much time fighting that he never gets his homework finished. They put so much energy into battles that they never learned how to read or write. They didn't leave us any written records of their lives. The only thing they left behind them were ruined cities. And so we know very little about Greece during the time that the Sea People and the Dorians lived there.

This time in Greece is called the Greek Dark Ages—because the history of the Dorians and the Sea People is almost completely unknown, or "dark," to us today.

Note: The Mycenaeans settled in Crete around 1450 BC/BCE. The Greek "Dark Ages" stretched from around 1200 to around 800 BC/BCE.

Chapter Seventeen
The Phoenicians

Phoenician Traders

When the Israelites walked from Egypt back up to Canaan, they weren't moving into an empty country. There were already people living in Canaan!

The people who lived up in the north of Canaan were called Phoenicians, and they were the greatest sailors in the ancient world. The northern part of Canaan wasn't a very good place to grow wheat, because it was rocky and sandy and dry. It wasn't a good place to raise animals, because there wasn't enough grass or water to make them fat and healthy. And it was hard to get into or out of—it was surrounded by steep craggy hills.

So the Phoenicians pushed their boats out onto the water and sailed around the Mediterranean Sea. They became traders. They cut down the tall cedar trees that grew in their homeland and floated the logs to other countries. They built beautiful furniture and sold it for a high price. They sold salt and dried fish and embroidered cloth. And they sailed around the coast of the Mediterranean and found the best places to dig up tin and other metals.

But the Phoenicians were best known for their glass.

Ancient glassmaking was a long, complicated process. First, the Phoenicians made a special chemical called *lye*

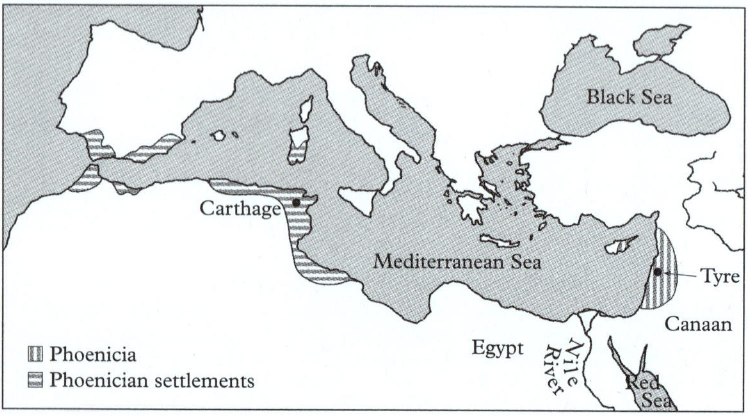

Phoenicia and Its Settlements

by pouring water over the ashes from a wood fire and collecting the liquid that oozed out. They mixed this lye with pure sand and melted the sand-lye mixture over a hot, hot fire. To get the fire hot enough to melt sand, slaves probably had to fan the fire with special pumps called *bellows* for hours and hours.

Once they had melted the sand and lye together, the Phoenicians would pour the mixture into special molds. When the sand-lye mixture cooled, it was hard, shiny glass. Sometimes the Phoenicians colored the glass by putting red, blue, and yellow dyes into it, or wound colored threads around the molds so that the finished glass had a pattern of threads all through it. Sometimes the glass even had gold and jewels in it.

Other ancient peoples made glass too. But the Phoenicians were the first glassmakers to invent *glassblowing*.

Have you ever blown bubbles in your milk through a straw? That's exactly what the Phoenicians did with their hot liquid glass. Instead of pouring the glass into a mold, a Phoenician glassmaker would dip a hollow pipe made out of thin metal into the sticky melted glass. Some of the glass would cling to the end of the pipe in a glob. Then the glassmaker would blow very gently through the pipe. The glass at the other end would puff out into a big round bubble. As long as the glass was still soft, the glassmaker could stretch it out so that bubble was long and thin, or twist it into different shapes. Finally, the glassmaker would cool the glass and break it carefully off the pipe. Blown glass was the most beautiful and expensive kind of ancient glass. All around the Mediterranean Sea, people were happy to pay the Phoenicians for this blown glass.

The Phoenicians were also known for making a beautiful purple dye out of snails. They collected snails, called *murex*, from the sea and boiled them with salt water and lemon juice for ten days. The boiling snails smelled awful. As a matter of fact, Phoenician cities like Tyre were famous for their stench—caused by the dye-factories that were boiling snails. "You stink like a man from Tyre" was a favorite insult in ancient times!

When the dye was finished, the Phoenicians dipped wool into it. The dye turned the wool a dark, beautiful purple. It took so many snails to make purple dye that the cloth made from purple wool was expensive. Sometimes it cost a whole year's pay to buy a purple cloak. So purple was often called "the color of kings" because only kings could afford to wear it.

The Founding of Carthage

The Phoenicians sailed all around the Mediterranean Sea. And they started *colonies*—little settlements of Phoenician people—in many of the places where they landed. One of the most famous cities was Tyre, over in Canaan. Another was Carthage, all the way over in North Africa.

Carthage was first settled around 814 BC/BCE. At first, Carthage was just a tiny village. But soon it grew to be a huge, busy city where merchants from all different countries came to trade their goods.

We don't know the names of the first Phoenicians who settled in Carthage. But later, a great writer named Virgil told this famous story about the beginnings of the city of Carthage:

DIDO WAS A PHOENICIAN PRINCESS, THE sister of the king of Tyre. She was a fortunate woman—she was married to a very rich man, and she lived in a luxurious palace.

But Dido's brother, the king, was jealous of her and of her husband's wealth. He wanted all that money for himself! So the king had Dido's husband arrested and put to death.

Dido was terrified. Would she be next? She gathered together all of her friends and left Tyre in the middle of the night. They pushed away from the shore in a boat and sailed away, never to return.

Dido and her friends traveled and traveled. Finally, they spotted land.

"Let's go ashore here, and build a new city!" Dido urged her friends. They agreed, but when they reached the place where Dido wanted to settle, they found that the land was already settled.

"We should go somewhere else," Dido's friends said. But Dido was determined to build her new city on that very spot. She wanted to live close to the water, so that ships would visit her new city and trade with her.

So she said to the owner of the land, "Will you sell me as much land as I can cover with the skin of a bull?"

"Of course!" the owner agreed. He thought that Dido would put her bull hide down over a little patch of ground, just large enough to stand on. But instead, Dido got out a very sharp knife and cut her bull hide into hundreds of long, thin strips. She laid the strips out, end to end, around a huge portion of land.

"There!" she said. "Now keep your promise and sell me this ground."

The owner of the land was forced to agree. So Dido and her friends built a tower on the ground and named their tower "Bull's Hide." They settled around the tower and named their city Carthage. Soon, ships from all over the world came to Carthage to buy and sell their goods. The city bought with a bull's skin became one of the most powerful in the world.

Note: The Phoenician civilization was at its height between 1200–700 BC/BCE.

Chapter Eighteen
The Return of Assyria

Ashurbanipal's Attack

Do you remember reading about Shamshi-Adad, the Assyrian king who wanted to rule the whole world? He led his armies out to conquer the cities all around him, and he built an empire—the Assyrian Empire.

But when they fought the Babylonians, the Assyrians lost. They became part of Babylon's empire, and had to obey the king of Babylon. But all the time they were thinking, "One day we will be free, and we will try to conquer the world again!"

Finally, that day came. The Assyrians rebelled against their masters, the Babylonians. They conquered the Babylonian soldiers. They dug canals through the city of Babylon and flooded it with water, washing the city away.

And then they started out to rebuild their empire. "We are like an evil rain that washes its enemies away!" they boasted. "We are like a net that tangles the feet of those who fight against us!"

The Assyrians raged up and down the Tigris and Euphrates rivers, taking over every city in their path. They stampeded over to Canaan and scattered the Israelites like dust; the Israelites were never allowed to return to their own land again. They marched up into Asia Minor and forced

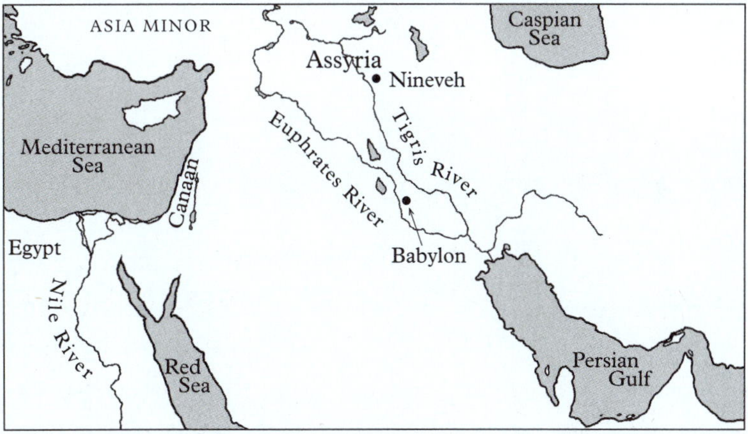

The Spread of Ashurbanipal's Empire

the people there to obey them. And one of the greatest Assyrian kings of all, Ashurbanipal, led his soldiers all the way down into Egypt—and took it over! After that, even the mighty pharaohs of Egypt had to obey Assyria.

Ashurbanipal became king of Assyria around 668 BC/BCE—over a thousand years after Shamshi-Adad first declared himself to be the King of the World. Ashurbanipal terrified his enemies. For fun, he went on lion hunts, chasing the lions down on horseback and shooting arrows at them. And when he led his soldiers into battle, he fought like an angry lion himself. With Ashurbanipal leading them, the Assyrians were almost impossible to beat.

Why were they so hard to conquer? The Assyrian soldiers fought in pairs. One man would hold a shield made out of baskets, tied together with leather. The other would shoot arrows from behind the shield. These basket shields were very light—but they kept arrows and spearpoints out. The Assyrians would put their basket shields side by side and march towards their enemies, like a moving wall

Ashurbanipal, the king who was as strong as a lion

with arrows spitting out from behind it.

Soon, the only way to escape the invading Assyrians was to hide inside a city with strong brick or stone walls. But Ashurbanipal, the king who was as strong as a lion, knew how to get over city walls. First, he ordered his soldiers to build a ramp out of dirt. They hauled buckets of earth up to a city's wall, holding their basket shields over their heads to protect themselves. They dumped the earth into a heap against the wall and went back for more. Slowly, the heap grew larger and larger until it reached all the way up to the top of the wall.

Then Ashurbanipal commanded his men to build a *siege tower*—a wooden tower on wheels. The soldiers pushed the tower up the ramp, towards the city walls. On top of the tower, Assyrian archers fired arrows into the city. A battering ram jutted out of the tower's front. The soldiers pushed it right into the wall, breaking up the brick and stone. Soon, a section of the wall tottered and fell. The Assyrian army poured through the gap, into the city. Another city had fallen to Ashurbanipal and his army.

Ashurbanipal was cruel and ruthless to the cities he conquered. He burned houses, smashed walls, and killed anyone who tried to disobey him. He scattered salt in their fields, poisoning the land so that no crops would grow.

He took captured people off to be slaves and never let them go home again. Most cities were too frightened to resist Ashurbanipal for long. They agreed to become part of the Assyrian Empire and to pay part of their money to the Assyrian king.

Ashurbanipal became very rich. He ruled the biggest empire that the world had ever seen. But all across Assyria, people hated him. The cities conquered by Ashurbanipal obeyed him because they were afraid, but all the time they hoped that Assyria would soon collapse. "When we finally hear the news of your destruction," one conquered man wrote, "we will clap our hands with joy! And no one will cry over you."

The Library of Nineveh

Ashurbanipal, the king of all Assyria, stood on his palace walls looking out over the city of Nineveh. He had spent years making Nineveh beautiful. It was his favorite city, and he was the strongest king in the world! He had built himself a magnificent palace, full of high, cool rooms hung with silk and painted with rich colors: royal blue, scarlet, and yellow as bright as the sun. The fifteen great gates of Nineveh's walls had been decorated with sculptures of bulls and lions and edged with gold. Carved pictures of Ashurbanipal's conquests lined the walls of Nineveh's greatest buildings. Canals brought water into the city, so that all Nineveh's people could drink; and throughout Nineveh, Ashurbanipal had planted gardens of strange and beautiful plants, so that his subjects could wander through green grass and admire the trees and flowers from far away.

Here is a story about what Ashurbanipal did next.

"I HAVE MADE THIS CITY OF NINEVEH BEAUTIFUL and strong," Ashurbanipal thought to himself. "But it isn't enough! How do I know that it will last after I am dead? A hundred years from now, how will anyone know of my greatness?"

"Excuse me, sir." A voice interrupted him.

He turned to see one of his chief scribes, holding a clay tablet. The scribe held the tablet out. Ashurbanipal saw that it was covered with writing.

"Have you brought me a new book to read?" he asked. Ashurbanipal's scribes, the men who were in charge of writing down all the events of his reign, knew that he loved to read. They were always on the lookout for new books for him. And in those days, books weren't written on paper. They were carved into clay.

"We've found you a wonderful book!" the chief scribe said. "It's a tale from the court of Hammurabi, the great king who ruled Babylon so long ago. No one has ever read it before! One of your men found it in the ruins of Babylon's old walls, and kept it safe until we could bring it here to you."

Ashurbanipal glanced down at the tablet. This was indeed a find—a story from the days of a famous king of old. Now he could look forward to a good long evening of reading.

That night, as Ashurbanipal sat in his room reading his new tablet by lamplight, he had an idea.

"How many of these tablets are left in the ruins of old cities?" he said to himself. "If they are not rescued, they will crumble away into dust. Then we'll never know these stories from old times. What if I were to collect them all together, and keep them here in my palace? That would be a great project indeed! And then I would become known as the king who collected books—and people could read my books hundreds of years from now."

Ashurbanipal set his new idea into action at once. He sent his scribes out into all parts of the vast kingdom of Assyria, ordering them to collect all the tablets they could find and bring them back to Nineveh. He commanded other scribes to go out and ask the people of Assyria to repeat the stories they had heard from their grandfathers and grandmothers. These stories had been told to children for centuries—but no one had ever written them down. Ashurbanipal's scribes wrote them on clay tablets, so that they could be kept forever.

He ordered the priests of Assyria to write down the words of their prayers. The court astrologers wrote down the movements of the sun, moon, and stars. The court doctors wrote down everything that they knew about illness and medicine. The court historians recorded all of the details of Ashurbanipal's reign, and everything that they knew about the kings who had come before him.

All of those clay tablets were thick and heavy. So Ashurbanipal built more and more rooms to

> keep them in. Soon he had collected thousands and thousands of clay tablets full of stories, prayers, instructions, history, science, medicine, and law. He had created the first library in the world.

And Ashurbanipal's wish came true. Although many of the tablets were destroyed in Assyria's wars with other countries, some of them still survive today, thousands of years later. They can still be read. And because we have Ashurbanipal's clay tablets, we remember him as the king who collected books—the first librarian ever.

Note: Assyria's expansion took place between 1300–1200 BC/BCE; it reached its greatest extent under Sargon II (721–705 BC/BCE). Ashurbanipal, the last great Assyrian king, ruled 668–627 BC/BCE.

History-Maker

The Story of Shammuramat, Warrior Queen of Assyria

Just as the Assyrian Empire was once again gathering itself to rule the world, Assyria had its very first queen.

Her name was Shammuramat.

As a young princess, Shammuramat married the Assyrian king Shamshi-Adad V. Shamshi-Adad V was the fifth Assyrian king to have the name Shamshi-Adad. (The V stands for "five" in the old Roman writing.) He claimed to be a distant descendant of the first Shamshi-Adad, who had long ago declared himself to be the "King of the World"—but Shamshi-Adad V was not nearly as great as his long-ago predecessor. In fact, after he and Shammuramat had several sons together, Shamshi-Adad V died without carrying out any famous deeds or amazing accomplishments.

He left Assyria to his son Adad-Nirari. Adad-Nirari was a very young man, but he was still considered to be a grown-up. He could have ruled Assyria all on his own.

But his mother Shammuramat had a different idea.

While her husband was alive, Shammuramat had been queen of Assyria. That didn't mean she had any power, though. Back in those days, women almost never had power to rule a country. This was especially true in Assyria, which was an empire of strong warriors. No woman had ever held power in Assyria—only men. Being the "queen of Assyria" just meant that Shammuramat was the wife of the king. She could have anything she wanted to eat, or wear. She could have beautiful rooms to live in, and servants to do errands for her. But she couldn't rule the country.

Now, Shammuramat decided to change that.

She wanted to help run the empire. She had ideas about how to keep all of Assyria's conquered cities loyal to the Assyrian throne. She was a strong, energetic woman who liked to ride and even fight—even though Assyrian women were never taught how to be warriors.

So for the next twenty years, Shammuramat ruled Assyria alongside her son. She helped him make laws for the country. She helped him decide how to spend money. She even rode out into battle with him! Together, they defeated rebels who tried to reject Assyrian rule. At the site of one of their victories, Adad-Nirari put up a stone memorial honoring the victory of "Adad-Nirari, king of Assyria, and of Shammuramat, queen of Shamshi-Adad, mother of Adad-Nirari." Shammuramat is the only Assyrian woman who ever got a victory stone telling about her strength as a warrior. (You can still see this stone at the museum in the city of Kahramanmaraş, in the modern country of Turkey.)

Shammuramat, Queen of Assyria

The Assyrians had never had a queen like Shammuramat. They didn't know how a woman could become so powerful. In fact, they started to make up stories about Shammuramat. A Greek historian named Diodorus wrote down many of these stories, hundreds of years later—because the stories about Shammuramat had been passed down through all of those years! Diodorus tells us that Shammuramat was the daughter of a fish-goddess. She was raised by doves, who fed her as a baby with cheese stolen from nearby shepherds and kept her warm with their wings. She invented a whole new kind of pants that could be worn into battle by both men *and* women. She built two enormous palaces at Babylon in only seven days. She dug out a whole new river to keep her people from becoming thirsty. And she marched into India and conquered an Indian army made up of wild elephants.

Of course, none of those things really happened. But when a woman or a man is very strong or very courageous, the people around them sometimes invent explanations to make sense of just *why* the heroine, or hero, is so different. The stories about Shammuramat don't tell us very much about who Shammuramat really *was*. But they do tell us that she was one of the most unusual Assyrian women who ever lived.

The legends about Shammuramat lived on. Many, many centuries later, playwrights and composers were still telling stories about Shammuramat. They used the Greek version of her name, Semiramis, and they wrote plays and novels and operas about her. Those plays and operas are still performed today!

Chapter Nineteen
Greece Gets Civilized Again

Greece Gets an Alphabet

For hundreds of years, Greece had been full of barbarians.

Do you remember those barbarians? They were the Dorians from up north, and the Sea People (also called the Philistines) who invaded Greece from the Mediterranean Sea. These people drove away or conquered the Mycenaean Greeks. The barbarians couldn't read or write. They weren't used to living in cities. Greek civilization had entered a "Dark Age"—and we don't know what happened during all of those years.

But something strange began to happen. The longer these barbarians lived in Greece, the more civilized they became. They were no longer wandering around looking for cities to attack. Instead, they settled into villages. They started to learn how to farm and fish. They were becoming less and less barbarian, and more and more Greek.

The Dorians and the Sea People lived in Greece for hundreds of years. They looked less and less like wild warrior tribes, and more and more like civilized merchants, farmers, and storekeepers. They started building fancier and fancier houses. Those houses had kitchens, rooms for taking baths, and separate rooms for men and women to entertain their friends. The villages where these houses were built grew even larger, into cities—each one with its own government and its own army.

The people in the cities learned how to grow olives, grapes, figs, and wheat and how to make wine from the grapes. Instead of riding out to kill their neighbors, they learned how to enjoy civilized sports like wrestling, chariot racing, and horseback riding. They loved to dance—at weddings, at funerals, at feasts, and at sports events. As a matter of fact, they soon invented over two hundred dances to use on all occasions.

The women no longer went out foraging for food, and they certainly didn't spend their time putting up tents, washing, and cooking like barbarian women. Instead, they spent their time indoors, away from the sun, so that their skin would remain pale and beautiful. They kept slaves to do all the hard work.

Now these barbarians were known, simply, as Greeks.

We know about these early Greeks because they soon learned how to read and write. They started to write down stories about their ancestors. They started to write down the myths and fairy tales that they told their children. And we still have some of this writing today.

The early Greeks didn't use the same alphabet that we use. They used their own letters. They probably learned some of these letters from the Phoenicians, who had one of the first alphabets. Here are some Greek letters:

α

This is called an *alpha*. If you think it looks like an *a*, you're right. It sounds like an *a* too. The alphabet that we use today borrowed many of its letters from the ancient Greeks. Here is a *kappa*, a Greek letter that makes the same sound as our *k*:

κ

Here is a *tau*, a Greek letter that makes the *t* sound:

τ

And here is a Greek *beta*, a letter that makes the *b* sound:

β

Our alphabet is named after the Greek letters *alpha* and *beta*. Can you hear the letters *alpha* and *beta* in the word alphabet?

Other Greek letters don't look anything like our letters. Here is a Greek letter called a *psi*. It makes the sound "ps"—that's a sound we don't use in English.

Ψ

The *psi* looks a little bit like a trident, a three-pronged weapon carried by the Greek god Poseidon, who lived in the sea. The letter is named after Poseidon too. Can you hear the *psi* sound in Poseidon's name?

Here is one more Greek letter. It is called a *theta*, and it makes the sound that our letters "th" make when you say them together:

θ

Even though some of the Greek letters are different from ours, we owe a lot of our alphabet to the Greeks. If you have an *a*, *b*, *e*, *h*, *i*, *k*, *m*, *n*, *o*, *p*, *t*, *x*, *y*, or *z* in your name, you are using a Greek letter whenever you write your name.

How would your name sound if the Greeks had never invented these letters?

The Stories of Homer

When the Greeks began to learn how to read and write, one of them decided to write down the old Greek stories that had been told out loud around Greek fires for years and years. His name was Homer, and he was the first great Greek writer. Tradition tells us that Homer was blind—so he listened to the stories he heard, and then told them to a scribe, who wrote them down using the Greek alphabet.

Homer told the story of a famous war—the Greek attack on the city of Troy. This war was called the Trojan War, and Homer describes it in his long poem, the *Iliad*. After he finished the *Iliad*, he composed another story, called the *Odyssey*. The *Odyssey* was about Odysseus, a Greek warrior who fought in the Trojan War. When Odysseus started to sail back home, he ran into all kinds of trouble!

Here is one of the stories from the *Odyssey*:

ODYSSEUS AND HIS MEN SAILED AWAY FROM Troy, looking forward to their return home. They praised all the gods of Greece for keeping them alive through the war. And they thanked the gods for their victory.

But they forgot to thank Poseidon, the god of the sea.

Poseidon was furious at being left out. He sent a strong wind to blow the ships off course, so that Odysseus would have a hard time getting home.

Odysseus and his men got lost, out there on the sea. After many days of sailing, Odysseus and his tired, hungry sailors saw a beautiful island. It was cool and shady, full of wheat and grapevines and wild goats that could be killed for food. So they landed their ships on the beach, got out their bows and arrows, and hunted. When they had killed enough meat, they lit fires, roasted the goats, and feasted. And the next morning, when the dawn lit the sky red, they got up to explore.

Around the other side of the island, Odysseus and his men found a huge cave, carved into a cliff. Laurel trees grew all around it. In front of the cave was a pen, walled with stone and filled with hundreds of sheep and goats.

"Who lives here?" Odysseus asked. "Let's go in and find out."

He took with him his twelve strongest men, along with a jug of sweet wine for a present. The rest of his men he sent back to the ships.

Odysseus and his twelve companions came up to the cave and peered in—but they could see no one. Carefully, they crept in. There they found pens of lambs and baby goats. The walls were lined with racks of cheeses, each cheese bigger than a man's head. Beneath them sat the bowls into which the cave's owner milked his goats, each bowl large enough for a man to lie down in.

When they saw this, Odysseus's men were terrified. "A giant lives here!" they said. "Let's take some cheese and some of the lambs, and get back to the ship before he returns!"

But Odysseus refused to run away. "We'll wait here and greet him when he returns!" he said.

So the men cut up some cheese and ate it for their dinners, after offering some of it to the gods as a sacrifice. They waited. Dark fell over the island.

And when it was completely dark, they heard footsteps, each one shaking the ground.

In through the door came the cave's owner. He was a giant, as tall as three men standing on each other's shoulders. He had only one eye, right in the center of his forehead. He was a Cyclops!

The Cyclops was herding his sheep in front of him. He carried over his shoulder three or four trees that he had pulled up for firewood. He flung them onto the floor of the cave with such noise that Odysseus and his men hid themselves in fright. When all the sheep were inside the cave, the Cyclops rolled a huge stone across the cave's entrance—a stone so heavy that twenty men couldn't have shifted it aside.

He milked his sheep and goats and got up to light his fire. When the flames roared up, the Cyclops saw Odysseus and his men, hiding at the far end of the cave.

"Well," he roared, "what do we have here? Robbers? Have you crept into my cave to take my sheep and my cheese?"

"No," Odysseus said, his voice shaking with fright. "We are merely travelers on our way home. Please, show us some kindness and hospitality—we are hungry and cold!"

"If you are travelers," the Cyclops said, "where is your ship?"

But Odysseus was afraid that the Cyclops might want to find the ship and destroy it. So he lied: "We were shipwrecked on your island," he said, "and our ship is destroyed."

Odysseus and the Cyclops

The Cyclops didn't answer. Instead, he snatched up two of Odysseus's men and ate them on the spot. And then he washed down his horrible meal with goat's milk, lay down on the floor, and went to sleep.

"Let's kill him while he sleeps!" Odysseus's men urged him.

But Odysseus refused. "If we kill him," he said, "who will let us out of the cave? That stone is too heavy for us to move. We would die in here!"

So Odysseus and his men spent the night huddled at the back of the cave, listening to the Cyclops snore as loud as thunder.

The Cyclops slept all night. When the red dawn came, he woke up, lit his fire, milked the goats, and grabbed two more of Odysseus's men for breakfast. After he ate them and drank some more milk, he pushed the stone away from the entrance to the cave and drove the sheep out. But before Odysseus and his men could dash out of the cave, the Cyclops rolled the stone back again, as easy as putting a lid on a jar.

Odysseus's men were terrified, moaning and crying. But Odysseus paced up and down the cave and thought hard. Finally he went to the pile of trees that the Cyclops had brought in for firewood. Several of them still lay beside the sheep pen, where the Cyclops had dropped them. One of the trees there was tall and green.

"Come on," Odysseus said to his men. "Be brave! Do what I say, and we'll escape. Let's cut a long piece off the end of this tree, about as long as a man is tall, and sharpen it. Don't ask why. Just do what I say."

The men cut the tree and sharpened it, and then Odysseus burned the sharp point in the coals of the fire until it was hard and black. He hid it underneath a pile of straw. And then he and his men waited, all day long, for the Cyclops to come back.

When the monster came back into the cave that evening, he drove his sheep and goats in, and again sealed up the door with the huge stone. He grabbed two more of the men and ate them, washing them down with goat's milk. And then Odysseus took his courage in both hands and went forward.

"Cyclops!" he said. "You've eaten so many of my men that you must be thirsty. Milk won't help that thirst! Here, I've got a jug of the best sweet wine you've ever tasted."

He held up the jug of wine that he had brought into the cave, and the Cyclops sniffed at it. It smelled so good that he drank a mouthful, and then another, and then another. Soon the whole jug of wine was gone. And the Cyclops was very sleepy.

"What's your name?" he growled. "Who's giving me this wonderful stuff to drink?"

"My name is Noman," Odysseus said.

"Noman, I'm pleased with your wine," the Cyclops answered. "So I'll eat you last!" And with that he sprawled over and went to sleep, right there on the ground.

Then Odysseus and four of his men dragged out the sharpened log they had hidden in the straw, and drove it right into the single eye of the Cyclops.

The Cyclops leaped up and roared with pain. He stumbled all around his cave, grabbing blindly for Odysseus and his men. But they got easily away from him, because he could no longer see them.

Soon, Odysseus and his men heard other footsteps outside the cave. The friends and neighbors of the Cyclops had come to find out what all the noise was about.

"Why are you making so much noise?" they called to the Cyclops. "You're keeping us from sleeping! Is someone attacking you?"

"Noman!" the Cyclops yelled. "Noman is trying to kill me!"

"No man?" the other monsters answered. "Well, then, go back to sleep!" And they all went away.

The Cyclops, groaning with pain, lay down until morning. Then he got up, feeling his way around with his hands, and rolled the stone away. He started to herd his sheep and goats out of the cave. But he reached down and patted the back of every animal that went past him, so that neither Odysseus nor his men could sneak out with the sheep and goats.

So Odysseus caught three fat sheep for every one of his men, and tied the sheep together in groups of three. He told each one of his men to hold on to the stomach fleece of the sheep in the middle of each group, and to let the sheep carry them out past the Cyclops. The Cyclops put his hands right on the sheep's backs—but he couldn't find the men who were holding on underneath.

When Odysseus and his men had gotten out past the Cyclops, they ran for their ships. The rest of the men saw them coming. Odysseus started to yell, "Pull for the sea! Pull for the sea!" And as soon as they had scrambled aboard, the oarsmen rowed the ships out into the water, safely away from the island of the Cyclops.

Then Odysseus began to shout, "Cyclops! Cyclops! See what happens to you when you eat guests who come to your house? You should have known better than to fall for my tricks!"

The blind Cyclops heard his jeers. In fury, he wrenched a huge boulder off the side of the cliff and threw it towards Odysseus's voice. Waves pushed the ship around, but Odysseus shouted again, "Cyclops, if anyone asks you who put out your eye and spoiled your beauty, tell them that it was Odysseus!"

"Curses on you!" the Cyclops yelled back. "I'm the son of Poseidon, the god of the sea! And I will ask him to send waves and wind that will sink your ship so that you'll never reach home alive!"

Odysseus ignored the threat. He told his men to row for the open water. As soon as they were far away from the island, their sails caught the wind and they headed for home.

But Poseidon heard the request of the Cyclops. He sent winds to blow Odysseus off course, and waves to batter his ship into pieces. It took ten long years and many dangerous adventures before Odysseus finally reached his home.

The First Olympic Games

The Greeks celebrated courage and strength by telling stories about brave, strong people like Odysseus.

They also celebrated courage and strength with a big festival, called the Olympic Games. The bravest and strongest Greeks came to the Olympics to compete for prizes.

The Olympics started when two cities in ancient Greece made peace, after fighting with each other for years and years. To celebrate the peace, they decided to have a festival—a big celebration—in honor of the god Zeus, the chief god of the Greeks. The festival was named after the town of Olympia, which was sacred to Zeus. The Greeks believed that Zeus and the other gods lived on the top of Mount Olympus, but Olympia was Zeus's second home. In fact, a gigantic statue of Zeus, more than forty feet tall and made of gold and ivory, sat in front of Olympia's temple to the chief god. The statue was so beautiful that it was known all over the ancient world!

At the festival, the Greeks feasted and made sacrifices to Zeus. And they also ran races. The winners of the races were given wreaths made out of olive branches to wear on their heads. The olive leaves represented peace.

The Greeks decided that they would get together every four years to have the Olympics, and to run races in honor of Zeus. As time went on, more and more Greeks from different Greek cities came to the Olympic Games. And the Greeks added more kinds of events to their games. Instead of just running races on foot, they started racing horses as well. They held boxing and wrestling matches.

They even invented a competition called the *pentathlon*, where the athletes had to do five different events. The winner had to throw a discus (like a metal Frisbee) and a javelin (a Greek spear) farther than anyone else. He also had to win a long-jump competition, a wrestling match, and a foot race.

But only men were allowed to compete in the Greek Olympics. Girls could watch, but they weren't allowed to race or to do any of the other events. And married women couldn't even watch. They weren't allowed anywhere near the Olympics, on pain of death. That's because the Greeks thought that only men could be truly brave and strong. They thought that the best way to honor the gods was for men to train their bodies to be as graceful and powerful as possible.

The Olympics were held every four years for over a thousand years. People came from all over Greece to compete in the games and to watch the other athletes. They all camped out at the games and spent their evenings feasting and listening to music. Poets would recite poems and stories out loud to entertain the crowds. These poems and stories were like movies to the ancient Greeks. Some of the poets probably told the story of the *Odyssey*. Others told the story of the attack on Troy. And others performed new stories and poems that they had written themselves.

The winners of the races and other competitions were treated like heroes. They were given banquets to honor them. And when they went back home, their own cities rewarded them with money and with free food for the rest of their lives.

Today, the Olympic Games are still held every four years. Hundreds of events take place—wrestling, running, and boxing, just like in ancient times, but also gymnastics, ice skating, soccer, basketball, swimming, and much more. Today, women can compete in the Olympics as well as men. Athletes come from all over the world, not just from Greece.

But the games are still called the Olympics, after Mount Olympus. And they still celebrate strength, grace, and courage—just like they did in the times of the ancient Greeks.

Note: Homer lived around 800 BC/BCE. The traditional date for the first ancient Olympic Games is 776.

Chapter Twenty
Sparta and Athens

Life in Sparta

The Greeks were very different from the other ancient kingdoms you've been reading about—the Assyrians and the Babylonians, the Egyptians and the Chinese. If you lived in Assyria, you obeyed the Assyrian king. If you lived in Egypt, you obeyed the Egyptian pharaoh. If you lived in China, you obeyed the Chinese emperor.

In Greece, though, there was no single king. The Greeks all spoke the same language, dressed the same way, and worshipped the same gods. They all came to the Olympic Games and feasted together. But each Greek city made its own laws. Each Greek city had its own army. And each Greek city had its own way of living.

The Greeks were horrified by the thought of obeying one, single, powerful ruler. They liked their independence.

Athens and Sparta were the two largest Greek cities, but the people of these two cities lived in very different ways. Sparta was ruled by warrior kings, and all Spartan men were required to be soldiers. Boys went to school, but they didn't learn philosophy, art, and music. Instead, when they were seven, they were sent away to special camps where they learned how to be obedient, disciplined fighters. They were taught to exercise so that their bodies would be strong. They were made to march long distances without socks or shoes, so that their feet would be tough. They weren't given very much to eat. And they were never allowed to complain. Spartan boys were expected to be tough and silent.

One story from Spartan times tells of a boy who was away at military camp, learning how to be a soldier. He was so hungry that he stole a live fox from someone else at the camp. He was planning on cooking and eating the fox! But just as he was getting ready to kill the fox, he saw some Spartan soldiers walking over to talk to him. He knew that they would beat him for stealing the fox, so he quickly hid the fox underneath his shirt. The fox immediately started biting him. But rather than admit that he had stolen the fox, the boy stood up and talked to the soldiers without showing any pain—even though the fox was chewing on his stomach. He suffered without showing it until the soldiers went away. All Spartan boys were supposed to be this brave and silent.

When they were twenty, boys had to pass a special test of fitness and bravery. If they passed, they were allowed to join the army. They would stay in the army until they were old men! Even if they got married, they weren't allowed to live with their families. Instead, they lived with the other soldiers in barracks. Boys who didn't pass the test weren't allowed to vote. They could never be full citizens of Sparta.

But what about the girls?

Girls were taught to exercise and be strong too, so that they could be the mothers of more boys who would fight for Sparta. In the ancient world of the Spartans, only fighters were truly important. Just like the Assyrians, the Spartans thought that women were weaker and more timid than men. So the women of Sparta were less important than the men.

Spartan Warrior

Spartan mothers were supposed to praise their sons for warlike behavior, and reward them for bravery. One Spartan mother told her son, who was leaving for battle, "Come back with your shield, or on it!" Since the losers of battles were forced to give up their shields, here's what she was really saying: "Either win the battle, or come back dead!" Spartans would rather die than lose a fight.

Sparta wasn't known for its art or storytelling, but the Spartan army was known and feared all over the world for its bravery and toughness. Today, we still call someone "spartan" if they suffer pain or disappointment without complaining.

Life in Athens

Spartans were expected to obey the warrior king of their city. But the Greeks who lived in Athens had a very different way of doing things.

Everyone who lived in Athens had a say in how the city was run, because Athens was a *democracy*.

That means that whenever a new law was proposed, the people of Athens could *vote* on whether or not it should actually be followed. Each citizen would have the chance to say, "Yes, this is a good law!" or "No, this is not a good law!" If more people voted Yes than voted No, the law would pass.

They also voted on their leaders, on how much tax they should pay, and on whether they should go to war. Whenever it was time for the citizens to vote about something, they would gather in the middle of the city, at a special meeting place called the *Agora*. (Later, the Romans would call this same kind of public meeting place a *forum*.) There, they would argue about whether to vote yes or no. After the arguments, they would make up their minds and then vote.

So that they could understand how to vote properly, the citizens had to be educated. They needed to know why taxes were important, and whether leaders were good or bad. They had to understand the laws of the city. If they were ignorant, they wouldn't be able to argue properly about the government of the city. And they wouldn't be able to make up their minds about how to vote.

So education in Athens looked very different from education in Sparta. The Spartans were expected to obey their king and to fight for him, so they were taught how to be brave, strong, and obedient. But Athenians had to learn about taxes, laws, and government. Athenian boys went to school, just like Spartan boys. But they didn't learn how to fight. Instead, they were taught how to read and how to write on wax tablets. They learned mathematics, so that they could count and add and subtract. They memorized the poetry of Homer. They learned how to play the flute and the lyre (an ancient Greek instrument that looked like a small harp). Like the Spartans, the Athenians were expected to be strong. But they exercised by wrestling and by racing with each other on foot.

Athenian girls were also different from Spartan girls. Athenian girls were taught to be housewives. Some girls learned how to read and write. But all girls learned, from their mothers, how to be *domestic*—how to manage a home, sew, raise a garden, take care of children, and manage slaves. Athenian women weren't allowed to vote. But they were expected to keep their homes running smoothly, while their husbands were away arguing in the Agora and voting about laws and leaders.

One of the most famous men in Athens was named Plato. Plato told the Athenians that a democracy had to have educated people in it! If they are ignorant, he said, people who know more than they do will become tyrants and tell them what to do.

Athenian philosopher Plato

Was Plato right?

Well, let's think about this. Imagine that you've never been taught anything about stealing or about ownership. You don't know that people have a right to own things and to keep them. And no one has ever told you what stealing is. You're completely ignorant.

Now imagine that you're on your way to the store with five dollars to buy a LEGO set. Along comes your neighbor.

She's bigger and older than you are, and she decides that she'd really like to have that five dollars.

"Hey!" she says. "Don't you know that it's Wednesday?"

"Why is that important?" you say.

"Well," she says, "on Wednesday, all smaller children are supposed to give their money away to larger children. It's a law! If you don't give me your money, you'll be breaking the law and you'll go to jail."

You want to do the right thing. And no one ever taught you that there was no such law! So you hand over your money, and your neighbor walks off with it.

That's just what Plato meant when he said that ignorant people will always obey tyrants. If you don't know what the law is, anyone can tell you what to do.

The Athenians didn't want tyrants to be in charge. So they were careful to educate themselves and their children. The Spartans wanted to be strong and victorious, but the Athenians wanted to be wise and educated. These two Greek cities were very different.

Note: The Greek city-states began to arise in the mid 800s BC/BCE. The Athenian and Spartan lifestyles described here date from the 400s.

History-Makers

The Story of Draco and Solon, The Two Lawgivers of Athens

THE PEOPLE OF ATHENS HAD A PROBLEM! Even though they voted for their laws, most of those laws were not written down. Once the laws were passed, they were memorized and then repeated *orally* (by person talking to person). And as the years went by, many, many, many laws were passed—too many for any one person to remember.

That meant that the rich and powerful men in Athens could take advantage of those who were poorer and weaker. They could misquote a law and take someone else's land. They could argue that the penalty for a crime was a heavy fine that had to be paid over to them. They could even make up a law and insist that it had been passed—even if that law had never existed.

The poorer people of Athens became more and more unhappy. Soon, they began to complain. They gathered in huge unruly mobs and insisted that there was only one way to make Athens a fair place to live. All of those laws needed to be written down. One Athenian, a poet named Euripides, said, "Only when laws are written can the weak and the wealthy be equal!"

Remember, the Athenians voted for their leaders as well as for their laws. So they gathered together and elected a man named Draco to be the one who took on the massive job of putting all those laws into writing.

Draco finished his task around the time of the Thirty-Ninth Olympic Games. Finally, Athens had a written law code. The Athenians gathered together once more—but this time they cheered! They were delighted to finally have written laws. Now, everyone, no matter how strong or weak, could know exactly what was right and what was wrong.

But then, they started to read through the laws.

Draco had written each law down with great accuracy. But what surprised all of Athens were the punishments for breaking each law.

Murder? The punishment was death.

Treason? Death.

Begging on the streets? Death.

Not working hard enough? Death.

Stealing a cabbage? Death.

You see, Draco had very strong ideas about what should happen when a law was broken! He told the Athenians, "Even the smallest of crimes deserves death. And there is no greater penalty than death for the bigger crimes."

The Athenians were furious over the harshness of these new laws. They began to hurl stones and bricks at Draco until he fled the city of Athens! He had to hide on a nearby island—which he never left again.

Another Athenian stepped forward to try to fix the mess that Draco had left behind. He was a young merchant named Solon. Solon believed that if laws were carefully written, people would *want* to follow them.

Solon worked hard and owned his own business, but he wasn't a very rich man who could get richer by cheating the poor, and he wasn't a very poor man who resented the rich. So both rich and poor Athenians agreed to elect Solon to rewrite Draco's laws.

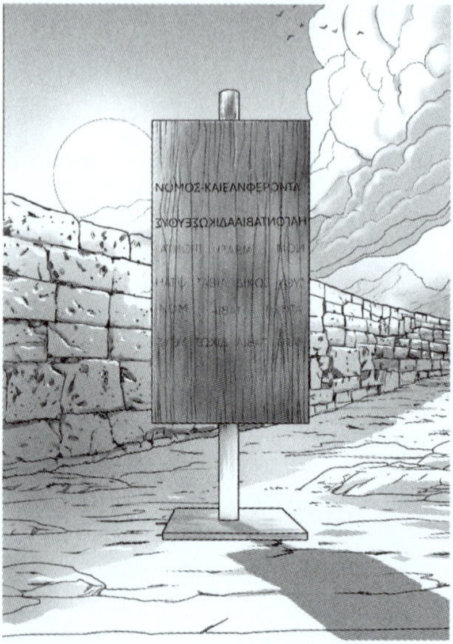

Solon's laws were carved on wooden posts. The letters were carved from left to right, and then backwards from right to left

Solon *revoked* (got rid of) all of Draco's laws except for the law that said murderers would be put to death. He rewrote all of the Athenian laws in order to protect the poor and to keep the rich from grabbing land and money for themselves.

One of Solon's friends warned him that these new laws wouldn't work. "Your laws are like spiderwebs," he told Solon. "The poor will get caught in them, and the powerful will tear them to shreds."

But Solon was sure that the people of Athens would understand and accept his laws. When he finished his task, he had the laws carved on wooden pillars and set up all around Athens. Then he announced that he would leave the city of Athens and travel the world for ten years. He thought that if he stayed in Athens, he would continually be asked to make changes to the laws, or explain them, or defend them. He wanted the laws to stand on their own.

Can you guess what happened?

The laws failed! The Athenians were no happier with Solon's laws than they had been with Draco's. Soon, Athens was in turmoil again.

Meanwhile, Solon visited Egypt, Phoenicia, and many other countries. One of his biographers, the Greek writer Plutarch, says that Solon and Aesop (the author of Aesop's fables), had a long and enjoyable visit!

When Solon returned to Athens, he was horrified to see all of the chaos and unrest. But he refused to try again to reform the laws. "I have done all I can to help my city," he told his friends, and he retired to live the rest of his life quietly in his own home, writing poetry.

Draco and Solon were very different men. Solon thought that women and men would be happy to obey good laws. Draco believed that they would not obey unless they were threatened with death! His punishments were so severe that even today, we call a horrible punishment for a small crime "draconian."

But for hundreds of years afterwards, the Greeks would speak in the same breath of "the great lawgivers Draco and Solon."

Note: Draco's laws were first published in 622-621 BC/BCE, during the Thirty-Ninth Olympiad. Solon's laws were completed c. 600 BC/BCE.

Chapter Twenty-One
The Greek Gods

The Golden Apple

The ancient Greeks may have lived in very different ways, but they all spoke the same language—Greek. And they all worshipped the same gods. The Greeks were polytheists. Remember: Polytheists believe in many gods. Monotheists, like the Jews, only believe in one god.

The Greeks believed in a whole family of gods. They thought that these gods lived up on the top of Mount Olympus, the highest mountain in Greece. And they also thought that the gods were very interested in what men were doing.

Sometimes the Greek gods were kind and helpful to men. But at other times, they were cruel. As a matter of fact, the chief god of the Greeks, Zeus, started a horrible war down on earth.

Here is the story that the Greeks told about Zeus and the beginning of that war.

Zeus sat on the top of Mount Olympus and looked down over Greece. All over the countryside, he could see men, swarming like ants. Men cutting down trees, men building houses all over the beautiful green fields, men pulling fish out of the sea. Men killing deer for food, shooting birds for fun, and blocking up streams for water.

Zeus sighed.

Zeus

"There are too many people on the earth," he said gloomily. "I should get rid of some of them."

He thought and thought. And finally he came up with a plan. He knew that the gods were all going to a big wedding, and that it would be the perfect time to start a fight.

So he made a golden apple, so beautiful that it made the sun look dim, and wrote around the top, "For the Most Beautiful." Then he called Eris, the goddess of strife.

"Here," he said, "take this apple to the wedding, and drop it on the floor in front of my wife Hera."

Eris liked to cause trouble. So she took the apple to the wedding, and waited until Hera and two other goddesses were standing next to each other, chatting. Then she rolled the apple over to Hera. It bumped against Hera's toes, and she picked it up.

"For the Most Beautiful!" she read. "Why, thank you! That's obviously me!"

But the two goddesses with her disagreed. Aphrodite, the goddess of love, twirled her shining golden hair around one hand and blinked her huge blue eyes.

"Hera, my dear," she said sweetly, "I think the apple must be for me."

"Oh, no," put in Athena, the goddess of war. She reached for the apple. "The apple is obviously for me."

"No!" Hera snapped, clutching the apple. "It's mine!"

The wedding guests all started to argue about which of the goddesses was the most beautiful. But then Hera said, "I know. Let's ask my husband to judge which of us deserves the apple. After all, he is the chief of the gods."

Zeus was standing innocently by the punch bowl. "What?" he said. "How can I judge my own wife? No, no. You must ask a mortal man to judge you. Ask Paris, the prince of Troy. He's the handsomest man on earth, so surely he can decide who is most beautiful among the goddesses."

Paris was lying happily on a mountainside, staring at the sky without a care in the world, when the three goddesses suddenly appeared in front of him with the apple in hand. They demanded that he judge them. Which was the most beautiful?

"Hmm," Paris said, wondering whether one of them would strike him dead if he chose the wrong goddess. "Well, let me see ..."

"Pick me," whispered Hera, "and I'll make you the king of the whole world of men."

"Really?" Paris said.

"No, no," hissed Athena. "Pick me, and I'll give you victory in every battle you ever fight!"

"That would be wonderful!" Paris said.

Athena

"Wait!" said Aphrodite. "Pick me, Paris, and I will give you the most beautiful woman on earth."

Paris's eyes lit up. "That's what I want!" he said, and gave the apple to Aphrodite.

Aphrodite went back to Mount Olympus, with Hera and Athena grumbling and complaining behind her. Once back at Mount Olympus, Aphrodite made Helen, the most beautiful woman in the world, fall madly in love with Paris. As soon as she saw him, she was his forever.

She ran away to live with him in Troy. But unfortunately, Helen was already married—to Menelaus, a Greek king!

Menelaus was furious. And he called on the gods to help him fight against Troy, defeat Paris, and get his wife back.

Hera was still angry with Paris, so she chose to fight against Troy. Aphrodite was on Troy's side. The sun god decided to be on Troy's side as well. Poseidon, the god of the sea, wanted to see Troy destroyed. And so it went; all of the gods lined up for or against Troy, as the Greeks sailed to attack it.

So the Trojan War began, and lasted for years and years of bloodshed and death—all because of Zeus and his golden apple.

Chapter Twenty-Two
The Rise of Rome

Romulus and Remus

In the stories that you've already read, the same thing keeps happening again and again and again. It happened in Sumer, and it happened in Egypt, and it happened in Babylon and in Assyria. A little village starts to get stronger. It becomes a city. A king or a warrior leads the city's people into battle and conquers the land around them. The city becomes a kingdom. And then the kingdom becomes a great empire!

The Egyptians and the Babylonians and the Assyrians all had great empires, but now we're going to learn about one of the greatest empires of all time. It grew to be the largest empire in the world, and it lasted for hundreds and hundreds of years. Over a thousand years after this empire fell, people were still learning its language, reading its books, and copying its government.

This empire was called Rome.

Like the other empires that you've learned about, Rome started out as just a tiny village—this time, in the hills of Italy. Go west from Greece and you'll see a piece of land that looks like a boot, jutting down into the Mediterranean Sea. This is called a *peninsula*, because it has water on three sides of it.

This peninsula is Italy.

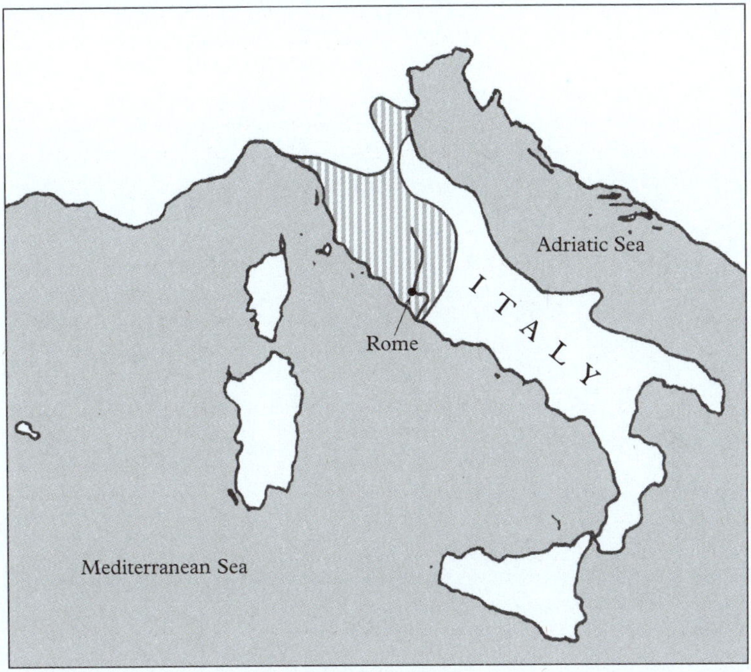

Rome and the Area Under Etruscan Rule

The people who lived in the Italian city of Rome told this story about the village's beginning:

Once upon a time a great king named Numitor had twin grandsons—strong, healthy baby boys, named Romulus and Remus. But Numitor also had a wicked younger brother who plotted against him and stole his throne. The new, evil king wanted to get rid of anyone who might claim to be the rightful king.

"Those babies might grow up to take my crown!" he said. "Go put them in the Tiber River!"

So a servant took the boys down to the Tiber River. But she felt sorry for them, and put them into a basket and pushed it out into the current.

The basket floated along the river until it got stuck in the root of a fig tree at the river's edge. That might have been the end of the two boys—but a wolf heard them crying. She peered around the trunk of the fig tree, and saw the basket with the babies in it.

Now, this wolf had cubs of her own. She felt pity for the two hungry babies, and so she tugged the basket up onto the bank and then back to her own den. There, she raised the babies with her own wolf cubs, as her own.

One day a shepherd, out looking for a lost lamb, heard a coo and then a gurgle from the brush surrounding the wolf's den. He pushed some branches aside—and there saw two fat, happy baby boys, playing naked among the wolf cubs.

The shepherd and his wife had no children of their own. So he took the boys home, and the two of them raised the babies to be tall, handsome young men.

Romulus and Remus

When Romulus and Remus were grown, they went back to the fig tree where their basket had landed, so many years ago. They looked around and saw seven hills. "This is the perfect place to build a town," they said to each other. "A town on top of these seven hills would be strong and hard to attack!" So they began to build a town.

Romulus declared himself the king of this new town. He put himself in charge of building a wall around it. "This wall will keep us safe!" he declared. "Anyone who climbs over my wall will instantly be killed!"

But Remus was angry with his brother. He thought to himself: "We built this town together! Why should Romulus be the ruler of it? I want to be the leader." So he walked up to the wall and vaulted easily over it.

"What kind of a wall is that?" he sneered. "Anyone can climb over it! How can *you* keep this town safe?"

Romulus was so angry that he drew his sword, charged at his brother, and killed him on the spot. Then he named the town Rome, after himself. He was Rome's first king.

What does this story remind you of? Do you remember the story of Sargon, the ruler of one of the very first kingdoms we studied? He floated down the river in a basket until someone rescued him. Ancient people liked these stories about their kings. The stories made the kings seem even more legendary—like great fairy-tale heroes who could do anything!

The Power of Rome

The legend of Romulus and Remus tells us that Romulus was the first king of Rome. Other stories about ancient Rome say that he was the first of seven kings of Rome. These kings fought with other tribes of people who lived in Italy. The kings wanted to take over more and more land, so that Rome would get larger and stronger.

The most important Italian tribe was called the Etruscans. The Etruscans lived north of Rome, in the hills and mountains of Italy. They liked music and art, and painted pictures that we can still see today. The Etruscans also grew crops, made weapons and jewelry out of metal, and sailed back and forth between Greece and Italy, trading with the Greeks. On these trips, the Etruscans learned how to use the Greek alphabet and worship the Greek gods.

The Roman kings fought with the Etruscans. But they also traded with them, and learned from them. The Etruscans taught the Romans how to dress like Greeks. They told the Romans about the Greek gods. The Romans learned about painting and music from the Etruscans as well. And they borrowed the customs of the Etruscan kings, who wore special robes called *togas*, with purple borders. The purple showed everyone how important the king was.

The Etruscan kings also carried a bundle of rods with an axe blade in it, as a symbol of royal power. The rods showed that the king had the power to punish anyone who did wrong. The axe blade showed that he could execute people who did very evil things. The Romans liked this symbol of power, which was called the *fasces*. Soon Roman kings, like Etruscan kings, wore special purple-bordered togas and carried fasces. Do you have an old dime? Look on the back of it and you will see a picture of the fasces. Or look for a picture of the Lincoln Memorial in Washington, DC. You will see the fasces on the arms of Lincoln's chair.

American courtrooms and government offices also sometimes copy this Roman symbol. They have a fasces in them to show that the judges have the power to punish criminals. The chamber where the United States House of Representatives meets, in the United States Capitol building, has two fasces on the wall, one on each side of the American flag.

The fasces showed how powerful the king was. But after seven kings, the people of Rome decided that the king had too much power. They didn't like living in a monarchy—a country where the king was in charge. Instead, they wanted Rome to be a place where the people could help make the laws and choose the leaders. So they drove out their kings and decided to make Rome into a *republic*.

A republic isn't the same as a democracy! The city of Athens was a democracy. All of the men who weren't slaves could vote about laws. But in a republic, only certain leaders can vote about laws. Those leaders *represent* the rest of the people—they are supposed to listen to the opinions of all the people who aren't voting directly for laws, and remember those opinions when *they* are voting.

In Rome, rich and powerful men called *patricians* were the representatives who voted for the laws. Two of these patricians were appointed by the other patricians to be the leaders of the city. They were called *consuls*.

The Romans thought that having two leaders, instead of one king, would keep any one man from getting too much power. The two consuls were supposed to keep an eye on each other! Neither one could do exactly what he pleased.

History-Makers

The Story of Tullia Minor and Tarquin the Proud, The Last King and Queen of Rome

Tarquin the Proud was the last of the seven kings of Rome, and Tullia Minor was his wife. But Tarquin didn't start out as heir to the throne, and at first he wasn't known as Tarquin the Proud. He was just Tarquin the Younger, because there were other, older men in his family named Tarquin.

Tarquin's father was from the Roman nobility, and when Tarquin grew up, his parents arranged for him to marry a princess. She was Tullia Minor, the daughter of the sixth king of Rome.

Tullia Minor was named after her father, King Servius Tullius. Back in those days, Roman girls didn't get to have their own names. They had a feminine version of their father's last name instead! We know from Tullia Minor's name that she was a younger sister—Servius Tullius's oldest daughter would have been named Tullia Major.

Tarquin the Younger and Tullia Minor were both ambitious. Both of them wanted more honor and respect than they already were given. But the Roman chroniclers say that, of the two of them, Tullia was the *most* anxious to gain more power! After she married Tarquin the Younger, she began to lecture and scold him, day and night. "I didn't marry you just to have a husband!" she told him. "I married you because I thought that you were worthy of wearing a king's crown! You can't just sit around and long to be mighty. It isn't enough to just *want* more power. You have to *act!* Do something!"

Tarquin and Tullia

After months and months of this, Tarquin the Younger began to agree with his wife. Together, they planned how they could seize the throne away from Tullia's father, Servius Tullius. And Tullia convinced her husband that violence was the only way to get what they both wanted. "You will have to kill my father," Tullia Minor urged her husband. "It is your only choice!"

One day, Servius Tullius was out walking in the garden when Tarquin the Younger broke into the throne room, sat down on the throne, and declared himself to be the king of Rome. When Servius Tullius learned that his son-in-law had seized his throne, he ran to the throne room and shouted, "I am the rightful king of Rome! How dare you sit on my throne while I am still alive?"

Tarquin the Younger leaped to his feet, grabbed the old king, and dragged him out into the street in front of the palace—where assassins hired by Tullia Minor finished him off. Some accounts even claim that Tullia Minor drove up to the palace in her carriage, saluted her husband as the new ruler of Rome, and then drove over her father's body on the way out!

Tarquin was now king of Rome, and Tullia Minor was Rome's queen. The new royal couple ruled with so much pomp and haughtiness that Tarquin earned himself the nickname "Tarquin Superbus"— Tarquin the Proud, or even Tarquin the Super-Arrogant! They stole land from their subjects, used Rome's wealth for their own comfort, and did exactly as they pleased. And because they had seized the throne by force, they were suspicious of anyone who might seem to be plotting to do the same. If they thought that courtiers were planning against them, or officials were scheming to take power for themselves, Tarquin and Tullia ordered them put to death—no questions asked. Their guilt had turned into cruelty.

After twenty-five years of tyrannical rule, the people of Rome could no longer stand this proud queen and king—and neither could the army. The generals and the soldiers rebelled. While Tarquin and Tullia were out of the city, the Romans closed the gates of the city and refused to let their rulers back in. Then, the army went outside the walls and chased Tarquin and Tullia away, far into the north of Italy.

The people of Rome had already been unhappy with the power of their kings. The evil deeds of Tarquin and Tullia convinced them Rome should never have a king again! It was only then that they decided to elect two consuls in place of having an eighth king.

There are many different versions of the story of Tullia and Tarquin, so we can't be completely sure that all of the details in this story are true. In fact, it seems likely that the tale of Tullia and Tarquin was actually a play that was performed in front of the Romans in order to explain why

Roman kingship came to an end and consuls were chosen to lead the Roman Republic instead.

But even if Tullia and Tarquin weren't exactly like the people in this story, they were real people who ruled in ancient Rome. And even though Tarquin the Proud was actually the evil king who brought about the end of the monarchy, later writers and historians were much more fascinated by Tullia Minor. Many centuries later, the playwright William Shakespeare used Tullia Minor as the inspiration for his character Lady Macbeth—a Scottish aristocrat who argued with and scolded her husband Macbeth until he agreed to kill their king and take the throne for himself. By the time of Shakespeare's plays, people still remembered Tullia Minor!

Note: Tullia Minor and Tarquin the Proud ruled Rome from 535-509 BC/BCE.

Chapter Twenty-Three
Babylon Takes Over Again!

Nebuchadnezzar's Madness

After Ashurbanipal died, the Assyrian Empire fell apart. And Assyria's old enemies, the Babylonians, were ready to take over. They made friends with another nearby nation called Media. Together, the Babylonians and the Medes stormed through Assyria's land.

Because the Assyrians had destroyed Babylon, the Babylonians wanted revenge! So now, with the help of the Medes, the Babylonians destroyed Nineveh, Assyria's most beautiful city. They broke down the walls and gates, ripped the doors off Ashurbanipal's great library, and smashed hundreds of his precious clay tablets. Fortunately, some of the books survived so that we can still read them today.

Then the Babylonians settled down to rule their own empire. The Babylonian Empire wasn't quite as big as the Assyrian Empire, because the Babylonians never took over Egypt. But it was almost as big. And for many years, the Babylonians were the most powerful people in the world.

Babylon, the city flooded by Assyria, was rebuilt. The great Babylonian king Nebuchadnezzar (who became king around 605 BC/BCE) spent much of his reign making Babylon beautiful again. He built huge walls all around the city, to keep it safe from invasion. In one of the walls, he built a great blue gate decorated with yellow and white bulls and dragons, and named it after Babylon's chief goddess, Ishtar. Underneath this gate, a great parade passed every year in honor of Ishtar. The gate became famous all through Nebuchadnezzar's empire.

Nebuchadnezzar was such a famous ruler that he became known as "Nebuchadnezzar the Great." But after his death, he was remembered a little differently. Later writers claimed that, during the last years of his reign, Nebuchadnezzar actually lost his mind!

One story about Nebuchadnezzar's madness is told in the book of Daniel, in the Jewish and Christian Bibles. The story says that Nebuchadnezzar was a little too pleased with himself and his accomplishments. He thought he was a god. He even made an enormous golden statue of himself, almost a hundred feet high, and told all of his people to bow down and worship it. Here is the rest of the story:

ONE DAY, THE GREAT KING NEBUCHADNEZZAR was walking on the roof of his palace in Babylon.

"Look at this beautiful city I have built!" he said to himself. "I am the most powerful king in the world! No one is greater than I am!"

As soon as he said this, a voice came from heaven. "Nebuchadnezzar!" the voice said. "You have become too proud! You think you are greater than God Himself. Now listen to your doom—you will act like an animal, and eat grass like a cow, until you admit that God is more powerful than you are!"

At once Nebuchadnezzar lost his mind. He ran out into the fields and lived like a wild animal. He walked on his hands and knees, until his knees were as tough as hooves and his fingernails were as long as a bird's claws. He drank from the river, slept under bushes, and woke up in the morning wet with dew. His hair grew long and shaggy, until he looked like a goat. And he ate grass like a cow.

His people gathered around at a distance and watched him. "What is wrong with the king?" they whispered. "He has gone mad!"

Finally Nebuchadnezzar looked up at the sky. "I am not a god!" he said. "I am only a man. And God is more powerful than I am."

At once Nebuchadnezzar was sane again. He stood up on his feet. He looked around him and knew that he was the king of Babylon, not an animal.

He returned to his palace in Babylon to rule his people once again. But never again did he claim to be a god. Now he knew that he was only a man.

The Hanging Gardens of Babylon

Have you ever heard the phrase The Seven Wonders?

The Seven Wonders of the Ancient World are things that ancient people made or built that we still think are incredible, even today. You have already read about two of the Seven Wonders of the Ancient World: the Great Pyramid of Giza, and the statue of Zeus at Olympia in Greece.

Another one of those Seven Wonders was found in Babylon. It was a huge garden, filled with trees, flowers, and waterfalls, built like an upside-down ziggurat. (Remember, a ziggurat was a pyramid that had steps on its sides so that priests could climb up to the top.) Each level of the garden overhung the level below. So these gardens became known as the Hanging Gardens of Babylon. People came from huge distances to see the Hanging Gardens.

Here is the story that has been passed down from ancient times about why these gardens were built.

NEBUCHADNEZZAR, THE GREAT KING OF Babylon, sat on his throne and worried. He had a great empire—but what if another country attacked him? He wasn't sure that his army could defend Babylon from invaders. And he was very worried about Media, a country to the east of Babylon. The Medes were expanding their own country. Their army was strong. He had heard frightening stories about Median soldiers!

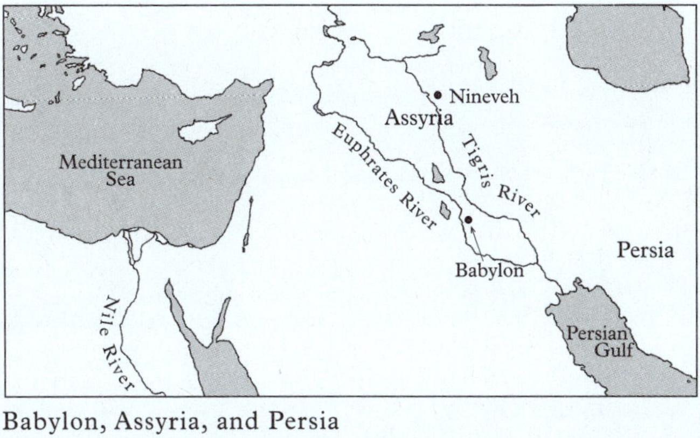

Babylon, Assyria, and Persia

"I know what I'll do," he thought to himself. "I will ask the king of Media if I can marry his daughter. Then he will be my father-in-law, and he won't want to attack me!"

Nebuchadnezzar had never seen the daughter of the Median king. But that didn't matter to him. He was willing to marry a stranger to keep Babylon safe. So he sent messages to the king of Media, offering to marry the princess.

Meanwhile, the king of Media was sitting on his throne, worrying about Babylon. "What will I do if Babylon attacks me?" he thought. "Their soldiers are such good fighters! I'm not sure that we could defeat them. How can I convince Nebuchadnezzar to leave me alone?"

Just then his servant entered with the message from Nebuchadnezzar. "Sir," he said, "the king of Babylon has sent you a message. He wishes to know if you will give him your daughter in marriage."

The king of Media was greatly relieved. "Of course I will!" he said. "Nebuchadnezzar would never attack his own father-in-law!" And he sent for his daughter, the princess Amytis.

"My dear," he said, "the king of Babylon wishes to marry you."

"But I've never even met him!" Amytis protested. "And I don't want to leave my home in the mountains to live in Babylon. It's down on flat land, where the air is still and thick."

"If you marry him," the king of Media said, "your home will be safe from attack. You will be helping your whole country."

Finally, Amytis agreed. She traveled to Babylon for the great wedding ceremony. As soon as Nebuchadnezzar saw her, he fell in love with her. He built her the most beautiful rooms to live in and filled them with lovely things. He gave her gold jewelry, clothes of silk, pet monkeys from China to play with, beautiful flowers to make her rooms colorful, and servants to do her every wish.

But Amytis wasn't happy. She missed the cliffs and valleys of the Median mountains. Most of all, she missed the gardens that her people built on the hillsides.

"I want to go home!" she said. "I don't want to live in Babylon anymore. It's so flat and dull here!"

"How can I make Amytis happy?" Nebuchadnezzar thought. And then he had an idea. He would build her a garden—a mountain garden, right in the middle of the city of Babylon.

Nebuchadnezzar set to work at once. He ordered his slaves to haul huge slabs of rock in from far away. Out of this rock, he built an enormous hill—an artificial mountain! He covered the rock with dirt and planted it thickly with trees, flowers, and bushes. He had plants brought from Media, so that Amytis could see familiar flowers again. Nebuchadnezzar's men even built a pump that would pull water up from the Euphrates River to the very top of the garden. Then the water ran down the garden, just like a mountain river. Nebuchadnezzar ordered paths built up and down the mountain. Then he brought Amytis out to see what he had done.

"My dear," he said, "you cannot return to Media. But I have brought a little bit of your homeland to you. Now you can walk in your hillside garden whenever you want."

Amytis's garden became known as the Hanging Gardens of Babylon. People came from all over to admire the mountain that Nebuchadnezzar had built in the middle of flat, hot Babylon. And every day, Amytis walked in her garden and pretended that she was back home.

Note: Nebuchadnezzar reigned from 605–561 BC/BCE.

Chapter Twenty-Four
The Medes and the Persians

A New Empire

Let's take a minute to review the story of the Assyrians and the Babylonians.

Earlier, we read about the Assyrian king Shamshi-Adad. He wanted to rule the world. He conquered the cities all around him and made them obey him. He put his soldiers in the conquered cities, and told them to punish anyone who disobeyed his laws. Soon the Assyrians ruled the whole northern part of Mesopotamia—the land between the Tigris and Euphrates rivers.

But the Babylonian kingdom ruled the southern part of Mesopotamia, and they were even stronger than the Assyrians. The Babylonian king, Hammurabi, marched his army up and took over Assyria. For a little while, the Assyrians had to obey the Babylonians.

The Assyrians didn't like belonging to the Babylonian Empire, though! Eventually, they rebelled and took their kingdom back. Now the Assyrians were in charge, and the Babylonians had to obey them.

The Assyrians went back to conquering all the cities around them. They fought their way all the way over to Canaan. They captured the Jews who lived there and made them leave their homes.

But then the Babylonians and the Medes joined together and destroyed Assyria. Now Babylon was in charge of the Assyrian lands, and Media was Babylon's powerful neighbor. This must have been a very strange time to live! The rulers of the world kept changing—first they were Assyrian, then Babylonian, then Assyrian, then Babylonian again.

The Babylonians and the Medes must have been pleased with themselves. They had finally gotten rid of Assyria. Now they were the most powerful nations in Mesopotamia!

But the Medes and Babylonians weren't in charge for very long. Another kingdom was becoming stronger and stronger—the kingdom of Persia.

Here is the story that the Persians told about their own kingdom's rise to power:

AT FIRST, THE PERSIANS WERE JUST A TRIBE of shepherds. They lived at the edge of Media. Their leader was named Cambyses.

The Persians were ruled by the king of the Medes, Astyges. Astyges wasn't a good man; he liked being king of the Medes and the Persians, and he would do anything to keep his power. He decided to send his daughter, the Median princess Mandane, to marry Cambyses, so that the Persians would remain loyal to Media.

Mandane and Cambyses had a baby boy—and one night, Astyges had a dream that scared him. He dreamed that his baby grandson would grow up, take his power away, and become the next king of the Medes. When he woke up, he was frightened! "If I don't do something about this," he thought, "my grandson will throw me off my throne, and become king in my place!" Astyges sat up all night, thinking about his dream.

In the morning, he called his chief adviser, a man named Harpagus. "I have a job for you," he said.

"I will do anything you tell me to, O King!" said Harpagus.

"Good!" Astyges said. "I am inviting my daughter and my grandson for a visit. Once my daughter has gone to bed, kidnap my grandson, take him out to the mountains, and kill him. And don't let anyone know what you're doing. Now go!"

Harpagus didn't want to do this terrible thing. But he was afraid to disobey the king. So when Mandane and her child had gone to bed, the first night of their visit, Harpagus took the baby and walked out to the mountains. "I have to obey my king!" he thought to himself. "I have to kill the baby. But I can't make myself do it!"

He looked around and saw a Persian shepherd, grazing his sheep nearby. He called the shepherd over. "Here," he said. "The king wants to get rid of this baby. You do it! If you do, I'll reward you with much wealth. But if you don't, I'll send the king's soldiers to punish you."

The shepherd looked at the baby, and had an idea.

"All right," he said to Harpagus. "I'll get rid of the baby." He took the baby and ran home to his wife, who had no children of her own. "Wife!" he said. "The gods have sent us a son! We can raise him as our own!"

His wife took the baby with tears of joy. And then the shepherd killed a goat, wiped his hands in the blood, and ran back to Harpagus.

"Look," he said. "I've done as you told me!"

So Harpagus went back to Astyges and told him that the baby was dead. But the shepherd and his wife named the baby Cyrus and brought him up there on the mountainside.

Cyrus grew up to be tall and strong. He was faster and smarter than any other shepherd's son. And he stood head and shoulders above every other boy his age. One day, the shepherd took him down from the mountainside into town to help with the selling of the sheep. While they were at the marketplace, Astyges, the ruler of the Medes, came by, along with Harpagus. As soon as Astyges saw the young Persian boy selling sheep, he knew that this was his grandson.

That evening he sent for Harpagus.

"You disobeyed me!" he said to Harpagus. And Harpagus admitted that he had given the baby to a shepherd, rather than killing him. Astyges was so furious that he tried to kill Harpagus and his whole family.

But Harpagus fled to the mountains and found Cyrus. "If you want to take the king's power away, and become king of the Medes yourself," he told Cyrus, "I will help you."

Together, Harpagus and Cyrus convinced the Persians to follow Cyrus, rather than Astyges. After three years of fierce fighting, Cyrus took power away from his grandfather and became the ruler of both the Medes and the Persians, just as Astyges had dreamed so many years before.

Now Cyrus, who had been raised by a shepherd on a mountain, ruled over the combined empires of the Medes and the Persians. But because of his love for his foster parents, he always thought of himself as a Persian.

Cyrus the Great

Cyrus was now the king of the Medes and the Persians. He was a great warrior—but he was also known as a good and fair king. He let the Median people stay in their own homes. He even let Median noblemen have some of the power in his new, combined empire. After all, his empire was so big that he needed help. He couldn't collect all the taxes, judge all the court cases, and settle all the problems himself! So he made both Persians and Medians officials in his kingdom. The Medians felt that they were being treated well—and so they didn't try to rebel against Cyrus's rule.

Cyrus the Great

Now Cyrus decided to make his empire even bigger. He wanted to conquer Asia Minor.

Asia Minor was ruled by King Croesus, who was the richest king in the world. He had more gold than anyone else. Cyrus knew that if he could conquer Croesus, he would be rich as well. So he marched his army up to the kingdom of Croesus and conquered it. He captured Croesus and made him stand up on the walls of his city and watch as Persian soldiers looted it. The soldiers went all through the city, carrying away armloads of treasures, gold coins, and jewelry. But Croesus just watched, calmly.

Finally, Cyrus said, "How can you be so calm? They are robbing you of all your gold!"

"No, they aren't," Croesus said. "The city belongs to you now. So they are actually stealing from you."

When Cyrus heard this, he stopped the soldiers at once and took all the gold back!

Next, Cyrus turned his army to the east. Cyrus marched the Medes and the Persians all the way over to the Indus River. Now he ruled all the land between Asia Minor and India. His empire was as wide as it was tall—and more and more, people spoke of it not as the empire of the Medes and the Persians, but simply as the Persian Empire.

Cyrus wasn't done conquering yet. There was one big enemy left for him: Babylon.

Remember, the Babylonians had been ruling in Mesopotamia for a long time! They were an old kingdom—and a very powerful kingdom. Cyrus wanted all that good, fertile land between the Tigris and the Euphrates rivers. But he knew that the Babylonian army was very strong.

However, Cyrus had one big advantage over Babylon. The Persians liked Cyrus, because he was a good, fair king. But the Babylonians hated their king. He had left the city of Babylon and had gone away to live in a distant desert. In his place, he had given his son Belshazzar control over the city. Belshazzar spent too much money on feasting and drinking, and not enough on the people of Babylon.

So when Cyrus marched his army to Babylon, he didn't meet much resistance. The Babylonians were sick and tired of their own king. They didn't fight very hard when Cyrus's army arrived at the walls. Some of the Babylonians even opened the gates from the inside and let him in!

When Cyrus took over Babylon, he also took over Canaan. Canaan (also called Palestine) had been the home of the Jewish people until Babylon and Assyria conquered it. The Babylonians and Assyrians had made the Jewish people leave their homes. But Cyrus was a merciful king. When he became the king of Babylon, he let the Jews go back to Palestine. And he let them go back to worshipping their own god. He even allowed them to rebuild their temple, and he gave them back some of the treasure that had been stolen from their first temple long ago. The Jews were so grateful to Cyrus that they called him the "Anointed of the Lord."

Now Cyrus was the greatest king in the world.

But there was still one country that didn't obey Cyrus: Greece. And soon the Greeks and the Persians would meet in battle.

Note: The earliest Persians lived around 700 BC/BCE. Cyrus the Great ruled 559–529 BC/BCE. Babylon fell to the Persians in 539 BC/BCE.

Chapter Twenty-Five
The Aryans of India

Life on the Ganges River

While the Greeks and the Romans and the Persians were all building their power near the Mediterranean Sea, another great civilization was growing in another part of the world—the Indus Valley.

Do you remember reading about Mohenjo-Daro, the mysterious deserted city of the Indus Valley? The citadel cities of the Indus Valley were deserted long, long ago. Maybe the cities were attacked by invaders. Maybe a long drought killed all the crops and forced the people to move away. Perhaps an earthquake destroyed the citadels. We'll never know for sure.

But India didn't just sit empty! After the people of the Indus Valley disappeared, new settlers came into India. They were called the *Aryans*, and they came down into India from the north, from the area we call *Asia*.

At first, the Aryans were nomads. But they soon settled down along the two big rivers of India, the Indus River and the Ganges River. They became farmers, just like the people who lived in the first villages of Mesopotamia. They grew crops for food. And like the people of ancient Mesopotamia, the Aryans raised animals, especially horses and cows.

Every year, the Ganges River overflowed its banks and left rich, dark soil all over the fields nearby, just like the Nile

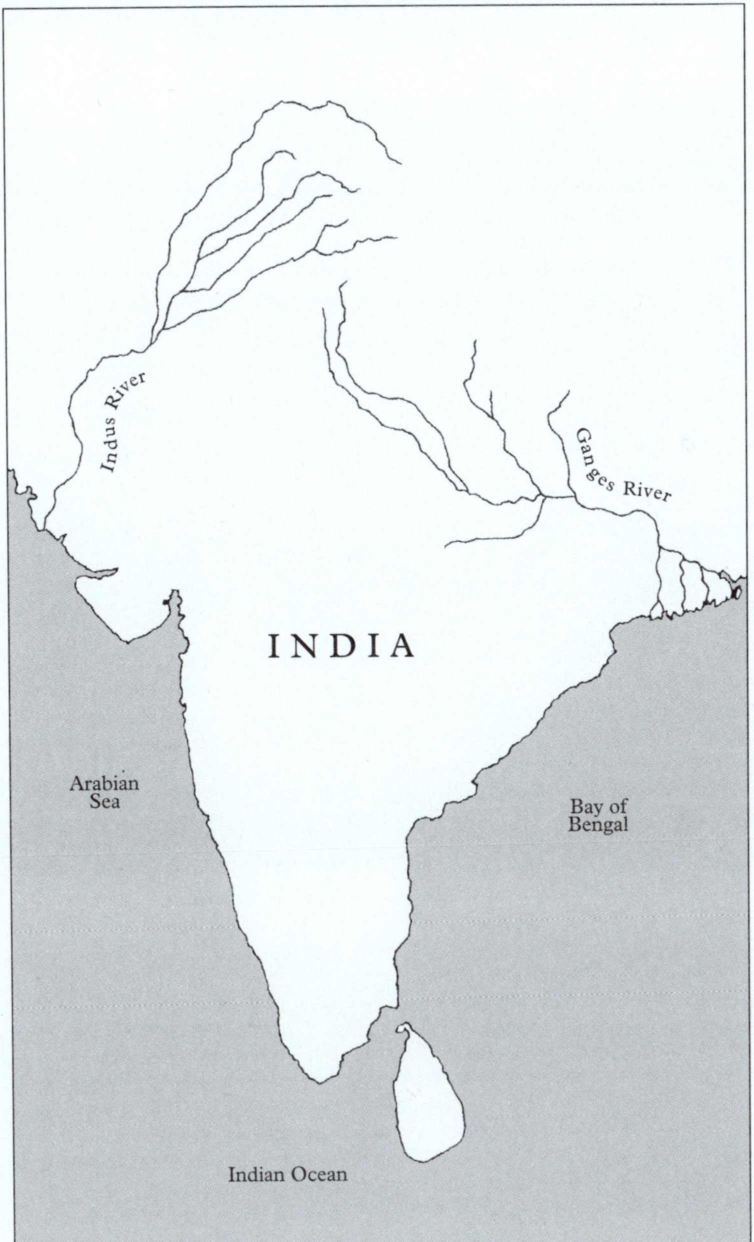
Indus River
Ganges River
INDIA
Arabian Sea
Bay of Bengal
Indian Ocean

India

River in Egypt. The people of ancient India grew wonderful crops in the dirt left by the Ganges River floods. They grew wheat, like the Mesopotamians, and rice, like the Chinese. Without the Ganges River, the people of India wouldn't have been able to survive. They believed that the river had been provided by their chief god, Shiva, the god of life.

Here is the story that the people of ancient India told about Shiva and the Ganges:

ONCE, THE RIVER-GODDESS GANGA LIVED IN the heavens. She never came down to earth at all; instead, she danced through the skies, bringing water to all who lived in the clouds, but ignoring the ground down below.

The good king of India, King Bhagiratha, grew more and more worried. How could his people survive without water? Surely Ganga would come down from the heavens and bring water to the people who lived on earth.

But Ganga refused to come down. She stayed up in the skies with her water—and the people of India were thirsty.

So King Bhagiratha called to Shiva, the god of life. "Shiva!" he cried. "We are dying of thirst! Please, please send Ganga to earth for us."

When Shiva heard Bhagiratha's cries, he called Ganga to his throne. "Ganga," he said, "the people of earth are thirsty. You must go down to the earth and take water to them!"

Ganga refused. "I will not!" she said. "I will stay here in the skies, my favorite place to be. Let the people of earth take care of themselves."

"But I command you!" Shiva answered, "and you must obey me."

At that, Ganga became furious. "Go to earth?" she yelled. "I'll go to earth all right—and drown everyone on it!" She balanced on the top of a cloud, ready to throw herself down to the earth with such violence that water would flood the entire surface of the ground.

But when Shiva saw what she was about to do, he leaped down to earth ahead of her. When Ganga came crashing down, she landed on his head, and her full weight came down on Shiva, instead of on the unhappy people of earth. Water flowed down Shiva's head in seven streams, down onto the thirsty ground beneath him. The seven streams came together into one mighty river—the Ganges River. And the Ganges River brought life and plenty to all the people who lived along its banks.

The people who believed in Shiva and Ganga were called *Hindus*. Today, their religion is called *Hinduism*. And many Hindu pilgrims still come to the banks of the Ganges. At dusk, they float lighted candles on the water and pray to the river-goddess, Ganga.

The Castes of Ancient India

The people of ancient India worshipped Shiva, Ganga, and many other gods. Their religion, Hinduism, taught that these gods had created life on earth. One of the holy books of Hinduism, the Rig Veda, tells this story about how life began:

LONG, LONG AGO, THERE WAS ONLY ONE gigantic man who lived in the whole universe. His name was Purusha. He had a thousand heads, a thousand eyes, and a thousand feet. The gods looked at Purusha and said, "Let's make a world from this enormous man!"

So the gods turned Purusha's head into the sky, and his eyes into the sun. They turned his legs into the Earth. His breath became the wind. And out of his body, they made four different kinds of people.

The first and most important people were the priests—the *brahmin*. They came out of Purusha's mouth. They were intelligent and wise; as they walked out onto the Earth, they became the most honored people in India. They were given the most delicious food, the finest clothing, and the biggest houses.

Out of Purusha's arms, the gods made the second kind of people—the noble warriors. They rode out onto the Earth on strong, beautiful horses. Their job was to protect the priests from enemies and to rule India. They too had good food and fine clothing, but not quite as fine as that of the priests.

Then the gods made traders and farmers out of Purusha's knees. The traders bought and sold goods; the farmers grew crops and raised their animals. They worked hard every day. They had enough food to keep them from going hungry, warm clothes, and dry houses. Their lives were harder than the lives of warriors and priests.

> Finally the gods came to the bottoms of Purusha's feet. Out of his feet, they made a humble group of people—the servants. Servants were not allowed to learn how to read and write. Instead, they spent their lives taking care of the priests, the warriors, and the traders and farmers.

These four groups of people became known as *castes*. If your family belonged to the farmer caste, you could only grow up to be a farmer. You could only marry someone who was also born to be a farmer. You could never be a warrior or a priest. And if your parents were servants, you were doomed to be a servant. Priests, warriors, farmers, and traders expected you to serve them for the rest of your life. You would never learn how to read, or to write. You would spend the rest of your life cooking, washing, and cleaning for someone else!

But the poorest people in India were those who didn't belong to the caste system at all. They were called "Untouchables." They weren't priests, or warriors, or farmers, or traders, or even servants. They belonged to the poorest, most miserable families in India. The "Untouchables" did all the dirtiest jobs in ancient India. They buried dead animals, cleaned the streets, worked in the fields, and picked up trash. They weren't allowed to drink water from public wells, or to use the same dishes as people from the four castes. These early Hindus believed that touching an Untouchable would make them unclean. And they didn't even want to look at the Untouchables who did the dirtiest jobs! Those Untouchables were called Unseeables. They were only allowed to do their work at night.

It was a terrible thing to be born into an Untouchable family! Untouchables were poor and badly treated. They weren't allowed to go to the doctor when they were sick. Children from Untouchable families couldn't go to school, or grow up to do jobs that they liked. They had to collect garbage and work in the fields, like their parents.

Thousands and thousands of people were Untouchables in ancient India—with no chance ever to be anything else.

Siddhartha

The priests, warriors, and rulers of ancient India lived well. They had good food and drink, soft beds to sleep in, beautiful clothes, and servants to do anything they asked. The traders and farmers of India weren't quite as well off—but they also had food to eat, decent houses to live in, and enough money to take care of themselves and their families.

But the servants who belonged to the lowest caste of India worked hard for very little money. They had to do the jobs that the priests, warriors, rulers, traders, and farmers didn't want to do. Servants didn't have nice houses or clothes. They weren't even allowed to learn how to read.

And the Untouchables were even more miserable than the servants. Untouchables couldn't even be friends with servants. They were only allowed to talk to each other. They spent their days doing dirty, disgusting jobs. And at the end of the day, they weren't even paid enough money to eat properly or to buy warm clothes.

But then one man saw how unjust this system was. His name was Siddhartha.

Here is the story that is told about his life.

LONG AGO, A PRINCE NAMED SIDDHARTHA lived in India. He didn't know how miserable the servants and Untouchables were, because he was surrounded by beauty and luxury every moment of his life. His proud father, King Suddhodana, built three palaces for his son! He gave Siddhartha a thousand servants to wait on him hand and foot. He hired the best tutors to teach his son how to write poetry, play music, fence, and wrestle. At night, Siddhartha slept on rich, soft sheets, while musicians played beautiful music to lull him to sleep. In the morning, servants brought him his meals in bed, while poets read to him and other servants burned incense to make his room smell sweet and fragrant.

But in time, Siddhartha became curious about the world outside. "What is outside the palace walls?" he asked his father. "I want to go and see the city around me."

"There's nothing that you need to see out there," his father answered. "Stay here in the palace. Eat the good food I've provided for you. Enjoy the music and the poetry!"

Siddhartha kept begging his father to let him go outside. Finally, Suddhodana agreed. But he told Siddhartha's chariot driver to stay only in the streets near the palace. He ordered all of these streets swept, and the fronts of the buildings scrubbed and repainted. He drove all the sick and poor away, into other parts of the city. At last, he allowed his son to go out.

At first Siddhartha was delighted. "The city is as beautiful as my palace!" he exclaimed. "How wonderful it must be to live in this city! And how fortunate its people are!"

But as his chariot turned a corner, Siddhartha saw an old, old man, dragging himself along with the help of two sticks.

"Who is that?" he asked his chariot driver. "What is wrong with him?"

"That is an old, poor man," the chariot driver said. "He can barely see or walk, and the only food he is given is the food that he can beg from generous people passing by. Everyone will grow old and feeble in time. Even you, Siddhartha."

Siddhartha had never before seen an old person. He was horrified. But he was even more distressed a few minutes later, when they passed a man sitting on the sidewalk, bent double in pain and pleading for help.

"What is wrong with that man?" he asked.

"He is sick," the chariot driver said, "and no one will help him, because he is an Untouchable. Soon he will die."

"What is death?" Siddhartha asked.

"Death is the end of life," the chariot driver told him. "We will all die. Even you, Siddhartha!"

Siddhartha returned to his palace, struck with grief and misery. He had never known that people lived in pain and suffering, or that all men will die. The luxuries all around him seemed false and wrong.

So he took off his fine clothes, put on the poor clothes of a beggar, and went out into the world. For years and years, Siddhartha lived the life of a beggar. He spent his time trying to find out why people must grow old and sick, and finally die.

One day, Siddhartha was sitting beneath a wild fig tree, thinking about the mysteries of life. Suddenly, he exclaimed, "I understand! Everyone, no matter how poor, sick, or miserable, can find happiness by leading a good life!"

From then on, Siddhartha was known as the Buddha. He taught his followers that they should be honest, make peace with their enemies, and avoid violence. The followers of the Buddha became known as *Buddhists*. Soon, many people in ancient India were Buddhists. Today, Buddhism is followed by many, many people, both in India and in other countries around the world.

A statue of the Buddha

Note: The Aryan people probably came into India around 1500 BC/BCE; their civilization reached a high point around 500 BC/BCE, when sixteen separate kingdoms existed in the northern part of India. Siddhartha Gautama (the Buddha) lived around 563–483 BC/BCE.

History-Maker

The Story of Ajatashatru the Expander, The First Empire-Builder in India

While the Romans were electing their first consuls, and the Persians were rising to power over the Babylonians, and the Greeks were trying to figure out how to write their law codes, the strongest kingdom in India was Magadha, on the Ganges River.

The king of Magadha was a descendant of the original Aryan settlers in the Ganges River valley. His name was Bimbisara—and he had a troublesome son.

This son was named Ajatashatru. From his youngest days, he was quick to fight, impatient to be a grown-up, and desperate to be king. He was his father's heir to the throne, but by the time he was a young man, Ajatashatru just couldn't wait for his father to die. Ancient stories tell us that Ajatashatru gathered soldiers around him, threw his father into jail, and allowed Bimbisara to starve to death. And when his father died, his mother also died, of grief.

This was not a good beginning—but now that Ajatashatru was the king of Magadha, he kept on killing and destroying in order to get what he wanted: a bigger kingdom!

The two kingdoms closest to Magadha were ruled by his cousin and by his younger brother. (Many of the Aryan rulers of India were related to each other.) Ajatashatru declared war on both his cousin and his brother. It took twelve hard years of fighting before he was able to defeat both of them and claim their kingdoms for his own.

He also attacked the kingdom just north of Magadha. This kingdom, the Licchavi, was ruled by two young princes who had an extraordinary tame elephant. He would spray the people of the court with water on command! The princes called him Seyanaga, which meant "The Sprinkler." Ajatashatru wanted to own The Sprinkler, but the two princes would not send him to Magadha. So Ajatashatru took this excuse to wage war on the Licchavi as well. This war took him sixteen years, but finally he won it as well.

During all of those years of war, Ajatashatru did three things for the very first time. He created the first professional army in India—the first army that was paid by the government to do nothing but fight. He invented a new kind of war chariot, a covered chariot with a swinging mace (a metal-headed club) attached to it. It was called the *rathamusala*, and it could drive through enemy troops and mow them down like a tank. And he also built a huge rock-throwing catapult that could hurl enormous pieces of stone. It was called the *mahashilakantaka*.

By the end of his rule, Ajatashatru had conquered thirty-six surrounding kingdoms! Because of that, he became known as Ajatashatru the Expander. He was the first Indian ruler to have a kingdom that looked more like an empire—a realm that stretched across many different peoples and territories.

But Ajatashatru the Expander did one more thing that we remember him for.

Siddhartha, the Buddha, lived most of his life in Magadha. In fact, Ajatashatru met with him personally.

Ajatashatru

The meeting between the Buddha and the murderous king is recorded on a carved pillar that Ajatashatru ordered to commemorate the occasion. The panels show Ajatashatru and his queen descending from their elephant and kneeling in front of the Buddha to honor him.

When the Buddha died, Ajatashatru at once claimed that Magadha had the responsibility to protect the Buddha's teachings. The Buddha himself had never written anything down. He simply spoke to his followers—and his followers repeated his teachings to others.

Ajatashatru wanted to make sure that the Buddha's teachings were properly remembered. So he ordered a council held in his capital, Rajagriha. He invited 500 of the Buddha's most dedicated followers, or *priests*. He built a huge hall for this council. He made it as beautiful as possible, and he spread out on the floor five hundred precious carpets, one for each of the priests who would attend the council. Each priest and his companions were responsible for memorizing and reciting a different set of the Buddha's sayings, and agreeing on the exact wording of each set of sayings.

This process is called the *canonization* of a piece of writing.

Imagine that you and your three brothers are all having a big fight about what your mother told you to do before she gets home. You say, "She told us to clean our rooms and finish our math homework."

Your oldest brother says, "No, she told us to finish our math homework and load the dishwasher."

Your youngest brother says, "She didn't say anything about math homework! She said to load the dishwasher and make up our beds."

And then your last brother says, "All I heard was, 'Clean your rooms.'"

You all remember something slightly different. So you have to agree together about what your mother *actually* said. Finally, you come up with, "Clean your rooms, finish your math homework, and load the dishwasher!" You all agree that your mother said that. You write it down on a piece of paper, put it on the refrigerator, and then you all get to work. You've "canonized" your mother's instructions!

Of course, when your mother comes home, she'll tell you whether or not you got her instructions right. But the Buddha was already gone, so the council at Rajagriha had the power to decide exactly which sayings would be attributed to the Buddha. Eventually, the sayings approved by this very first Buddhist council would become the Pali Canon, the first written account of the Buddha's sayings.

But that wasn't the end of Ajatashatru's story. When he was an old man, his son murdered him to take his throne, just as Ajatashatru had murdered his own father. And after Ajatashatru, the next five kings were each murdered by their own sons.

Ajatashatru made sure that the Buddha's sayings of peace and harmony were passed down to future generations—but at the same time, his own family was tormented by violence and unrest for many, many years.

Note: Ajatashatru ruled Magadha from c. 492-460 BC/BCE.

Chapter Twenty-Six
Writing, Fighting, and Thinking in China

Calligraphy in China

The Aryans came down into India from central Asia. If you were to put your finger on India, on your map, and then move it up to the north, then you would be in central Asia. And if you move your finger right on the map, you'll go into the eastern part of Asia—China. We've already learned a little bit about the farmers of ancient China, and about the pictograms used by the ancient Chinese.

Pictograms are picture-words that look almost exactly like the words they represented. But as Chinese writing continued to develop, its pictograms looked less and less like the words they stood for. In later Chinese writing, you can often still see a picture. But the picture is harder to find. This kind of Chinese writing is called calligraphy, and the pictures are called characters.

Here are some modern Chinese characters. Do they look like the words they stand for?

Mountain (can you see the peaks of the mountain?)

山

Fire (can you see the flames leaping up?)

火

Man (he has two sets of arms!)

夫

Horse (does this look like a horse to you?)

馬

Writing Chinese characters is more like drawing a picture than writing a word. Chinese calligraphers—people who spent many years learning how to write in Chinese—use seven different kinds of lines to write their characters. They call these lines the "Seven Mysteries." The first three lines are easy:

Horizontal Line:

Dot: 

Vertical Line: 

Can you draw these lines?

The next three lines that belong to the Seven Mysteries are a little more difficult:

Downward Stroke 1: This line is like a slope down from a flat place.

Downward Stroke 2: This line has a little point at the top.

Sweeping Downward Stroke: This line goes the other way!

丿

Can you draw these three lines?

The very last line is a Hook that can be drawn two different ways:

like this:

乙

or like this, like a big "L":

乚

Chinese calligraphers put these lines together to form Chinese characters. This character, for "field," uses three Horizontal Lines and three Vertical Lines:

田

It represents a farmer's field. Can you see the rows in the field?

Here is a character that uses a Vertical Line, a Horizontal Line, a Downward Stroke, and a Sweeping Downward Stroke. Can you guess what it is?

木

It's a tree. The Chinese word for "forest" is three trees, put together like this:

木
木木

Now let's look at one last character. It uses a Horizontal Line, a Sweeping Downward Stroke, and a Hook:

女

This is the character for "woman." It is supposed to look like a mother with a baby on her lap. Do you see anything that looks like a baby? Remember, Chinese characters aren't the same as pictures. Sometimes it is very difficult to see a picture in them.

In ancient China, calligraphy was done with a special sharp paintbrush, made out of animal hairs. Calligraphers made their own brushes by tying the hairs together into a little bundle with a silk thread. Then they glued the hairs into the end of a tube made out of a tiny piece of bamboo.

If the calligrapher wanted to paint very small, thin lines, he made his brush out of mouse hair, because the hairs are so little! If he wanted to paint medium-thick lines, he would use rabbit hair. And if he wanted to paint big, broad lines, he would use sheep hair—or wolf hair.

Painting each Chinese character took a long, long time. Can you imagine writing a whole book this way? Eventually, the Chinese people decided to find a quicker way to write books. They carved their characters into blocks of wood. First, the calligrapher would write the character on the block of wood. Then, a craftsman would carve away the wood from around the character, so that it stood out. Then the calligrapher would coat the raised Chinese character with ink, turn the wood block over, and press it down on a piece of paper. Now he could copy the character over and over in seconds, just by dipping the wood into ink and pressing it down.

This process is called "printing." With printing, books can be made more quickly and cheaply. The Chinese were the first ancient people to use printing. The oldest printed book in the world is called the Diamond Sutra. It was printed in China over a thousand years ago, but we can still read it today!

Confucius: China's Wise Teacher

When we studied India, we read about a prince who left his palace to wander through the world and look for the secret of happiness. He was named Siddhartha, but he became known as the Buddha. His followers are called Buddhists.

The Buddha taught that a good, virtuous man can be happy, even if he is poor. He taught his followers to be peaceful, honest, and kind, and to avoid doing any kind of violence, even to animals or insects.

At the same time that the Buddha was teaching people in India, another man in China was teaching the Chinese people that they too could learn to be happy, even if they were poor. His name was Confucius.

Confucius was born to a noble Chinese family. He had the chance to go to school, where he learned music and archery. But his family was poor. And all around him, Confucius saw war and turmoil.

He lived in China during a time called the Period of the Warring States. In those years, China was ruled by strong warriors called "warlords." Each warlord had his own, separate kingdom and his own army. There were at least seven strong warlords in ancient China—and at least seven different Chinese kingdoms. China wasn't one country. It was a whole handful of different countries, all fighting with each other!

Confucius hated war. He wanted the Chinese people to live in peace. He offered to work for the government of his own Warring State. He wanted to help the rulers make peace. But the rulers rejected his advice.

So Confucius became a teacher instead. He told all those around him his ideas for bringing peace and happiness. More and more people listened to his teachings.

Confucius taught his followers that each person should respect the authority of those who are greater. Children ought to listen to and obey their parents. Women should obey their husbands. Husbands should do whatever the rulers tell them to do. Rulers should obey the laws of the gods.

He also taught that people in authority should be kind to those who are beneath them! So rulers should be kind to men, men should treat their wives well, and parents should take care of their children.

Confucius's sayings were collected together into a book called The Analects of Confucius—written in Chinese calligraphy.

Here are some of his most famous sayings:

Do not do unto others what you
would not want others to do to you.

Can you think of something you would not want done to you? Should you do it to someone else?

Here is another saying:

If you make a mistake and do not correct it,
this is called a mistake.

This means that, whenever you make a mistake, you should try to fix it. If you don't, you have actually made two mistakes! Can you think of a mistake you made recently? Did you try to fix it?

It is the wiser person
who gives rather than takes.

Giving is more fun than getting! Do you enjoy watching other people open the gifts that you give them?

He who aims to be a man of complete virtue
does not seek to gratify his appetite in his food.

Good people are not greedy! Eating whatever you want whenever you want it shows that you don't have self control.

Even though the Period of the Warring States was a hard, violent time to live in China, Confucius offered the people of China a way to have a quiet, peaceful life—by living well, being honest and thoughtful, and following the rules. The followers of Confucius knew that they didn't have any power to make the Warring States stop fighting. All they could control was their own behavior!

Note: Confucius lived around 551–479 BC/BCE. The "Period of the Warring States" stretched from approximately 500 until 230 BC/BCE.

History-Maker

The Story of Mencius, The Greatest Follower of Confucius

ABOUT A HUNDRED YEARS AFTER THE DEATH OF Confucius, a baby boy was born on the eastern coast of China. His name was Meng-tzu, but we usually call him by the Latin form of his name: Mencius.

Mencius grew up in the little Chinese state called Zou, on the Shandong Peninsula. (Remember, a peninsula is a piece of land that juts out into a sea or ocean, so that it has water on three sides.) Zou wasn't one of the important

Mencius

Warring States—it was tiny and powerless, and Mencius's family wasn't wealthy or influential. And then, when he was only three years old, his father died.

His young mother had to move out of her husband's house—and decide how to raise her toddler son on her own. First, she settled down in a little house next to a cemetery. But after a year or two, she realized that while little Mencius was playing in the yard, he was imitating the funeral rituals that he saw people carrying out in the graveyard next door.

She didn't think this was a good way for a young boy to play! So she moved to an even smaller house, next to a marketplace. It didn't take long for her to realize that Mencius was now entertaining himself by pretending to be a salesman, shouting out to passersby to come and buy goods—just like the sellers in the marketplace.

So she moved for a third time, to a tiny house near a school. There, her growing boy started to copy the example of the teachers he saw every day. He began to read everything he could find, study with diligence, and learn about the world. Finally, Mencius's mother was content.

When Mencius was a young man, he began to study with Confucius's grandson, a teacher named Zisi. Mencius spent the rest of his life learning about Confucius's thoughts. He wrote down his own ideas, his conversations with other students and teachers, and many stories about his mother in a long book that was named after him. Centuries later, the book Mencius wrote would become one of the most widely read texts for students of Confucian thought. Mencius brought Confucius to future generations!

Mencius taught two very important ideas. The first was that people are essentially good. Mencius wrote that everyone is born with "sprouts of virtue" inside. Every boy and girl can water and fertilize these sprouts of virtue by having a good attitude and trying hard to do the right thing. Then, the "sprouts" will grow up into full-grown flowers of virtue, and bring joy and gladness. To illustrate this idea, Mencius often told the story of his mother's choice to live next to a school. When young Mencius imitated the teachers he saw, he was watering his sprouts of virtue and becoming a better person.

Here is another story he told about these sprouts of virtue. "Imagine that a little boy falls into a well," he told his listeners. "Everyone who sees the child fall will rush over to the well and try to get him out. They don't do this because they want to please their neighbors, or make the parents happy, or because the child is bothering them by making too much noise. They try to get him out because of the sprouts of virtue inside them. They want to do the right thing!"

But in the time of the Warring States, many people seemed to be evil. They acted violently and selfishly. So not everyone agreed with Mencius that people are good.

His second idea was even less popular!

The Warring States were full of war leaders who called themselves kings. But Mencius taught that a king could only rule if the "Will of Heaven"—divine power—approved of him. The Will of Heaven didn't talk out loud, though. It didn't announce from the sky, "This is a good king!" Instead, to find out the Will of Heaven, you had to talk to the people in the ruler's kingdom. If they were happy, safe, had enough to eat and drink, and had good places to live, that proved that the king had the Will of Heaven on his side. But if they were poor and miserable, the Will of Heaven was not on the side of their king.

When that happened, Mencius believed that the people could remove the king from power and choose someone else who would actually carry out the Will of Heaven.

The kings of the Warring States hated this idea! They didn't want their power to be questioned by anyone. Mencius offered to become an adviser to several different Warring States—but all of the kings turned him down. They didn't want Mencius in their state, telling people that if they were wretched, they could rebel against their king.

So Mencius went back to the town where he grew up. When he died, he was buried there in a special place called the Forest Grove of the Second Sage.

Today, Mencius is remembered as one of the very first teachers to argue that kings and governments are supposed to serve their people—not the other way around!

Note: Mencius lived c. 372-289.

Chapter Twenty-Seven
The Wars of the Greeks

Greece's War with Persia

The Greek cities of Athens and Sparta didn't have much in common except for their language and their gods. They *did* have something in common with the Warring States of China—they spent a lot of time fighting each other! Sometimes the Athenians attacked Sparta. Sometimes Sparta attacked Athens. The two cities went on fighting, off and on, for years.

But then something frightening happened. The Persians started to invade Greece.

Remember, the Persians became a great empire under the rule of Cyrus the Great. Now the Persians were ruled by another great king—Darius the Great. By the time of Darius's rule, the Persians had conquered almost all the rest of the land around them. Greece was one of the few countries that didn't obey the Persian Empire.

The Persians wanted Greece too.

At first, the Persians just sent messengers to Greece. The messengers came to Athens and Sparta and announced, "We are from the great king of the Persians! He wants you to be part of his empire. If you agree, send him back some earth and some water from your cities. Then he won't attack you."

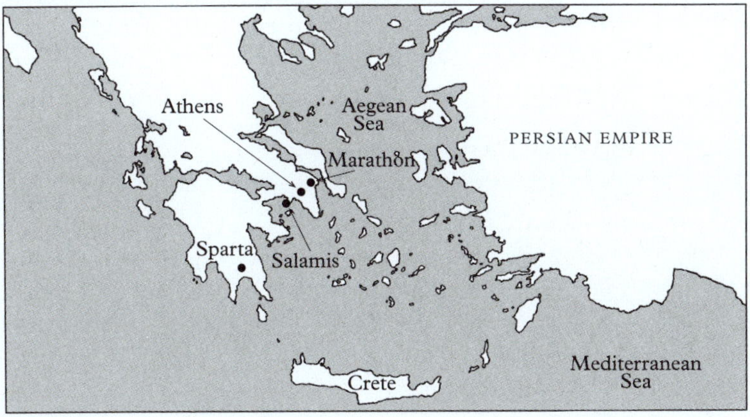

Greece's War with Persia

The Athenians and the Spartans were furious. How dare the king of the Persians demand that they surrender without even a fight? So they grabbed the messengers and threw them down a well. "There!" they said. "There's plenty of earth and water for you down there!"

After that, Persia was determined to attack. The Persian army advanced on Greece. Athens and Sparta decided that they had better stop fighting each other, and become allies, so that they could defend themselves against the Persians.

The war against Persia began around 500 BC/BCE. It dragged on for years and years, as Athens and Sparta fought battle after battle against the Persian invasion.

One of the most famous battles of the war was the Battle of Marathon.

Marathon was a little village near the coast of Greece, close to the Aegean Sea. One day in the year 490 BC/BCE, a ship came to Athens with frightening news: The Persians were coming! They were sailing from Asia Minor across the Aegean Sea, straight for the village of Marathon. The Athenians knew that if the Persians could land all of their soldiers at Marathon, the Persian army could march into Athens and destroy it.

So the Athenians sent a message to Sparta, saying "Come and help us!" But the Spartans were having a religious festival, and refused to leave Sparta until the festival was over.

The Athenians were outnumbered. There were too many Persian soldiers for the army of Athens to defeat alone. But the men of Athens had no choice. They marched from Athens to Marathon and waited for the Persians to land.

When the Persian army landed, they launched thousands of arrows at the Athenian army. But the men of Athens charged through the arrows and attacked the Persians. The Persians were so startled and disorganized that they lost the battle. They were forced to retreat.

When the Athenians saw that they had won the battle, they sent a runner back to Athens, to tell the people who were anxiously waiting at home that the Persian threat had been driven back. The runner, Pheidippides, ran over twenty-six miles, up steep hills and through rough country, to reach Athens. When he arrived at the city, he gasped out, "We have won!"

And then—according to legend—he died of exhaustion.

Today we have a race named after the village of Marathon. The race is a little over twenty-six miles long, and it is called a *marathon*. It is run in the Olympics in honor of the brave Athenian who ran from Marathon to Athens with the good news of victory.

The Battle of Marathon didn't end the war, though. The Persians and Greeks went on fighting until the Greeks finally defeated the Persians, once and for all, in a great sea battle at a place called Salamis.

After the Battle of Salamis (which took place in 480 BC/BCE) the Persians finally gave up attacking Greece. The Greek cities would remain free and independent from Persia.

The Greeks Fight Each Other

Now Greece was at peace. Instead of putting all their time and energy into fighting the Persians, the Greeks were able to do other things. They became famous for their *architecture*—the way they designed and built buildings. The Greeks built enormous buildings from marble. One of the most famous Greek buildings is called the Parthenon. The Parthenon was a temple built in honor of Athena, the Greek goddess of war. Its ruins still stand in Greece, in the city of Athens, on a hill called the Acropolis.

On both the inside and outside walls of the Parthenon were pictures, carved in marble, of different scenes from Greek history. These pictures were called *friezes*. One of the friezes shows a legendary battle between the Greeks and an army of centaurs. Centaurs are imaginary creatures that are half man and half horse.

The soldiers and centaurs on the friezes look very real. You can see the muscles in the arms of the soldiers, and the expression on the faces of the soldiers. The Greeks tried very hard to make their pictures and statues look like real people. The faces of their statues look like the faces of real men and women. And the folds of their clothing look like they are made from real cloth. It is hard to believe that they are carved from stone.

With the Persians defeated, Athens and Sparta no longer had to fight. The Greeks could have gone on making their beautiful buildings and creating their statues in peace.

But they didn't.

Sparta and Athens were both afraid that the other city would become too powerful. So instead of remaining on friendly terms, Sparta and Athens began to fight with each other again. This new war between Sparta and Athens began in 431 BC/BCE. It had a very long name—the Peloponnesian War. And the Peloponnesian War went on for a long time, over twenty-five years.

At first, Sparta gathered all its armies together and marched towards Athens to invade it. But the Athenians responded by building a high, strong wall all around the city—so fast that the people of Athens used every stone they could find, including columns from buildings and even tombstones! "We will fight with the 'Long Wall' of Athens!" the people said. Instead of fighting with swords, they would let the strong wall around the city protect them.

When the Spartan army arrived, they couldn't get past the wall—so they turned around and went home. But this certainly didn't bring an end to the war. Both the Athenians and the Spartans tried to claim control of the other Greek cities. The Spartans accused Athens of wanting to rule the whole world. The Athenians insisted that the Spartans hated democracy. The two armies fought battles with each other—and neither city gained the upper hand.

Then, a terrible thing happened in Athens. A dreadful sickness broke out, inside the city walls.

We don't know exactly what this sickness was, but it was probably spread either by fleas on rats, or by lice. But the Athenians didn't know this. They just knew that people were getting sick and dying all over the city. A historian named Thucydides, who lived in Athens during the great sickness, tells us that the people of Athens "died like sheep," and that the houses of the city were filled with bodies.

By the time the sickness ended, the greatest Athenian general, a man named Pericles, and many of the strongest young men of Athens had died. Athens was forced to make peace with Sparta. The city just didn't have enough men to keep on fighting.

But that peace only lasted for six years.

The Athenians and the Spartans simply refused to admit that either city was stronger. They refused to stop fighting. And one man, an Athenian named Alcibiades, took advantage of this ongoing hatred for his own gain.

Alcibiades was desperate for power and glory. Even though Athens needed to rest and recover from the horrible years of sickness, Alcibiades convinced the Athenians to send what was left of their navy back into battle again. He even volunteered to be one of the generals in charge of the attack.

But as the Athenian navy sailed towards its target, Alcibiades realized that the coming battle would be a huge disaster. He deserted the Athenians—and went to Sparta! There, he promised the Spartans that he would show them how to defeat the Athenians. Meanwhile, almost all of the Athenian navy was either killed or captured, and almost all the Athenian ships were destroyed.

With the help of Alcibiades, Sparta attacked Athens again. Even though Athens was weak, the Athenians defended their city with determination. So Sparta and Athens kept on fighting—for eight very long years!

Finally, when they realized that they could not conquer Athens, the Spartans kicked Alcibiades out. Alcibiades, who had collected a lot of treasure over his years away from Athens, wrote to the Athenians and offered to come back, with all of his gold, to help the city out.

The Athenians certainly didn't want Alcibiades back again! But they wanted to defeat Sparta, and they wanted the treasure Alcibiades offered. So they agreed to make Alcibiades commander of a new Athenian navy, as long as they could use his money to build new ships and hire new sailors. Alcibiades agreed. He returned to Athens, gave the Athenians his money, and claimed his new title as admiral of Athens.

The ruins of the Parthenon in Athens

Can you guess what happened next?

The rebuilt Athenian navy sailed into battle—and was wiped out. In August of 405, 171 Athenian ships sank in a single day! After the defeat, Alcibiades deserted the Athenian navy. He turned up a few years later in a village ruled by the Persians. He died there, in a house fire, and no one was sad about his death.

Now Athens had no money left, and only a few ships. But Sparta was not much better off. Most of the Athenian men and many of the Spartan soldiers had died in the long, long Peloponnesian War. Greece no longer had the men they needed to keep other invaders away. The Greek cities had spent all their energy fighting each other; they had none left to defend themselves.

And soon, invaders would come.

Note: The Peloponnesian Wars were fought 431–404 BC/BCE, with a brief peace in the middle.

Chapter Twenty-Eight
Alexander the Great

Philip and His Son

If the Greek cities had stayed friends and allies, like they were when they fought against the Persians, Greece would have been a strong country. But instead, Sparta and Athens kept on quarreling. They were like sisters and brothers who were too busy arguing with each other to notice that a bully is coming.

In this case, the bully was a king named Philip, who ruled a country called Macedonia.

Philip noticed that Athens and Sparta had become weaker and weaker after years of battle. And so he came down into Greece with his army and conquered the Greek cities. They barely had enough energy to resist.

Now Philip ruled Macedonia and Greece. But he wanted even more cities. He wanted to sail across the Aegean Sea to Asia Minor and take over the Persian Empire as well. But before he could attack Persia, Philip died. And his son Alexander took over his throne.

Do you know what the name *Alexander* means? It means "protector of men." In the ancient world, you protected someone by ruling over them. Alexander became the most famous ruler of men ever. He was known by the whole world as "Alexander the Great."

Alexander had always been an unusual boy. Even as a child, he was strong and brave. Nothing scared him. Here is a story that the Macedonians told about Alexander's childhood:

When Alexander was still a small boy, he went with his father Philip to look at a warhorse that Philip wanted to buy. The horse, a huge black stallion named Bucephalus, bucked and kicked constantly. No one could ride him.

"He's too wild," King Philip said. "I don't want him. I would never be able to manage him."

"I can ride him!" Alexander said.

"Nonsense!" Philip said. "You're too little."

"But I can!" Alexander insisted.

"If you can ride him, I'll buy him for you," Philip promised.

Alexander had been watching Bucephalus carefully. He noticed the horse kicked and reared whenever the sun threw his shadow on the ground in front of him. Alexander thought that the huge stallion was frightened of his shadow. So he walked fearlessly up to the horse, took his bridle, and turned him so that he couldn't see his shadow.

Instantly, Bucephalus stood still. He allowed Alexander to mount him and ride him around.

So Philip bought the horse for Alexander. And when Alexander became king after his father's death, the great black stallion Bucephalus always carried him into battle.

We don't know if Alexander actually tamed Bucephalus when he was only a child—but we do know that he loved his warhorse. He even named a city after his horse. He called it Bucephela!

Alexander had many opportunities to ride that warhorse into battle. His father, Philip, had conquered Greece, but Alexander had even larger goals in mind.

He wanted to rule Persia.

The Persians had given up trying to conquer Greece, but their empire was still the largest in the world. It stretched all the way from Asia Minor to India. And Alexander wanted it. When Alexander met the Persian army in Asia Minor, he used his cavalry—soldiers riding on horseback—to push the Persians back.

Asia Minor was now his. But could he conquer the rest of the Persian Empire?

Here is another story that Alexander's men told about his conquests.

Alexander and Bucephalus

ONE DAY, riding across his newly conquered lands in Asia Minor, Alexander stopped at the city of Gordium. There, he saw something odd in the city's center—a chariot tied to its axle with a huge, complicated knot of rope, larger than a man's head.

"What is that?" he asked.

"That is the Gordian Knot," the people told him. "We have a legend about it. The man who loosens that knot will rule all the rest of Asia. But it is impossible to untie the knot. Hundreds of men have tried, and no one has ever succeeded!"

Alexander studied the knot carefully. Then he took out his sword and sliced the knot in half.

"There," he said. "I have loosened the knot."

No one had ever thought of doing that before. But the prophecy of the knot came true—Alexander conquered all the rest of Asia.

Whether or not Alexander did actually slice through the Gordian Knot, he *did* carry out the prophecy—and even more! He went south into Egypt and was crowned the pharaoh of Egypt. And then he came back up into Mesopotamia and took over the rest of the Persian Empire.

Now Alexander was king of more land than anyone else had ever ruled. He was truly "Alexander the Great"—the ruler of the largest empire the world had ever seen.

Alexander's Invasions

Once Alexander the Great arrived at the edge of the Persian Empire, he wanted to keep going. He wanted to conquer all of India.

Alexander's army began to invade India. Alexander learned how to use elephants in combat. And his soldiers won most of their battles.

But the Indians who fought against Alexander were fierce warriors as well. Even though the soldiers from Macedonia won many battles, more and more of them died claiming these victories.

Finally, Alexander's army mutinied. After a particularly difficult battle, in which over a thousand soldiers were killed or badly wounded, the army refused to go any farther. "Be content with what you have!" they told Alexander. "We don't want to go on dying to make your empire bigger."

Alexander didn't want to stop. He stayed in his tent, sulking. He refused to see anyone, hoping that his army would change its mind.

But the men were firm: They would not fight in India any longer.

Finally Alexander agreed. He gave up trying to take over the rest of India. Instead, he put his energy into running the huge kingdom he already had.

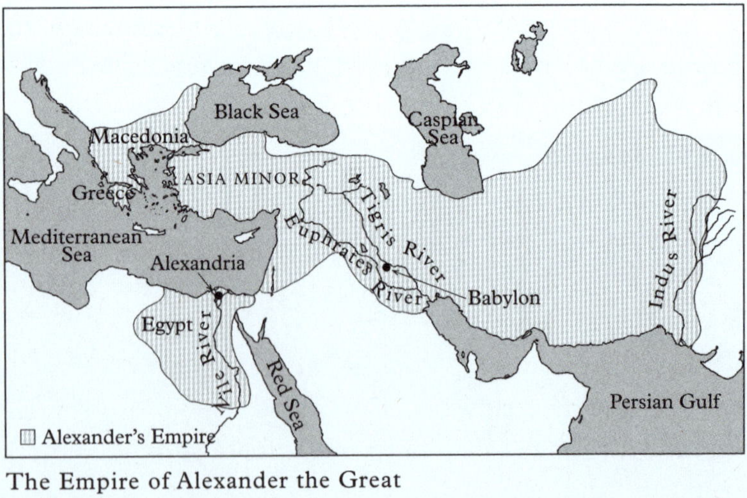

The Empire of Alexander the Great

Alexander wanted the people of the future to remember what a great ruler he was. And he knew that cities last for years and years. So he built new cities all over his empire. He named many of these cities after himself: Alexandria. Some of these cities still stand today. Just as Alexander intended, they remind us that Alexander the Great was the greatest conqueror of ancient times—and ruled over the hugest empire that the world had ever seen.

The most famous city called Alexandria is in Egypt. This Alexandria was built near the Nile River and the Mediterranean Sea, so that merchants could reach it easily by ship.

Alexander himself marked out the city's walls, but he died before he could see any of the city's buildings. But after his death, Alexandria became the greatest city in the world. Many famous scholars and writers lived in Alexandria. It became a center for art, music, and learning. Today, Alexandria is still a big and important city.

Just outside Alexandria was the biggest lighthouse in the world. It was called the Pharos, and it was 330 feet tall. Ships could see it from miles away. They used its light to sail safely into the harbor of Alexandria.

Do you remember reading about the Seven Wonders of the Ancient World? These were seven amazing sights of ancient times. We learned that the Hanging Gardens of Babylon, the Great Pyramid, and the statue of Zeus at Olympia are three of the seven wonders. The Pharos is the fourth. No one had ever seen a lighthouse as large as this one.

The Pharos was destroyed long, long ago. No pictures of the Pharos survive from ancient times. But only a few years ago, divers found huge chunks of stone at the bottom of Alexandria's harbor.

This stone may be all that is left of the Pharos.

The Death of Alexander

Alexander the Great became king when he was only twenty. Most people today haven't even finished college when they are twenty. But at this young age, Alexander inherited a throne and all the responsibilities of a ruler.

It only took Alexander eleven years to spread his empire all across the ancient world. One story tells us that when Alexander was still young, he burst into tears one day because there was no more of the world left to conquer. He had already seized it all.

What would Alexander the Great have done next?

We will never know, because Alexander died suddenly when he was only thirty-two. He was planning on taking an expedition with his army when he began to feel weak. He decided to wait a day or two until he felt better.

"Go ahead and make all the preparations," he told his generals. "We will go as soon as I recover from my sickness."

But that day never came.

Alexander got weaker and weaker. Finally, he was too weak to speak. His generals came to see him, but Alexander could only move his eyes. The next day, Alexander the Great died.

No one knows exactly why he died. Some people think he might have been poisoned by one of his generals who wanted his power. Others say that he probably died of malaria—a fever caused by mosquitoes who carry certain kinds of germs. We will never know for sure.

Alexander's body was put into a glass coffin and taken back to the city of Alexandria. The coffin was placed into a stone sarcophagus, there in Alexandria.

Alexander's generals knew that no one else could keep control of Alexander's large empire. Only Alexander could manage to rule such a huge kingdom. So they divided it up.

One of the generals took Macedonia and the northern part of Alexander's kingdom in Asia Minor.

Another general, named Ptolemy I, took over Egypt. His family would rule Egypt for three hundred years. Ptolemy was responsible for finishing the city of Alexandria; he built a huge library in Alexandria and filled it with books.

A third general, named Seleucus, took over the southern part of Asia Minor and Alexander's lands in Asia, almost all the way over to India. The descendants of Seleucus were called the Seleucids, or the Syrians.

Now Alexander's great empire had become three separate kingdoms, with three kings fighting for power. Alexander had brought a very brief time of peace by uniting different cities and nations into one country. But that time of peace was over. Alexander's three generals and their descendants would spend the next hundred years fighting over control of different parts of Alexander's old kingdom.

Note: Philip conquered the Greek city-states in 338 BC/BCE. Alexander the Great ruled from 336–323 BC/BCE.

Chapter Twenty-Nine
The Mauryan Empire of India

The Empire United

When we read about Egypt, we learned that Egypt was divided into two parts—Lower Egypt and Upper Egypt. The Lower and Upper Egyptians fought each other until King Narmer made them all into one country. After the Egyptians stopped fighting each other, Egypt grew to be rich and strong.

When we read about the Akkadian Empire, we learned that Sumer was full of lots of independent cities. Each one had its own army, its own king, and its own way of doing things. But Sargon, the first great Akkadian king, united all the cities into one empire with one king and one set of laws.

Sargon and King Narmer did the same thing: They made people who were quarreling and fighting with each other be friends and allies.

We also read about two cities that refused to be allies. The two great Greek cities, Athens and Sparta, fought with each other for years and years, until both cities were weak and tired. After Athens and Sparta were finished fighting each other, the Macedonians came down and conquered both cities! Athens and Sparta were too worn out to resist.

All of these countries were weak when they were divided, and strong when they were united.

India was no different.

When the Aryans first settled in India, they built many different cities. The cities belonged to many different small kingdoms. Each kingdom was independent, and the kings of these little kingdoms spent many years fighting each other—just like the Warring States of China.

But one family of Indian kings wanted India to be a strong, unified country. They united the different Indian cities together into one empire—the Mauryan Empire. This empire covered the whole northern part of India.

The most famous Mauryan emperor was named Asoka. He became king around 268 BC/BCE. Asoka conquered cities throughout India in a war that killed thousands of people.

But when Asoka visited the defeated cities after his great victories, he saw the suffering that his soldiers had caused.

Asoka renounced war after seeing the suffering it caused

"I will no longer fight with an army," he announced. "Instead, I will draw people into my empire through honesty, truthfulness, and mercy. I will follow the teachings of the Buddha and give up violence from now on!"

Asoka carved these ideas on stone monuments and pillars and set them up all around his empire. We can still read them today. He tried to reason with his subjects, rather than giving out strict, harsh commands. He tried to act kindly and mercifully to all his people. He had trees planted along the roads, so that travelers could walk in the shade. He built hospitals for sick people and for sick animals as well. He even made laws to keep people from being cruel to animals, and he became a vegetarian (someone who doesn't eat meat) so that no animals would be killed for his food.

Asoka became famous for his ideas and for his just, merciful rule.

The Jataka Tales

King Asoka gave up fighting and stopped eating meat because of the teachings of the Buddha. Many of these teachings are written down in one of India's most famous books. It has a very long name—the *Mahayana Tripitaka*.

This book contains all sorts of writings, but some of the best-known writings are called the Jataka Tales. According to legend, these tales were told by the Buddha to show the people of ancient India how to live. The stories explain that goodness, patience, mercy, honesty, and friendship will bring happiness.

One of these stories, called "The Hare," teaches that generosity will be rewarded. Here is how the story goes:

ONCE UPON A TIME, A HARE, AN OTTER, A jackal, and a monkey lived together in a deep wood near a village. Through the deep wood wound a long, dark path. Many travelers walked along the path, traveling to the village on the forest's other side.

One night, the hare, the otter, the jackal, and the monkey sat together around their evening meal.

"Tomorrow is a special day in the village on the other side of the forest," the hare said. "We should be ready to give food to anyone who is traveling to the village. Let's be generous and give our best to any traveler who asks."

The otter, the jackal, and the monkey agreed. The next morning, the otter went out to the river nearby to hunt for food. Now, that same morning a fisherman had caught seven red fish and buried them in the damp sand to keep them fresh. Then he had gone off downstream to fish some more. The otter smelled the fish and dug them up. "Whose are these?" he asked, looking around. "I don't see anyone to claim them. I'll take them home and eat them myself."

The jackal went out to the edge of the village on the other side of the forest and sniffed around a poor man's hut. In the poor man's kitchen, he found two pieces of meat and a jar of milk.

"Well, I don't see anyone in this hut!" he said. "So I'll just take these home and eat them myself."

The monkey climbed up a forest tree and picked mangoes for himself. He scurried back down the tree and hid the mangoes in his own bed. "Later," he said, "I'll eat these myself."

The hare went out into the field and started to pick grass. Grass was his favorite food. But then he stopped and thought, "A traveler will not want to eat grass! What else can I feed a hungry man who asks for food? I have nothing else! If someone begs me for a meal, I will offer myself for his dinner."

From up above, the god Sakka heard the hare's promise. "Can this be true?" he said to himself. "Will this hare really be so generous and unselfish as to give his own life? I will go down to the earth and see."

So Sakka disguised himself as a priest and went down to the earth. He walked along the forest path. Soon he saw the monkey.

"Monkey, monkey," he cried, "I am so hungry! Will you give me food?"

"I could share a mango or two," the monkey offered.

"Thank you," said Sakka. "I'll come back for it tomorrow."

Next he saw the jackal. "Jackal, jackal," he cried, "I am so hungry! Will you give me food?"

"Well," the jackal said, "you can have one of my pieces of meat, and a drink of my milk."

"Thank you," said Sakka, "I'll come back for it tomorrow."

A little further along the way, he saw the otter. "Otter, otter," he cried, "I am so hungry! Will you give me food?"

"You can have two or three of my fish," the otter suggested.

"Thank you," said Sakka. "I'll come back for it tomorrow."

Finally, Sakka met the hare. "Hare, hare," he said, "I am so hungry! Will you give me food?"

"All I have is myself," said the hare, "but you are welcome to eat me."

"But I am a follower of the Buddha!" Sakka objected. "I cannot kill an animal for food!"

"Then light a fire," the hare said, "and I will jump into it myself. Then I will be roasted for you to eat—and you won't have to kill me."

So Sakka built a fire. The hare shook himself, crouched down, and jumped into the flames. But although the fire licked at his fur, he felt no heat. "Why isn't this fire hot?" the hare asked. "It won't roast me so that you can eat!"

"Because I am no priest," Sakka said. "I am the god Sakka, come down to earth to see whether you would be as generous as you promised. Now, good and generous hare, live happily the rest of your life with my blessing."

And he made the hare a nest of soft grass and returned to his place in the sky. The hare lived happily ever after. When he died, Sakka drew his picture on the moon so that all could see it. Today, you can still see the picture of the hare on the surface of the moon!

Note: The Mauryan Empire lasted from 321–185 BC/BCE. Asoka ruled from 268–232 BC/BCE; the Mauryan Empire began to disintegrate after his death.

Chapter Thirty
The People of the Americas

The Nazca Drawings

We have been reading about the people who lived in Europe, Africa, and Asia. But over on the other side of the world, other ancient civilizations lived.

Like the people of ancient Africa, the people of the Americas didn't leave written records behind them. So we don't know as much about them as we know about the Egyptians, the Babylonians, the Assyrians, and the Greeks.

But the people of the Americas did leave artifacts behind them—ancient buildings, ruined villages, and mysterious earth mounds.

If you put your finger on the Fertile Crescent again, and this time go *left* (remember, left is *west*), you'll go across the Mediterranean Sea and out into the Atlantic Ocean. And if you keep going across the Atlantic Ocean, you'll come to two *continents* (big masses of land) linked together in the middle by a narrower strip. These are the Americas. The top continent is called North America, and the bottom continent is called South America. We call the strip in the middle Central America.

South America has mountains all along one edge and flat, fertile land in the middle. Tribes of ancient people lived both in the mountains and down in the jungles of the flat lands.

Like the people of ancient Mesopotamia, the people of ancient South America grew crops, kept animals, hunted, and caught fish. Just like the people of ancient Africa, they ate root vegetables every day. The African roots were known as yams, but South Americans grew a very similar root known as *cassava*. They learned how to dry the cassava roots and grind them up into a powder. They used this powder to make a kind of pudding that you may have eaten yourself—tapioca pudding. (If you haven't eaten it, ask your parents or your grandparents what it tastes like!)

One of these South American tribes was called the Nazca. They lived along the rivers of South America in a place that is now called Peru. The Nazca left behind them one of the strangest mysteries of ancient times.

More than two thousand years after the Nazca lived in South America, an airplane flew over Peru. The pilot looked down. He saw a drawing of a monkey—a drawing that covered hundreds of feet of ground. The lines of the drawing were scraped into the earth. From down on the ground, the drawings couldn't be seen. The lines just looked like old roads, or gashes in the ground. But from up in the air, those lines made pictures.

Soon, other fliers discovered more enormous pictures: a spider, a pelican almost one thousand feet tall, a hummingbird, and flowers. They also found spirals, squares, and other patterns carved into the ground. There were over a thousand line drawings and patterns there on the earth!

Because there is very little rain in the area where the Nazca drawings were made, the lines have lasted for over a thousand years. A highway was built across some of the drawings, and others have been damaged by cars driving

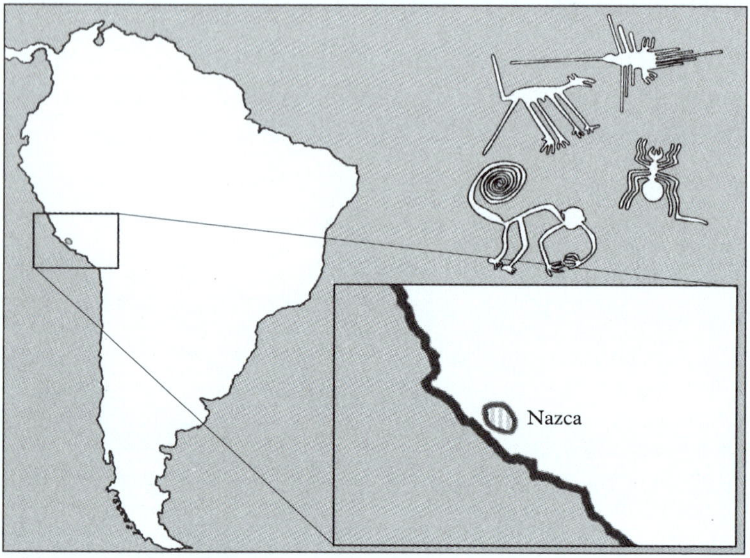

Nazca Line Drawings in South America

across them or by people scuffing at the lines with their feet. But many of the drawings are still intact. Look on this page for a map of the drawings. Can you tell what they are?

So how did the Nazca people make these drawings? After all, they couldn't fly. They couldn't get up in the air to see what their finished drawings looked like. Making a line drawing on the ground must have been like drawing with your eyes closed. Do you think you could draw these pictures with your eyes closed? It probably wouldn't look much like a bird when you were finished.

No one has been able to solve the mystery of the Nazca drawings. The best guess we can make is that the Nazca people were very good at mathematics. They could figure out how long each line should be, where it should turn, and where it should meet the next line through doing calculations. Another theory is that the Nazca artists used the position of the stars to help them with their drawings.

But the Nazca civilization ended about 1,500 years ago. So we will never know the answer to this question.

The Heads of the Olmecs

Just above South America is Central America, which is sometimes called *Mesoamerica*. Earlier, we read that *Mesopotamia* means "between the rivers" because *potamia* means "rivers" and *meso* means "between." (Remember the hippopotamus? *Hippo* means "horse" and *potamus* means "river," so a *hippopotamus* is a "river horse"!) Well, since *meso* means "between," *Mesoamerica* means "between the Americas." Central America is between North America and South America.

The Olmecs were the first civilization in Central America. They built a big city, now called San Lorenzo, in the country that we now call Mexico. The city stood up on top of a huge hill. The most important people—leaders, priests, and rich men—lived up in the city. Poor people and farmers lived down at the foot of the hill, on the plain. They grew crops on the plain and sent them up for the important people to eat. If you were an Olmec, it was much more fun to be rich than to be poor.

At the center of the city, on top of the hill, the Olmecs built a huge pyramid of dirt and clay. The platform was so high that it could be seen by someone standing miles away. Every single bit of clay that was used to build the pyramid had to be hauled up the hill in baskets. The Olmecs built the dirt pyramid basketful by basketful,

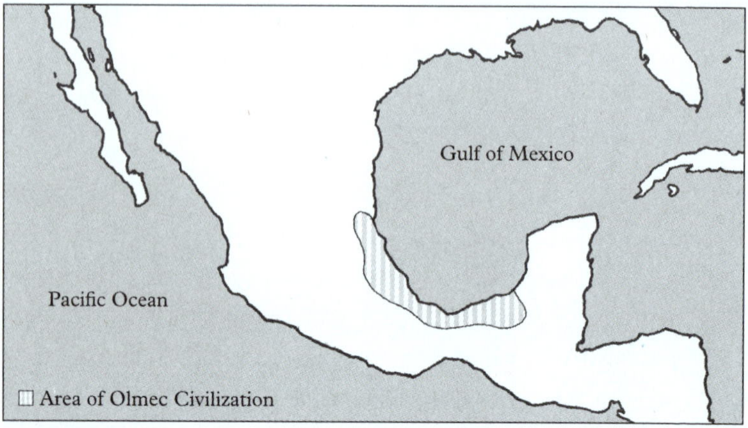

Mesoamerica

just like the Egyptians, who built their stone pyramids by hauling stone blocks one by one.

Up on top of this clay and dirt pyramid, the Olmecs built a temple to their gods. That means that the temple was the highest place in the whole city. We don't know what the Olmec gods were called, but we know what they looked like. One was a snake with feathers. Another was half human, half jaguar. A third was a dwarf-like creature who lived in waterfalls.

The temple of the Olmecs disappeared long, long ago. But the statues that stood around the temple still exist. They aren't statues of people. They're just statues of heads.

The Olmec heads are probably sculptures of important rulers. But none of these stone rulers has a body. The heads sit directly on the ground, as though an enormous stone person had been buried in the dirt up to his neck. And the heads are enormous—as big as eleven feet tall. That's taller than the biggest person you know, and probably higher than your ceiling. The eyes of the heads are bigger than your whole head. You could put your entire hand up their noses! If you were standing next to one, your head would only come up to its cheek.

An Olmec head

What if these huge heads had bodies? They would be stone giants, as tall as a four-story building. Their hands would be big enough for you to sit in. A grown-up's head wouldn't even reach to one of their knees.

The huge heads sat in a circle around the temple on top of the clay pyramid. What were they for? No one really knows. Perhaps the Olmecs, like the Egyptians, thought that their rulers were gods and wanted to honor them. Maybe they carved the giant heads to remember their rulers, the same way that we name airports and roads and buildings after our own leaders. Some archaeologists have suggested that the giant heads were used for altars, or for thrones.

But we will never know the answer. The Olmec heads, like the Nazca drawings, will remain mysterious.

Rabbit Shoots the Sun

Now let's travel up from Central America into northern America.

Today, North America contains the countries of Canada and the United States. But back in ancient times, tribes of people roamed all through this big continent.

Way, way up north, where the weather is very cold, ancient North American people hunted and fished to survive. It was too cold to grow crops, so they lived by trapping the animals all around them—seals, polar bears, birds, and caribou. (*Caribou* is another word for reindeer, which are horned animals like elk or antelopes.) They gathered and ate the special kinds of mosses and lichens that grow in the cold north. Some of the bravest even went out onto the icy seas in boats that were made out of skins. They fished and chased whales. A whale could provide enough meat for an entire village. And its blubber, or fat, made good oil for oil lamps.

In the middle of North America, ancient tribes grew corn and other grains. They followed the huge herds of buffalo that roamed around from meadow to meadow. They ate buffalo meat (the tongue was one of their favorite parts!). They used buffalo skins for clothes and for blankets and tents, and sharpened the buffalo's horns into knives. Tribes who lived near the oceans and rivers also fished and trapped.

The ancient North Americans didn't settle down in one place and own houses. Instead, they lived like nomads. They moved from place to place, eating whatever the land could give them. They didn't make written records, or leave great stone buildings behind them. Instead, they left us stories that were passed down from fathers and mothers to children for hundreds and hundreds of years.

Many of these stories try to explain something about nature. "Rabbit Shoots the Sun" tells us why rabbits are so timid:

IT WAS THE HOTTEST DAY OF SUMMER. THE rays of the sun beat down on the ground and turned it brown and dry. The grass withered in the heat. The animals were too hot and weary to run, hunt, or play. They lay in the shade, gasping for breath and wishing that the sun would set.

Rabbit had been trying to find water all day. Every puddle he came to was dried up into hard, black mud; even the stream had trickled away into dust. His throat was sore and dry. Even his eyes were dry! He sat down in the middle of the dry stream bed and yelled up at the sun, "Stop shining! Stop drying everything up! We need to cool off!"

But Sun paid no attention to Rabbit. He went on shining. The ground kept right on drying up, and Rabbit got hotter and hotter and thirstier and thirstier.

"Sun needs to learn a lesson," Rabbit grumbled. "I know what I'll do. I'll take my bow and arrows and go east, to the place where the Sun comes up every morning. And when Sun puts his head up tomorrow morning, I'll shoot him!"

Now, in those days, the Sun did not rise slowly, coming up over the edge of the world a little at a time. Instead, he jumped up into the sky with a great bound. And Rabbit knew that he could shoot an arrow directly into the middle of the Sun. So he grabbed his bow and arrows and loped off towards the east. As he ran, he sang:

Rabbit, great Rabbit,
Rabbit, enemy of the Sun.
The Sun will learn my strength.
Ho! Rabbit is coming!

When he reached the edge of the world, he sat down under a tree and waited. The sky grew dark. Rabbit waited all night long with his bow in his hands.

In the morning, Sun sprang up over the edge of the world. He laughed out loud and stood looking around him. At once, Rabbit jumped to his feet and shot an arrow straight into Sun's center.

At once, the arrow ripped a great hole in the Sun. Fire poured out all over the world. The tree above Rabbit's head began to smoke and crackle. The grass at his feet went up into flames. Rabbit's fur began to scorch. In a panic, he threw down his bow and arrow and ran away. As he ran, he called out,

Rabbit has shot the Sun!
Fire is over the world!
Watch out, watch out for the flames.
Ho! The fire is coming!

"Over here!" a little voice called. "Quick! Jump under me and you will be safe! I am so little that the fire will sweep right overtop of me!"

Rabbit looked and saw a tiny green bush. At once he jumped beneath it, buried his head beneath his paws and put his nose into the ground. The fire swept over him with a huge roar. When it had died away, Rabbit put his nose out from underneath the bush and looked around him. The fire was gone, but the world was brown and burnt. And the bush was no longer green. Now it was yellow, scorched by the fire. We still call it the yellow bush, because although it is green when it first grows, it turns yellow when the sun sweeps over it.

Rabbit crept quietly away. To this day, Rabbit runs and hides when the light of the sun falls over him. As for the Sun, he was never as bold as before. Instead of leaping up over the edge of the world, he creeps carefully up, little by little, looking all around him for Rabbit and his bow.

Note: Most of our detailed knowledge of South, Central, and North American native peoples dates from medieval times. The Mayans, the Aztecs, the Incas, the Native American tribes of North America, and the native peoples of South America will be covered in more detail in the second volume of *The Story of the World*, since in most cases their civilizations reached their highest points after AD/CE 400. This chapter is a first introduction to the Americas and highlights the most memorable tribe of each of the Americas in order to lay a foundation for later learning.

The Nazca civilization flourished around AD/CE 200. The Olmec civilization flourished between 1200–900 BC/BCE (roughly corresponding to the Assyrian expansion, the Greek Dark Ages, and the New Kingdom of Egypt).

Chapter Thirty-One
The Roman Republic

The Roman Builders

Let's go back to a city we haven't visited for a while—the city of Rome, now the center of the Roman Republic.

Do you remember the last king and queen of the kingdom of Rome? Tullia Minor and Tarquin the Proud were driven out of the city, and two consuls were chosen to replace them. The Roman Republic was no longer a monarchy.

But Rome was still warlike! The Romans weren't content just to stay in their little city of Rome. The bigger the city got, the more land the Romans wanted. And the best way to get land was to take it from other towns and tribes.

So the Romans attacked their neighbors and conquered them. The more land they conquered, the richer they got. Soon, the Roman Republic controlled the whole Italian peninsula.

Now, the Romans needed to be able to travel easily from one end of the peninsula to the other. So they began to build roads.

Most roads in the ancient world were rough, muddy tracks filled with holes and blocked by rocks and fallen trees. But the Romans built roads that were easy to travel on. First, they dug a wide ditch and filled the ditch with sand. Then they poured small stones on top of the sand. Next, they poured concrete over top of the stones. Finally, they laid wide, smooth paving stones on top of the concrete. Along the road, the Romans put up stone pillars and carved on them the distance between towns. A traveler on a Roman road could look at these *milestones* and know exactly how much farther he had to go!

The Romans became famous for their beautiful roads. The most famous of all Roman roads was called the Appian Way. It led from Rome to several large Roman cities in Italy. The Appian Way can still be used today. Roman roads were so well built that they lasted for hundreds of years. Today, many roads in Italy still follow the tracks of the old Roman roads.

And the Romans were the first ancient people to use concrete. They discovered that if they mixed volcanic ash, water, and lime, the soupy mixture would dry as hard as stone. They used this concrete to cement large stones together into both roads and buildings. In fact, the Romans built whole apartment buildings out of concrete. Some of these ancient apartment buildings were five stories high! One Roman writer tells the true story of an ox who escaped from his owner on market day and ran into an apartment building. It kept climbing up higher and higher and higher, until it reached the top floor. And then it jumped out of a window.

Unfortunately, some of the apartment buildings weren't very well built—and they collapsed, sometimes killing the people who lived inside. Others were slums, without any water or toilets. Whole families lived in one room. They dumped their waste out the windows into the streets.

As the Roman cities grew larger and larger, the people who lived in them needed more and more fresh water. So the Romans designed special channels for water, called *aqueducts*. The aqueducts were like narrow stone bridges with water pipes that ran across the top of them. Through these aqueducts, the Romans could bring water into the cities from springs thirty miles away.

The Romans needed water for drinking and cooking, but also for taking baths. Baths were very important to the ancient Romans! Most of them took a bath every day. But they didn't bathe in a bathtub, like you do. Instead, they went to the public baths, which were more like swimming pools. People gathered at the public baths to get clean. They rubbed oil or animal fat on their skin, and then scraped themselves clean with special curved blades. Then they could swim in cold or hot water, brought in by the aqueducts.

Today, the ruins of Roman roads, buildings, baths, and aqueducts can still be found in the places where the Romans lived—even though they were built more than two thousand years ago.

The Roman Gods

The Romans went to Greece to buy and sell. In Greece, they learned about the Greek gods, and heard Greek myths. And when they came back to Italy, they adopted the Greek gods as their own.

But they called these Greek gods by their own, Roman names. Do you remember Zeus, the king of the Greek gods? He made the golden apple so that he could start the

Trojan War on earth. In Rome, Zeus was called Jupiter. He controlled the sky, the moon, and the weather: wind, rain, and thunder. Today, we call one of the planets in our solar system Jupiter, after the Roman name of the king of the gods.

The planet Mars is also named after a Roman god—the god of war. (In Greece, Mars was called Ares.) And do you remember the Greek god of the sea, Poseidon, who tried to keep Odysseus from getting home? The Romans called this sea god Neptune. Our solar system also has a planet named Neptune.

The Romans told stories of their gods to explain the natural world. One story, about Ceres and her daughter Proserpine, tries to show why winter and summer come every year.

One day Ceres, the goddess of the harvest, and her daughter Proserpine were roaming through the woods. Wherever Ceres stepped, ripe grain sprang up; whenever she touched a tree, fruit blossomed beneath her hands. Her daughter followed along behind her, as beautiful as springtime.

Ceres stopped for a moment to drink from a cool stream. While she drank, Proserpine wandered away to a beautiful clump of lilies nearby. As she bent down to pick them, the ground suddenly opened beneath her and she disappeared! When Ceres looked up, Proserpine was gone.

"Proserpine!" Ceres called. "Proserpine! Where are you?" But there was no answer.

For fourteen days, Ceres wandered the earth, looking for her lost daughter. Finally, Ceres met a

Pluto stole Proserpine away

nymph who whispered, "I have just come from the Underworld, land of the dead. I saw your daughter there! She was stolen by Pluto, the king of the underworld, to be his wife! When he saw her, he fell in love with her, and the ground opened up beneath her so that she could walk through it into the land underground."

When Ceres heard this, she was furious. "I have helped the ground to bear crops!" she shouted. "And this is how it rewards me! I will curse it until it is dry and empty of all life!"

Instantly the trees around her began to turn brown, and the leaves fell from them. The grass died, and the flowers withered. In great rage, Ceres turned and climbed up into the heavens, all the way to the palace of Jupiter, king of the gods.

"Jupiter!" she said. "Force Pluto to return my daughter to me! If you don't, I will never again let spring come to the earth. There will never be fruit, or grain or grass again. The earth will always be as dead and hard as my heart without my daughter!"

Jupiter thought about this.

"Very well," he said at last. "I will tell Pluto to let your daughter go—on one condition. She can leave the underworld as long as she hasn't eaten or drunk anything in the palace of Pluto.

But if she ate or drank with him there, she will have to stay."

Suddenly the earth cracked open. There stood Proserpine, beside a tall dark man in a black cloak—Pluto, lord of the underworld.

"My daughter!" Ceres exclaimed.

"Wait," Jupiter said. "Proserpine, have you eaten or drunk anything in the underworld?"

"Hardly anything," the girl said. "I only ate six seeds from a pomegranate, just a few minutes ago."

"Then you must stay with Pluto," Jupiter said.

But Ceres refused to give in. "If I don't get my daughter back," she warned, "spring will never come again."

Jupiter considered the case carefully. At last he said, "She only ate six seeds. So for six months—half of the year—she must stay in the underworld with Pluto. But for the other six months, she can come and live with her mother in the world above."

And so Proserpine spends six months of every year in the underworld. When she is in the palace of Pluto, her mother Ceres mourns and weeps. The leaves fall from the trees, the grass turns brown, and the flowers die. But when Proserpine comes back to her mother each spring, Ceres rejoices. The leaves of the trees begin to grow; the grass turns green again, and flowers begin to bud and bloom.

Note: In Greek mythology, Pluto is known as Hades; Ceres is called Demeter; and Proserpine is known as Persephone. The Broadway musical *Hadestown* tells the myth using the Greek names.

The Roman Gladiators

Today we're going to read a story about a man who became a Roman gladiator—someone who fought with other men as a game. The man in the story, Servius, is imaginary. But there were thousands of men just like him in ancient Rome.

SERVIUS LIVED IN A SMALL VILLAGE NEAR THE sea. He spent his days working with metal—he made plows and hoes for the farmers who lived near him, and fishhooks for the fishermen. He liked his work. At night, he would sit with his friends around a fire and talk, sing songs, and tell stories. Servius was happy.

One day, as Servius was heating the metal to make a new hoe, he heard a thundering noise. He looked up, wondering if it was about to rain. But the noise wasn't thunder! It was the sound of horses' hooves. Around the corner of the peaceful village rode a group of men with swords, shields, and spears. They wore helmets and red cloaks.

"We are Romans!" the biggest man shouted. "We claim this village for Rome! Now you must obey us!"

Servius looked around for a weapon, but all he could see was a hoe, hanging on the wall! He grabbed it and swung it at the man, but he missed. Two other Roman soldiers leaped from their horses and seized Servius from behind.

"You are our prisoner!" the big man said. "You'll return with us to Rome."

They put Servius on a horse and made him ride with them for days and days down a broad, wide road of stone. Finally Servius saw the wall of a city ahead. It was the highest wall he had ever seen. A man standing on another man's shoulders couldn't even see over it.

The soldiers took him through a small gate in the city wall. When they came out the other side, Servius found himself in a narrow, crowded street full of people. Little wooden booths lined both sides of the street. Inside the booths, men and women were selling fruit, pieces of cooked meat, bread, cabbages and carrots, and jugs of cheap wine. Children ran down the middle of the street, chasing a mangy dog. Women hung laundry out on wooden balconies above the street. He could hear babies crying, men shouting, women talking to each other, horses and donkeys neighing. He had never seen so many people in one place at the same time.

Soon, the street grew wider, and the houses grew bigger. Servius began to see green gardens, fountains, and houses made out of white marble. There were fewer people here, and they were dressed in fancier clothes—white togas with borders of red and blue. They were approaching the center of Rome.

"Where are you taking me?" Servius asked one of the soldiers who rode beside him.

"To the gladiator school," the soldier said. "You're big and strong, and you have courage. You'll make a great fighter, once the trainers at the school have taught you what to do."

Servius felt his mouth go dry with fright. He had heard about the notorious gladiators of Rome—fierce men who fought with each other and with wild animals while a cheering crowd looked on.

"But what if I don't want to be a gladiator?" he said.

"You don't have any choice," the soldier answered. "You're our prisoner. Go to the gladiator school, or be executed."

They stopped at a high stone wall, and two Romans took Servius through the gate. Inside, a large courtyard was full of men, training for their gladiator matches. At the center, a man wearing only a loincloth and a belt was trying to throw a fishnet over his opponent. He brandished a three-pointed spear in his other hand. The man who fought against him was waving a short sword and defending himself with a large round shield. His helmet was covered with pictures of fish.

"The man with the net is called a net-fighter," one of the soldiers told Servius. "The other one is a fish man. The net-fighter is trying to catch him in the net and stab him. Maybe, if you're lucky, you'll learn how to be a net-fighter!"

Servius's knees were shaking with terror. If this was just the training camp, what would it be like to fight a real gladiator fight, in the arena? How could he ever survive?

The Gladiator School

At the gladiator school, Servius lived in a cell just like a prison cell. But he was taken out every day for gladiator training. First, he had to pass a test to see how fit he was. Two trainers—big men with scars on their faces, wearing armor and carrying short, sharp swords—walked all around him. They poked him and squeezed his arms. Then they pointed to a post, a hundred feet away. "How quickly can you run to that post and back?" one asked.

Servius scowled at the man. He didn't want to learn how to fight, but if he didn't, he would be killed. Finally he turned around and ran to the post and back.

"Very good," the trainer said. "Now let's see how you do for endurance."

For the rest of the day, the two trainers forced Servius to run, jump, wrestle, and climb. By night, he was covered with sweat and mud, and was so tired he could hardly drag himself back to his cell. But he had passed the test.

The next day, Servius stood in the courtyard along with five other new prisoners.

"You will be gladiators!" one of the trainers shouted. "Repeat after me the oath of the gladiator! 'I undertake to be burned by fire, to be bound in chains, to be beaten by rods, and to die by the sword.' To be a gladiator is a wonderful privilege! You are indeed lucky!"

Servius swallowed nervously. He didn't feel lucky. But all around him, the other prisoners were repeating the gladiator's oath. So he took the oath as well.

The next thing he knew, they were being marched off to their first training exercise—swinging wooden swords at straw men, propped up against the gladiator school wall.

The trainers had once been gladiators. They taught Servius and the other new recruits sword-fighting moves. When Servius had learned the moves, he then fought against one of the other gladiator students. They both had wooden swords, so no one got killed. But Servius didn't parry quickly enough, and the other student's wooden sword crashed against his side. He was sore for days, but the trainers just laughed at him.

"You'd better learn to be tough," one of them said. "We don't care if it hurts. Just keep fighting. You'll get hurt worse than that when you fight in the arena."

In the arena! Servius's heart sank. He already knew that his first fight in the arena was only a week away. He was to be a *secutor*, a gladiator who chased net-fighters around the arena. He had already practiced fighting with his real weapons and armor—a short, strong sword, a large shield, and a metal leg-guard that covered his left leg. On his head he wore a round helmet with two tiny eyeholes. He could barely see out of the helmet! How would he ever catch a net-fighter? What if the net-fighter caught him first?

On the day of the fight, Servius was taken to the arena—a large bare space near the outer walls of Rome. Wooden seats had been built all around it. They were filled with men and women, and even children. All of them were cheering and shouting. They were enjoying this!

Servius's trainer put his helmet on and tightened his armor. "Go get him!" he said, and pushed Servius into the arena. The metal helmet was hot and tight. Servius felt like he could barely breathe. He turned his head and caught sight of his opponent—a net-fighter, creeping towards him from the other side of the arena. The net-fighter threw his net. Servius felt it strike against his shield. He advanced forward, waving his sword. The net-fighter backed away. Suddenly he turned and began to run.

"He's as frightened as I am!" Servius thought. He started to chase the net-fighter. His heavy armor slowed him down. The net-fighter wasn't wearing armor. He was getting away.

Suddenly the net-fighter tripped and stumbled. Before he knew it, Servius was standing right over top of him. He could hardly believe it. He had won the match! He put his foot on the net-fighter's chest and looked around him. The crowd was booing and making the thumbs-down sign.

Servius knew what that meant. They wanted him to kill his opponent. If the net- fighter had been brave and bold, the crowd might have had pity on him and turned their thumbs up. Then, Servius could show mercy and let the other man live. But he was supposed to do whatever the crowd said.

Servius looked down. The net-fighter knew what the thumbs-down meant. He had closed his eyes. He thought he was about to die.

Servius stepped back and put his sword back in its sheath. "Get up," he said. "I can't kill you. I am not an animal! I know that it would be wrong to kill a man for sport."

The net-fighter scrambled away from him, hardly able to believe his ears. The crowd was booing louder and louder. They wanted to see blood!

But Servius turned around and walked back towards his trainer. He knew he would be punished. Maybe he would even be killed. But he knew now that he could not kill another man.

The Romans were an accomplished and powerful people, but they were also bloodthirsty. They liked to see men hurt. They enjoyed seeing blood.

Some of the historians who lived in Rome thought that this bloodthirstiness was wrong and evil. They wrote about men like Servius who refused to kill their opponents in the arena. Some even killed themselves so that they would not be forced to kill other men. The Roman philosopher Seneca the Elder wrote, in a letter to a friend, "The show was even better to watch when this happened—because the men in the audience learned that it is more decent to die than to kill."

History-Maker

The Story of Spartacus, The Rebel Gladiator

The gladiators of Rome lived harsh, difficult, short lives. Some of them rebelled against this life by refusing to kill. Others tried to win every fight so that they could live as long as possible. And still others tried to creep out of the camp and escape back to their homes.

But a gladiator named Spartacus chose another way to rebel. He assembled an army of gladiators to defy the Romans!

We don't know very much about Spartacus's early life. He was originally from Thrace, which was a nation north of Greece. The Romans thought that Thracians were barbarians, so when they took Thracians captive, they treated them like slaves. Spartacus must have been captured when his village was overrun by Romans.

The historian Plutarch says that Spartacus was educated, and cultured. Maybe he was a schoolmaster, or a merchant, or even a historian himself! But that didn't matter—because when he was captured by the Romans, he was sent to a gladiator training school in the city of Capua.

Capua was south of Rome, and the gladiator school there had a reputation for being one of the most horrible of all gladiator schools. Plutarch says that the gladiators there "had done nothing wrong, but, simply because of the cruelty of their owner, were kept in close confinement until the time came for them to engage in combat."

Spartacus endured life in the gladiator school as long as he could. But the locked cells, the lack of food, the vicious instructors, and the violent training exercises were finally too much for him. He gathered up seventy-eight of his fellow gladiators, and convinced them to break out of the camp.

The gladiators didn't have any weapons, because those were all locked up by the trainers. Instead, they raided a butcher shop nearby for kitchen tools—knives and spits and giant forks and pokers. Then, they ambushed a shipment of gladiator weapons bound for the training school, and took those as well. When Roman troops chased the escaped prisoners down just outside the city, Spartacus and his gladiator friends managed to drive them back with the kitchen implements and stolen gladiator swords and spears.

Spartacus

Now Spartacus was the leader of a gladiator army! And a full-blown war began between the Romans and the escaped gladiators. It became known as the Gladiator War.

Spartacus knew a lot about military strategy—maybe from his studies before he was captured. When he found out that three thousand Roman soldiers were assembling to attack the rebel gladiator camp, he made a plan.

When the Roman soldiers approached, the gladiators fled from them, up a nearby mountain. The Romans thought they were winning! There were only two ways off that mountain—down a sheer cliff on the other side, or back through the three thousand Roman attackers. The Romans advanced with confidence. The gladiators were trapped!

What Spartacus knew, though, was that the sheer cliff was covered with thick, ropy vines. The gladiators hauled the vines up, cut them off, and made ladders out of them. Then, they dropped the ladders off the cliff, scrambled down them, and then ran around behind the attacking Romans and trapped *them* on the mountain instead! The Romans had to surrender.

Spartacus led the gladiators in more and more victories. They were joined by other escaped gladiators, fleeing slaves, and unhappy conquered peoples who didn't want to be under Roman rule. Eventually, Spartacus had seventy thousand men under his command.

But then, Spartacus began to lose control over his army.

You see, Spartacus knew that the gladiators couldn't conquer Rome. Rome was too powerful and too large. The Romans would win in the end. So Spartacus just wanted the gladiators to claim their freedom. He tried to convince his army to leave the Roman Republic, march up to the north of Italy, and go over the mountain range called the Alps. Then, all of them could scatter and go back to their homelands.

But now that the gladiators had a taste of victory, they didn't want to leave. They wanted to keep on attacking Roman cities and taking booty for themselves.

As more and more Roman cities suffered from gladiator attacks, the two Roman consuls decided to send an enormous army against Spartacus and his men. Spartacus had to lead his gladiators in retreat. He went towards the coast of Italy, and paid a pirate fleet to pick up the gladiators and sail them away across the water to safety.

But the pirates weren't honest pirates! They took Spartacus's money, and then abandoned the gladiators on the beach.

The Roman army started to build a wall to trap the gladiators where they were. But then, Spartacus had a bit of luck. It started to snow—and the snow became heavier and heavier. Spartacus led his army through the snowstorm, which was so heavy that the Romans couldn't see through it, and the gladiators escaped.

The Romans must have felt that Spartacus couldn't be defeated! And Spartacus himself began to plan out a final escape from Italy for his men. Meanwhile the Romans brought even more troops.

And then the story came to a tragic end.

The gladiators had become so confident in their own power and strength that they ignored Spartacus's instructions. If they'd followed Spartacus's plans, they might have won the Gladiator War. Instead, they mounted a hasty, rash attack on the strengthened Roman lines—and were finally defeated.

Spartacus himself did his best to drive back the Romans. He drew his sword and fought his way through the Roman soldiers, making his way straight for the general of the Roman troops, calling to his own men to follow him. Instead, in fear they deserted him—and the Romans surrounded and killed him.

The gladiator rebellion had failed. Spartacus was dead, and the Romans put almost all of his followers to death as well.

But Spartacus had fought bravely and honestly until the very end of his life. His fame and his nobility lived on in stories for centuries. In fact, a very famous movie was made about Spartacus that people still watch today!

Note: Spartacus lived 103-71 BC/BCE. There was more than one gladiator revolt against the Romans; the Gladiator War is also known as the Third Servile War (73-71 BC/BCE).

Chapter Thirty-Two
Rome's War with Carthage

The Punic Wars

Rome took over all of Italy. But the Romans still weren't happy. They wanted more!

Unfortunately, another city, Carthage, also wanted more. Do you remember reading about Carthage? The Phoenicians built the city of Carthage on the northern coast of Africa. They sailed their trading ships in and out of Carthage for hundreds of years.

Carthage made a lot of money trading with cities all around the Mediterranean Sea. They wanted to keep on trading with these cities, and they didn't want Rome to get in the way! But the Romans also wanted to trade with these same cities, without Carthage interfering. So Rome and Carthage began to fight. They fought for years and years and years. These wars were called the Punic Wars. They began in 264 BC/BCE. And they didn't finally end until 146 BC/BCE, over a hundred years later.

At first, Carthage had the advantage because it had a navy—soldiers who knew how to sail ships. Rome didn't have a navy. But when a Carthaginian ship wrecked on the coast of Italy, the Romans took it apart and figured out how to copy it. They built ships of their own and learned how to sail them. Soon the Romans could match the Carthaginians in a sea battle.

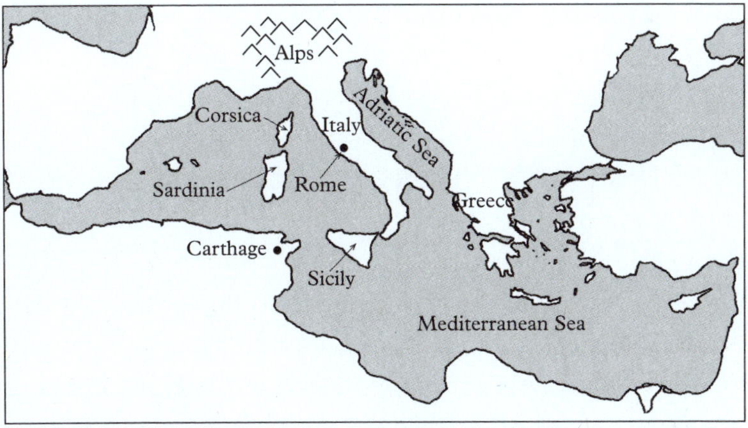

Rome and Carthage

But Carthage was a tough enemy. The Romans had to work hard to beat them. They made lots of sacrifices to their gods, asking for victory. One Roman general named Claudius Pulcher actually took sacred chickens with him on his ship! He hoped that the sacred chickens would give him good fortune in battle. And he also thought that he could foretell the future by watching the way the chickens ate.

Unfortunately, the chickens got seasick and wouldn't eat at all. This was a very bad sign. The Roman soldiers on Claudius Pulcher's boat got more and more nervous. "The gods are against us!" they whispered. "We can tell, because the chickens aren't eating! We are doomed to fail!"

Claudius Pulcher got more and more irritated. Nothing he could do would make those chickens eat. So finally he ordered, "Throw the chickens overboard!"

Sure enough, he got badly beaten in the next battle. And all of his soldiers thought that they were defeated because they had thrown the sacred chickens into the sea.

The Carthaginians and Romans fought back and forth for a long time. Neither side could win. And then, one of the Carthaginian generals got a wonderful idea.

Instead of attacking the Romans with ships, he would attack them with elephants!

Roman soldiers were camping near the Alps, up in the north of Italy, when they heard strange noises. They peered out of their tents into the swirling snow and mist. Suddenly, huge dark shapes loomed up in the snow. The ground shook. A herd of wild elephants was charging through the camp.

The Roman soldiers fled in terror. Many of them had never seen an elephant before. And these were no ordinary elephants. They were specially trained for battle. When they were told to attack, they spread their ears wide out to make their heads even larger. Their heads and ears were painted red, white and yellow, to make them look even more terrifying. Some of them were pulling carts full of armed Carthaginian soldiers, shooting arrows at the Roman troops. Others were carrying wooden boxes that contained even more attacking soldiers.

Some of the Romans did try to fight back. They ran for their horses and mounted, ready to attack the thundering beasts head on. But the horses were stricken with terror. They bolted, carrying the Roman soldiers off into the dark.

The Carthaginian general who planned this attack was named Hannibal. Hannibal saw that the ongoing fight between Carthage and Rome at sea was a stalemate—no one was winning. So while the two navies fought with each other, Hannibal took his army and forty elephants around the Mediterranean Sea by land. He surprised the

Romans by coming down over the mountains into Italy. His invasion took place in 218 BC/BCE.

Once Hannibal had gotten into Italy with his elephants, he roamed up and down Italy, burning villages and leaving Roman soldiers dead all through the countryside. The Romans were terrified. And they were afraid that Hannibal would come all the way to the city of Rome and burn it too.

Hannibal, the Carthaginian general

Then a Roman general named Scipio thought of a plan to defeat Hannibal and his men. He gathered together the best Roman soldiers, sailed down to Carthage, and attacked the city itself.

The city of Carthage wasn't expecting to be attacked! And all the best Carthaginian soldiers were over in Italy. So the people of Carthage sent a message to Hannibal: "Come back to Carthage and help us!"

Hannibal left Italy and sailed across the Mediterranean Sea to defend his hometown. But his soldiers were so worn out from burning and sacking towns in Italy that they were defeated! Hannibal himself ran away and hid, in Asia Minor.

Finally, the city of Carthage was forced to surrender to Rome. When Hannibal heard this news, over in Asia Minor, he drank poison. He could not bear to think that his great city, Carthage, had been beaten by the Romans who were afraid of his elephants.

Note: The First Punic War was fought 264–241 BC/BCE; the Second Punic War took place 218–202 BC/BCE.

Chapter Thirty-Three
The First Dynasties of China

The First Emperor and the Great Wall

We've learned about several different countries that had to be united by strong kings. King Narmer made Upper and Lower Egypt into one country. Over in Sumer, Sargon the Great united all the different, fighting Sumerian cities into one country. And in India, the different cities were all independent until the Mauryan Empire united them all into one country.

Exactly the same thing happened in China!

Remember, this time in China was called the "Period of the Warring States" because China was filled with different kingdoms ruled by warlords. The Warring State all the way to the west was called Qin (pronounced "Chin"). Its warlord, Qin Zheng, had an army with one million men in it.

The other Warring States didn't like the Qin. They thought the Qin people were barbarians—uncivilized people who didn't care about reading, writing, or art. But the Qin army was the strongest army in China. The Qin conquered the other Warring States, one at a time, until Qin Zheng ruled all of China.

In 221 BC/BCE, Qin Zheng declared himself the first emperor of *all* China. Of course, China had had other rulers who called themselves *emperor*. But Qin Zheng claimed to be the first *true* emperor of all Chinese people. He even changed his name to Shi Huangdi. In Chinese, this name means "First Emperor." Qin Zheng, now called Shi Huangdi, wanted his subjects to remember his claim to be the most powerful ruler China had ever had, every time they spoke his name.

Shi Huangdi knew that the conquered warlords would try to rebel against him. So he forced all the warlords and former rulers of the Warring States to move into his capital city. As long as they lived near him, he could keep an eye on them and make sure they weren't planning to overthrow him. He took all their weapons away, melted them down, and turned the metal into twelve enormous statues, which he put in his own palace. He built wide, straight roads so that his soldiers could travel quickly to fight anyone who might try to rebel against him. He executed anyone who might be planning treason. And because he was afraid that Chinese writers might encourage the Chinese people to get rid of him, he ordered thousands and thousands of books burned.

Some of these books were printed. But many were written by hand. Calligraphers had spent years and years laboring over their pages. But Shi Huangdi didn't care. He wanted those books

Shi Huangdi, China's "First Emperor"

destroyed so that no one would get rebellious ideas from them. His prime minister even announced that anyone who discussed books in public would be executed in the marketplace.

Shi Huangdi kept his new empire together. But he used burning, destroying, and killing to keep his power. Even though he gave his name to the country of China, many Chinese people despised him for his cruelty.

One day, the First Emperor sat on his throne, thinking about his new empire. He had been careful to stamp out rebellion inside his borders—but his kingdom wasn't secure yet. Outside the borders of China, ferocious tribes roved through the wild mountains and plains of the north. For years, these northern barbarians had attacked the Warring States, trying to take over their land. They were the earliest of the tribes which were later called Mongols.

The Mongols rode swift horses and shot arrows with deadly precision. So some of the Warring States had built walls to keep the Mongols out. These walls were still standing, but parts of them had crumbled away into dust. And between the walls were huge gaps.

"The Mongols could come through those gaps at any time," Shi Huangdi thought. "They could sweep down and take over parts of my empire. How can I protect China from the Mongols? If only I could build a wall along the whole northern side of my empire!"

Then Shi Huangdi had an idea: a stupendous, incredible idea. "Perhaps I can build a wall along China's northern border!" he exclaimed. "A wall thousands of miles long! A Great Wall!"

So Shi Huangdi summoned his architects and builders. "All along the northern part of my empire," he told them,

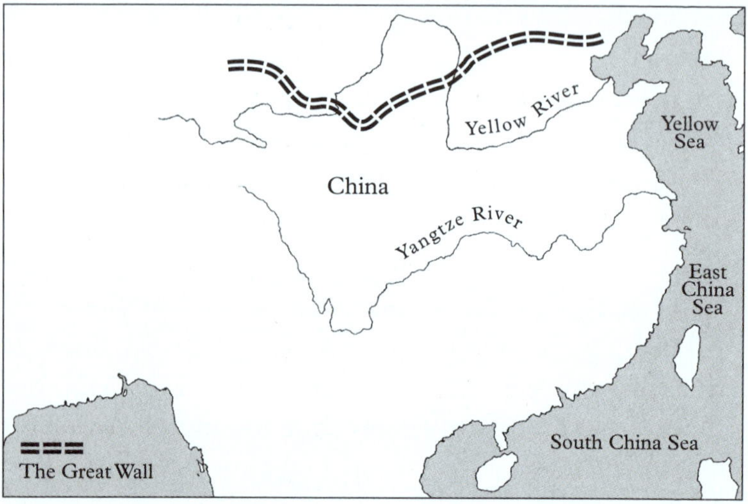

The Great Wall of China

"old walls are falling down. I want to repair these walls. And then I want to build a new wall, connecting all the old walls together into one huge barrier that will keep the Mongols out of my kingdom."

"But, Emperor," the architects and builders protested, "there is not enough stone in the far reaches of your kingdom to build a Great Wall!"

"Then think of another way to do it," Shi Huangdi ordered.

The builders and architects labored for weeks, trying to think of a way to build the wall in places where stone was scarce. Finally, they discovered a way. The builders made a wooden frame, as high as a man's waist and as wide as a wall. They set this frame upon the ground and filled it with loose dirt. Then workers stamped and packed the earth until it was only four inches high and as hard as concrete. They lifted the frame up, set it on top of the packed dirt, and filled it again. They could build a dirt wall as hard as stone, four inches at a time!

When Shi Huangdi saw the dirt wall, he was pleased. "Now it is time to build!" he commanded. And he ordered thousands and thousands of men out to work on the Great Wall. He sent peasants who had no choice but to obey. He sent his enemies and his prisoners out to work on the Wall, forcing them to labor day and night. He declared that every grown man in China must work on the Wall for one month out of the year. And he sent his armies out to guard the workers from attack as they built the Wall.

For years, the people of China worked to finish the Wall. They built up over mountain ridges and down into valleys. As the Wall grew higher and higher, they were forced to haul dirt up to the top in small baskets. It took days and days to complete even one section of the Great Wall.

When Shi Huangdi died, the Wall was still unfinished. But over the next few hundred years, each Chinese emperor who came to the throne sent men to work on the Wall. Guard towers were built every few miles, so that watchmen on top could see the Mongols coming long before they reached the Wall. Brick and rock reinforcements were added to the dirt sections. Eventually, the Wall was three thousand miles long, long enough to reach from one side of the United States to the other!

Today, long stretches of the Great Wall of China still stand. Although some parts of it have collapsed, others are still strong and high enough to walk along. People come from all over the world to walk on the Great Wall of China.

The First Emperor's Grave

In 1974, before you were born, two men were digging a well. They were farmers who lived near the city of Xi'an, in the middle of China. The morning was hot; the sun beat down, and the two men were sweating and thirsty.

"Let's stop for a drink," one of the farmers said to his friend.

"Oh, let's just dig a little longer," his friend answered. "We're bound to hit water soon."

So they kept digging. The ground was hard, and the dirt they turned up was red and rocky. Soon their shovels began to turn up pieces of broken pottery.

"Someone broke a pot here," the first farmer said.

"Those pieces are too big for a pot!" his friend said. "And look. That piece looks like … an arm!"

The two friends kept digging. They found broken arms and legs made out of clay—and even a head, wearing a helmet! Soon, word of their discoveries spread to the city of Xi'an. Archaeologists living in the city hurried out to see what the farmers had found. They began to dig deeper and deeper.

They found a huge underground pit filled with three thousand soldiers, made out of clay baked hard. The soldiers were life-sized! And buried along with the soldiers were sharp, shining weapons, full-sized horses also made out of clay, and wooden war chariots. The horses wore clay saddles, and harnesses made from gold and bronze. As the archaeologists uncovered each soldier, they saw that every single face was different—molded to look like a real person. No two soldiers were the same! And all the soldiers were facing east, as though they were guarding something behind them. What were they guarding?

They were guarding the tomb of Shi Huangdi.

You see, the First Emperor of China wanted to live forever. He spent the last part of his life looking for the Water of Eternal Life, a legendary drink that would keep him from dying. He made five different trips into the mountains of China, looking for this Water.

But he never found it. And when he knew that his death was near, he ordered a great underground city, more than five miles wide, built for his tomb. He hoped that his body would stay forever in this city. Shi Huangdi ordered his crown, robe, and royal bed to be placed in one of the chambers. He commanded his servants to enter the chamber every day, even after his death, to make the bed and bring water and food—just as though he were still alive!

So far, archaeologists have found three pits filled with clay soldiers. At the center of the underground city, a huge burial mound rises up above the ground. Underneath this burial mound lies the tomb of Shi Huangdi. Ancient Chinese writers, describing Shi Huangdi's underground city, tell us that the tomb itself is far, far below the mound—almost a hundred feet below the surface of the ground. The tomb is made of stone, covered with melted copper to keep the water out.

What is inside the tomb?

We don't know for sure, because archaeologists have agreed to keep the tomb sealed. But shortly after the death of Shi Huangdi, an ancient Chinese historian described the burial chamber like this:

> *Rare treasures and jewels, removed from various palaces, towers, and halls, filled the grave. Craftsmen were ordered to set arrows on crossbows, which would shoot automatically at anyone breaking in. Rivers and seas in miniature were dug and filled with mercury, made to flow by mechanical devices. On the ceiling, stars and planets were set. Candles were lighted, burning fish fat, so that they might keep the grave chambers lit for a long time.*

Does the burial mound really contain all of these wonders? Well, archaeologists have already discovered that the ground around the mound contains mercury—a silver metal that flows like water. This mercury must have come from inside the mound.

One day, archaeologists may be able to use technology to peer inside the tomb without breaking its seal. That way, we might be able to see what's inside it—while we avoid those automatic crossbows!

The Han Dynasty and the Silk Road

Shi Huangdi, the First Emperor, wanted his dynasty to rule China for centuries. But the Qin dynasty—the first to rule all of China—lasted less than fifteen years.

After the First Emperor died, his son, the Second Emperor, copied his father's harsh methods. He killed everyone he suspected of plotting against him—until the Qin army mutinied against his cruelty and made his young nephew the Third Emperor in his place. But the Third

Emperor only ruled for forty-six days before a full-scale war broke out!

Remember, the Warring States of China had only been conquered by the First Emperor twenty years before. They weren't used to being part of one China. They were very ready to break apart and go back to being separate Warring States instead.

But an army general named Liu Bang wanted to see the dream of one China come true.

Liu Bang had been born a peasant, but he worked his way up through the army to become a well-liked general. He was a kind and generous leader, and he was more merciful than the Qin emperors. In fact, one story about Liu Bang says that when the Second Emperor ordered him to put hundreds of prisoners to death, Liu Bang managed to set those prisoners free, because he knew that they were innocent. He could have been put to death for this, but instead, he did what he thought was right and fair.

When Liu Bang announced that he would try to keep the Warring States together in one nation, his men followed him and fought on his side. Liu Bang was able to claim the title of emperor of China! He built a capital city at Chang'an, just south of the Qin capital; he gave himself the royal name Gao Zu; and he announced that his dynasty would be known as the Han.

The new Han emperor wanted to hold onto his throne—but he knew that he couldn't be as severe as the Qin emperors. If any of the Warring States tried to revolt, Gao Zu marched the Han armies in to defeat them. But he also told them that no one would be accused of a crime, or punished, without plenty of evidence. He told his supporters that they wouldn't have to pay any taxes, as a sign of his gratitude for their loyalty. And when he did conquer rebellious armies, he pardoned everyone who fought against him, as long as they hadn't cursed his name and said that he wasn't worthy of being emperor.

Imagine that you have six friends. The seven of you are all members of the same club—maybe it's a Scouting troop, or a sports team, or a chess or craft club. But the seven of you are always fighting with each other. You fight about what games you'll play. You fight about what you'll have for lunch. You fight about who's the best at skating, or dancing, or softball. You fight about everything all of the time.

Now imagine that the grown-up leading your club sits you all down and says, "The next person who starts a fight gets thrown out of the club forever, AND is grounded for a full year—you can't leave your room or do anything other than schoolwork—and no desserts!"

You might be able to avoid fights for a while. But finally, you would just all quit the club. It's too much stress to think about a year of being grounded with no games or desserts!

But what if the leader of the club said, "If any of you get into a fight, the two of you who are fighting will have to go off together and figure out a solution and then come back and tell me what it is. If you're able to find a good solution, we'll all go out and have ice cream together!"

Which approach might work better?

The first approach was the one that the Qin used; the second was the Han emperor's strategy. And the Han emperor succeeded.

In fact, he was so successful at reestablishing the single country of China that myths grew up around him. One story claimed that his father was actually a dragon god.

Another story says that he killed a gigantic white serpent threatening the Chinese people. Yet another story says that the First Emperor, when he was still alive, was told by a fortuneteller that a Son of Heaven (an emperor) would arise from Liu Bang's hometown!

When Gao Zu died, he was succeeded by his son, Wendi. Wendi followed his father's example. He was as kind and lenient as he could possibly be; he gave the different Warring States plenty of freedom to take care of their own people, as long as they didn't fight against him. He ruled for over twenty years, and when he died, the Han crown went first to his son Jing, and then to his grandson Wudi.

By the time of Wudi's reign, the Warring States had begun to forget the old, divided past. Wudi's subjects had begun to think of themselves as "Chinese." The Han Empire was no longer a patchwork of fighting warlords. It was a stable country with a strong, efficient ruler.

So for the first time, travelers from the west began to visit China, and discover all of the wonderful things that the Chinese people made and sold. They finally felt safe enough to make their way to the Great Wall and through its gates.

Today, we call the paths that these travelers took—from Europe, past the Mediterranean and into China—the "Silk Road." This name isn't quite accurate! Merchants who traveled from Europe to China did buy silk—but that was only one of the many, many things that Europeans found in China. They also bought perfumes, gold, jade and lacquer, rare and beautiful flowers, spices like cloves and ginger and cinnamon, and rugs with rich, complicated patterns.

And the Silk Road wasn't just one road! It was a whole network of paths, roads, and sea passages that led from Europe into China.

As more and more travelers made their way along the Silk Road, they brought with them European goods to sell in China as well—such as horses that were larger and stronger than the native horses of China. The people of the Han Empire called these "heavenly horses"!

The trade along the Silk Road brought Chinese goods to Europe, and also made China richer and richer. Even though the Qin dynasty gave its name to China, the Qin emperors ruled for just a few brief years. But the Han dynasty, which turned China into one of the wealthiest nations in the world, would survive for nearly 400 years.

Note: The "Period of the Warring States" began around 500 BC/BCE. Qin Zheng's forced unification began around 230 BC/BCE; the first united Chinese empire dates from the beginning of the First Emperor's reign in 221 BC/BCE. The burning of the books took place in 213 BC/BCE. Construction of the Great Wall of China began in 214 BC/BCE and continued for several centuries. After the First Emperor's death in 209, seven years of unrest led to the foundation of the Han dynasty in 202 BC/BCE. The Han dynasty ruled China until AD/CE 220.

History-Maker

The Story of Zhang Qian, Hero of the Silk Road

NEAR THE END OF THE REIGN OF THE FIFTH HAN emperor, a young man named Zhang Qian lived in a small village in the center of China.

He was a strong, generous young man, much loved by his friends and his family. He could have stayed home and lived a peaceful, prosperous life. But Zhang Qian longed for excitement and adventure. So he joined the Han army and learned how to fight. Soon, his commander saw his skill and his strength, and sent Zhang Qian to the capital of China so that he could serve in the emperor's court.

This was the beginning of an extraordinary adventure for Zhang Qian!

Just as he arrived in the capital city, the Han emperor died, and his son Wudi was crowned emperor in his place. The new Emperor Wudi knew that a few travelers were beginning to arrive from the West. He knew that bringing more merchants and visitors into his empire would help make the Han stronger and more important.

But it was still very hard for visitors to find their way from the lands around the Mediterranean all the way past the Great Wall, because the network of roads from west to east was so complicated. And there was an even bigger problem: barbarians! Nomads called the Xiongnu roamed along the border of the Han Empire. They captured and even killed travelers on their way into China. Trade couldn't happen if the merchants were afraid of dying!

Wudi had already heard about the strong, trustworthy young soldier named Zhang Qian. So he summoned Zhang Qian into his royal presence.

"I will send ninety-nine other soldiers with you," he told Zhang Qian. "This band of one hundred has two important tasks. First, travel to the edges of my empire and find a way to drive off the Xiongnu. Second—go west and map out better ways for the people there to travel into our country."

This was exactly the sort of adventure that Zhang Qian had been longing for. He immediately agreed to lead ninety-nine other men into dangerous, unknown lands. He would have to travel thousands of miles across unknown deserts and mountains to reach his goal. He couldn't wait!

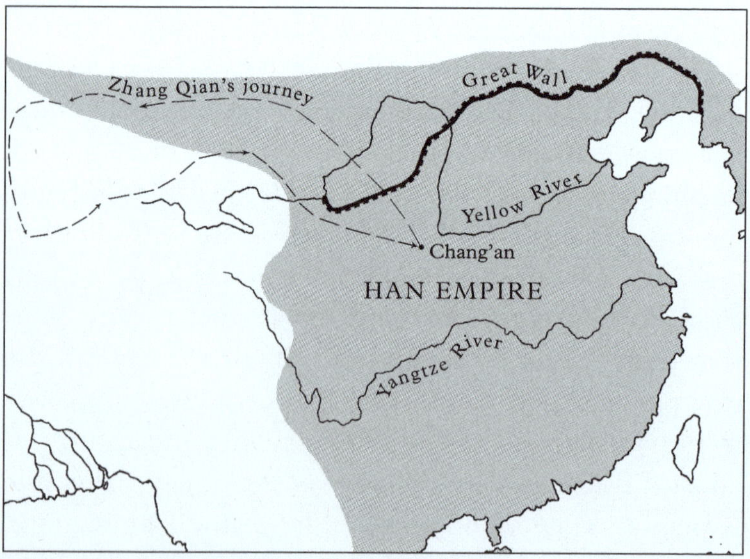

The Journey of Zhang Qian

Zhang Qian

He set off with his company as soon as they could gather food, drink, and supplies. They trudged through rough wild lands for many, many weeks, heading for the border of the Han Empire.

And then—disaster!

The Xiongnu descended on Zhang Qian's expedition. Most of the men scattered and ran, and the Xiongnu took Zhang Qian captive and hauled him back to the camp of their leader.

But the Xiongnu leader, a man known as the *chanyu*, or chief, took a liking to Zhang Qian. Like the young man's friends back in China, he found Zhang Qian to be generous, honest, and kind. So he did not order Zhang Qian put to death. Instead, the *chanyu* decided to keep him captive—but gave him a house, and even a wife.

For the next ten years, Zhang Qian lived with the barbarians. He became one of them. He and his wife had a young son. He earned their trust. They thought he had become one of them.

But finally Zhang Qian realized that the Xiongnu had stopped watching him so closely. Late one night, he packed up his bags, and led his wife and his son out of the Xiongnu camp, to freedom.

Together, the little family continued on the original journey to the West—ten years later! They traveled through the countries north of India, all the way over towards the coast of the Mediterranean Sea. Zhang Qian kept careful notes about the countries and kings that he met along the way.

Finally, more than twelve years after he set off on his journey, Zhang Qian returned to the capital city of the Han. He was greeted with great cheers and applause. Emperor Wudi had long ago given him up for dead—but instead, Zhang Qian had returned with hundreds of pages of written accounts about the kings and countries to the West.

Zhang Qian was a hero. And because of his amazing journey and all of his adventures along the way, the young men of Han China wanted to be just like him. All of the strongest and most ambitious courtiers begged Emperor Wudi to send *them* on journeys to the West, so that they could be like Zhang Qian.

More and more expeditions from Han China traveled west, mapped out the roads to the Mediterranean, and showed other travelers how they could come east to China. With better maps and better knowledge, the Han army was able to travel along those routes and drive away barbarian threats. The Chinese even began to establish army posts along the roads to protect travelers from attack.

Because of Zhang Qian and the young men who followed him to the West, trade began to flow along the roads between the West and the Han Empire—the roads that would become known as the Silk Road. European traders bought silk from Chinese traders, of course, but they also bought jade stones, beautiful beads, oils and spices, tea, stoneware and porcelain dishes, and also the amazing Chinese *lacquerware*—vases, plates, bowls, and cups made out of wood and layered with the sap of the

Chinese lacquer tree. This sap dried to a glossy smooth coating that could be painted, carved, layered with stones or shells, or even dusted with gold.

In return the Chinese bought goods from the West. They bought exotic pearls, elephants, lions, and ostriches, but also new vegetables and fruits: sesame seeds, peas, cucumbers, and grapes, which had never been seen in China before.

Zhang Qian spent the next years of his life traveling back and forth along the roads between the Han Empire and the West, and marking out paths for many, many others to follow him. Because he was the first to open up the Silk Road, he is still remembered in China as one of its greatest ancient heroes.

Note: Zhang Qian's first journey west was c. 138-126 BC/BCE.

Chapter Thirty-Four
The Rise of Julius Caesar

Caesar Is Kidnapped

One day, a baby boy was born to a rich family in Rome. The family was known as the Caesars, and they named their new baby Julius.

Remember, Rome had become a strong republic, ruled by two consuls who were elected by the citizens of Rome. The great city of Rome had become one of the richest cities in the world. People from far away knew about Rome. They admired its beautiful buildings and splendid roads. They came from all over to trade in Rome, to watch the gladiator fights, and to admire Roman art. The Romans were the most powerful and prosperous people anywhere.

The parents of little Julius Caesar were important, wealthy Romans. They claimed to be descended from Romulus, the founder of the city of Rome. Julius's father was a rich nobleman who helped to make the laws of Rome. And Julius's uncle was a consul, one of the two rulers of Rome. "My little boy will accomplish great things!" Julius's father declared. "He will become one of the most famous men in Rome!"

As soon as Julius was old enough, his father sent him to school to learn reading, writing, mathematics, and *rhetoric*—the art of speaking in public. Julius Caesar became very good at speaking in public. He grew up to be tall and strong, with keen black eyes and a deep, powerful voice. Whenever he made a speech, crowds gathered to listen to him.

Soon Julius decided that he wanted to help govern Rome. He threw big parties for the people he needed to vote for him. He did favors for them. He became more and more popular.

But Julius decided that he needed even more lessons in rhetoric, so that he could convince even more Romans to vote for him. And the most famous rhetoric teacher of all lived in an island in the middle of the Mediterranean Sea. So Julius Caesar hired a ship to take him out to the island.

"It'll cost you extra," the captain of the ship told him. "There are pirates all over the Mediterranean. Their ships are faster than anyone else's. They steal cargo and kidnap important people. No one can control them. Are you sure you want to go?"

"I'm not afraid of pirates!" Julius answered. He paid the captain of the ship and got on board.

But no sooner was the ship out of sight of land than another ship came into view behind it—a sleek, fast ship.

"Pirates!" the captain shouted. He tried to sail faster, but the pirate ship gained on him. All the sailors ran up to the deck to fight, but the pirates boarded the ship and took it over. They stole the cargo—and then they saw Julius Caesar, standing in the middle of the captured sailors. They could tell by his clothing that he was a rich, important man.

"We'll keep you for ransom," the pirate captain said. "Who are your relatives? We'll tell them that we'll send you back as soon as they pay us $100,000!"

Julius Caesar burst out laughing. "Is that all?" he said. "I'm worth at least $250,000!"

"You think you're so important?" the pirate said. "Very well, we'll keep you and see how much money we can make from you!"

"I'm warning you," Caesar said, "as soon as I'm free, I'll return and execute all of you."

The pirates laughed; they didn't take Caesar's threats seriously. They took him back to their ship and kept him for more than a month. But Caesar treated them as though *they* were the prisoners. "Savages!" he would call out. "Be quiet! I'm napping! And be sure that the food I'm served for supper is better than what I had for lunch!"

The pirates thought Caesar was funny. Finally, Caesar's family managed to put together the ransom and sent it to Caesar's captors. The pirates took the money and told Caesar goodbye.

"Go back to Rome, little boy," they mocked him. "Go back to where it's safe! The sea belongs to us."

But as soon as Caesar got back to Roman territory, he convinced the Roman navy to lend him three warships and several troops of soldiers. He sailed back out into the Mediterranean. Sure enough, he found his pirate captors anchored near a beach, waiting for their next victims.

This time Caesar was ready. He told his soldiers, "Get ready to fight!" He circled his warships around and met the pirates head on. The soldiers and pirates fought hand-to-hand, climbing from one ship to another, until the pirates were defeated.

"Now who does the sea belong to?" Caesar said to the pirate captain. He took the pirates back to Roman land, and had them all executed.

After this, everyone in Rome knew who Caesar was. They knew that he was a strong leader and a fierce fighter. Julius Caesar's name was on everyone's lips. The people of Rome were ready to vote for Caesar!

The Consuls of Rome

Once he was back in Rome, Julius Caesar decided that he wanted to be a consul—since the consuls were the most powerful men in the Roman republic.

But there was a problem: Rome already had two consuls. There was no room for Caesar.

Instead, Caesar was given the job of governing the Romans who lived all the way over in Spain. Many Romans had settled there, and they needed a Roman leader to run their colony.

Governing Spain was not Caesar's idea of an important job! But he knew that he could not become consul in Rome yet. So in 69 BC/BCE, he gathered together his men and his possessions, and set off for Spain.

He traveled up through Italy, over the Alps. On the way through the Alps, Caesar and his friends came to a tiny, shabby village high up in the mountains. The streets were made of mud. The people were dressed in rags. Goats ran around between the houses, and the children played barefoot in the dirt.

"What a disgusting place to live!" one of Caesar's friends exclaimed. "Can you imagine spending your life here?"

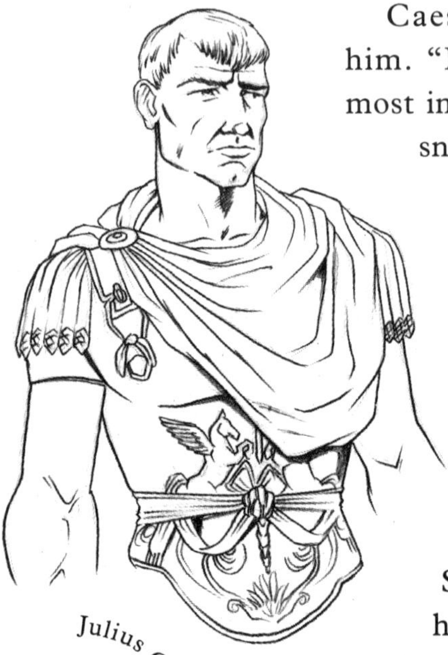

Caesar turned around to him. "I would rather be the most important man here," he snapped, "than second in command in Rome."

They traveled on to Spain. In Spain, Caesar worked hard and became popular. He drove away the mountain bandits that kept attacking the Roman cities in Spain. But all the time, he longed to go back to Rome and become powerful there, in his hometown.

One day, he was sitting in his library reading about the life of Alexander the Great. His friends were there with him, talking about life in Spain and when they might be able to return to Rome. Slowly they noticed that Caesar had stopped reading. He sat with his book on his knee, staring out the window. On the page in front of him was a picture of Alexander the Great, riding his great warhorse Bucephalus, with hundreds of cheering soldiers following him into battle.

Suddenly Caesar burst into tears.

His friends had never seen him weep before. "Caesar! Caesar! What is wrong?" they asked.

"Don't you think I have reason to be sad?" Caesar asked them. "By the time he was my age, Alexander the Great was already the king of five or six different countries! And I haven't done anything remarkable yet! I should weep and be sad! When will I have the chance to become famous?"

Finally, Caesar finished his job in Spain and went back to Rome. And he did something extraordinary—he convinced the two consuls who ruled Rome that he should become consul as well!

Now three powerful men ruled Rome—and Caesar was one of them. The three rulers were called the *triumvirate. Tri* means "three." How many wheels does a tricycle have? Three. How many children are there when triplets are born? Three. Triumvirate means "three leaders."

But Caesar became more and more popular with the people of Rome. They knew that he was a good general and a strong fighter, and they thought that Caesar could keep them safe. Before long, no one paid much attention to the other two consuls.

Caesar was the only one who mattered.

Caesar and the Senate

Julius Caesar was popular with the people of Rome. But he wasn't quite so popular with the Roman Senate.

The Senate was a group of rich, powerful men who made laws and decided what enemies Rome would fight next. The consuls were supposed to listen to what the Senate said and follow the Senate's decisions. But Caesar didn't pay very much attention to the Senate. Instead, he did what he pleased.

The Senate was deeply unhappy about this, and very, very suspicious of Caesar. "What if he wants to become king?" they asked each other. "What will happen to Rome? What will happen to us? One man should not rule Rome. We should govern Rome together, so that no single man has all the power in Rome! If only Caesar were like Cincinnatus!"

Who was Cincinnatus? He was a legendary Roman who represented the ideal ruler of Rome. Here is the story of Cincinnatus:

ONCE UPON A TIME, CINCINNATUS WAS A consul of Rome. But he lost his wealth, retired from his high position, and became a farmer instead. He spent his days planting wheat and tending grapes. But he was so wise and well-loved that Romans came to him from all over to ask his advice.

Now, Rome was the strongest city in the world. But one day, Rome heard disturbing news: A tribe of barbarians was headed towards Rome, burning and plundering everything in their path. They had sworn to conquer Rome and kill its people.

The Romans weren't afraid—yet. After all, the Roman army was the most powerful in the world. So Rome sent out its most skillful soldiers to stop the barbarians. The soldiers rode out of the city, splendid in shining armor and scarlet cloaks. The women and children cheered and waved. "Come back in glory and triumph!" they called out. "Come back in victory!"

They waited day after day after day. Finally, they saw dust in the distance: horsemen were approaching the city. But what had happened to the Roman army? Only five dirty, bloodstained soldiers were returning. They galloped through the gates into the center of the city and told their story, gasping with pain and weariness.

"The barbarians are too strong for us!" they said. "They attacked us at a narrow mountain pass! They came at us from behind and from ahead. And meanwhile they threw rocks at us from the hills above us. Send help to our army at once, or Rome will fall!"

The Senate was terrified. "All our strongest soldiers have already gone!" the senators said to each other. "We only have boys left. Who can lead them into battle?"

Suddenly one senator said, "Cincinnatus! Let us send for Cincinnatus. He is our only hope!"

Cincinnatus was out working in his fields when the senators arrived at his house. He washed the dirt off his hands and listened to their pleas. "If you will lead the reinforcements into battle," they promised him, "we will make you the king of Rome."

So Cincinnatus returned to the city with them and became the leader of the reinforcements. He armed the boys and taught them how to fight, and then led them out towards the mountains to rescue the Roman army. Cincinnatus was so wise and crafty that this troop of boys beat off the barbarians, drove them back to the mountains, and brought the rest of the Roman army home! They marched back into Rome with trumpets blaring and people cheering.

"Be our king, Cincinnatus!" the people of Rome begged. "We will give you all power! You can do whatever you want!"

But Cincinnatus took off his armor and gave his banner back to the Senate. "No," he said, "Rome does not need a king. I give all my power back to the senators. They should make your laws."

And he went back to his fields and his grapes, leaving the Senate in charge of Rome.

The Senate thought that Cincinnatus was the ideal Roman. He served his city when he was needed, but then he gave his power back to the Senate.

But Caesar wouldn't behave like Cincinnatus. He kept on gathering power. He became more and more popular.

"One day," the senators said to each other, "Caesar will try to become king of Rome. Then what will we do?"

Caesar Fights the Celts

Caesar didn't have any intention of going back to his fields, like Cincinnatus. He wanted to be the single—and most powerful—ruler of Rome.

But he knew that the Roman people wouldn't make him ruler yet. Before that could happen, the Romans would have to love him and trust him even more.

So Caesar set out to be the greatest war hero ever. If he won many battles and conquered a great deal of land for Rome, maybe he could convince the people of Rome to make him the leader of the entire republic.

Caesar took good care of his army. He trained them to fight. He paid them well and gave them plenty to eat. The soldiers weren't used to being treated so well. Soon they were completely loyal to Caesar. They followed him into battle against Rome's neighbors.

Caesar didn't always win his battles, but he didn't let the people of Rome know that. Instead, he only sent them messages about his victories! He pretended that he never lost a fight.

The country Caesar wanted to conquer most was called Britain. Caesar thought that Britain would be easy to conquer. But he had to build ships and sail his army across the water to get to Britain's shores.

He built the ships and put the soldiers onto them. The ships set out for Britain. But some of them got lost on the way. And the soldiers who were still with Caesar were cold, wet, and tired. They were sick of the ocean and ready to get back to dry land.

"Look!" one of them shouted at last. "Land!"

The soldiers clustered at the side of the boat, anxious to see Britain for the first time. They saw a misty green island—with an army waiting for them on its shore.

The people who lived in Britain were called Celts. They were tall, muscular, warlike men. They were so proud of their height and strength that they went into battle naked! They wore only metal collars and tall metal helmets that made them look even bigger. They carried heavy iron swords and wooden clubs. And they painted their bodies blue all over, because they thought that the blue lines would magically protect them from swords and arrows.

The Romans stared up at these huge, painted warriors. They began to murmur among themselves: "We can never beat them! They are too big and fierce!"

When the boy who held Caesar's flag heard the soldiers murmuring, he jumped out of his ship, into the shallow water near the beach. He started to wade ashore, holding the flag high. He wanted to show how loyal he was to Caesar.

The other soldiers didn't want to see Caesar's flag captured, so they leaped in after him. The Celts attacked. They fought there, ankle-deep in the water, for hours.

Finally the Celts retreated. The Romans landed triumphantly on the beaches of Britain.

But the Romans only stayed in Britain three weeks. A huge storm wrecked many of the Roman ships. More Roman soldiers were ambushed and defeated. Finally Caesar decided to leave Britain and come back with a bigger army.

He came back a year later with more soldiers. This time he was able to stay in Britain longer. He forced some of the Celts to pay money to the Roman army as tribute. But the other British tribes remained free of Roman control.

Caesar hadn't exactly conquered Britain. But he didn't tell the people in Rome about his defeats! Instead, he kept sending messages of victory back to Rome. He even wrote a book about his wars in Britain and in the nearby land known as Gaul (modern France), called *The Gallic Wars*. In his book, Caesar hardly even mentioned the times when he was defeated. He only talked about his successes. He didn't exactly tell lies, but he certainly talked about his battles in a way that made him sound even more victorious and successful than he was.

Note: Caesar was born in 100 BC/BCE. Caesar's campaigns in Britain took place 55–54 BC/BCE.

Chapter Thirty-Five
Caesar, Ruler of Rome

Caesar Crosses the Rubicon

Caesar's victories made him a hero to the people of Rome—but the senators were afraid of Caesar.

"If he comes back to Rome now," the senators said to each other, "the people will want him to be ruler of Rome! And then what will happen to us? We won't be able to run Rome anymore!"

Two of the senators decided that they would try to make one of the other consuls, Pompey, turn against Caesar. This was hard to do, because Pompey had married Caesar's daughter. But Pompey was jealous of Caesar. He knew that Caesar was much more popular than he was.

So Pompey decided that he would listen to the senators. "Listen," they said to him. "Tell the people of Rome that Caesar is a traitor! Tell them that he isn't loyal to Rome. Take away Caesar's position of consul before he gets back to Rome. Then you will be the strongest man in the whole city."

Pompey agreed to this plan. He sent a message to Caesar, telling him that he would be arrested when he returned to Rome. He told Caesar to give up command of his army. And all the people of Rome were told that Caesar was a traitor.

Far away in Gaul, Caesar got the bad news. His own city was calling him a criminal and a traitor, and the Senate wanted to arrest him and put him on trial! What should he do?

Caesar knew that the Senate didn't want him to have *any* power in Rome. But he was convinced that the Roman people still thought of him as a great hero. So he took his army and marched back towards Rome.

Soon Caesar came to the Rubicon River. The Rubicon was the border of Roman land. Caesar knew that as soon as he crossed over the Rubicon, he would be in the land controlled by the senators. The senators would try to arrest him, and he would have to fight them. His army would end up fighting against other Romans. So if he crossed over the Rubicon, he would start a *civil war*—a war that a country fights against itself. Should he do it?

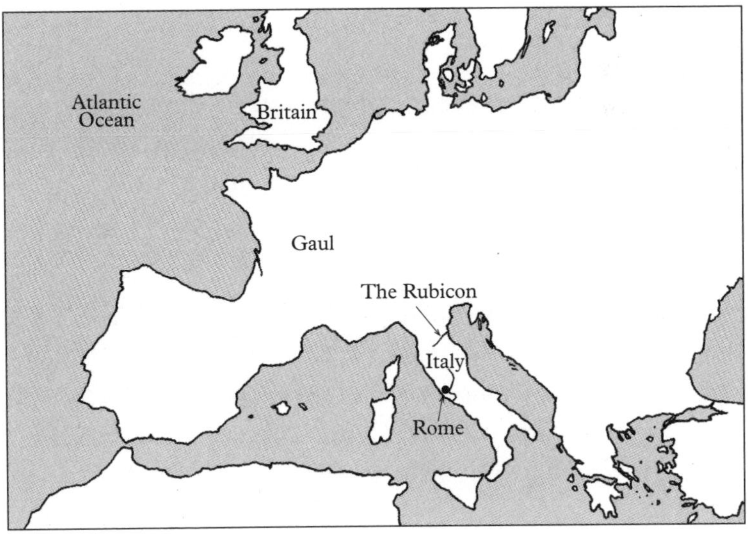

Caesar, Britain, and the Rubicon

He stood at the river for a long time, staring at the bridge.

"Even yet," he said to the captain of his army, "we may turn back. But once we cross that little bridge ... we will have to settle this with our swords."

Finally Caesar drew his sword and stepped onto the bridge.

"My enemies have forced me to do this!" he announced. "We will march into Rome. Let the die be cast!" He crossed the Rubicon on January 10, 49 BC/BCE. His army followed him towards Rome.

Back in Rome, Pompey and the senators were trying to raise an army of their own. But no one wanted to fight against Caesar's soldiers. After all, Caesar's army had spent years battling in foreign countries. They were tough, strong, and loyal to their leader. When Caesar and his army came in sight of Rome, all of Pompey's soldiers ran away. And before Caesar could enter the city, Pompey fled as well.

Caesar marched triumphantly into Rome. No one dared to arrest him. Now the Senate had to admit that Caesar was too powerful to drive away. Caesar wasn't the king of Rome, but he was the strongest man in the whole nation.

Today, when someone has to make an important decision, people still say "You're about to cross the Rubicon." *Crossing the Rubicon* means that you're about to do something that you can't undo. We get this expression from the story of Julius Caesar's return to Rome.

Caesar and Cleopatra

Caesar now ruled all of Rome and all of Rome's territories. The army obeyed him. The people loved him. And the Senate couldn't drive him out.

But Caesar still wanted to get rid of Pompey. He knew that Pompey had run away to Egypt. And down in Egypt, Pompey was trying to convince the Egyptians to help him attack Caesar and take Rome back.

"I can't leave him down there!" Caesar thought to himself. "He'll come marching back up here with a whole army of Egyptians and attack me again. As long as Pompey is free, this civil war will never end. I'll have to go down to Egypt and arrest Pompey and put him in jail before I can have any peace."

So he started down to Egypt. But the Egyptians were having troubles of their own. They had two pharaohs—a queen named Cleopatra VII and her brother, Ptolemy XIII. Cleopatra and her brother Ptolemy were supposed to rule Egypt together. But they didn't get along with each other. They fought constantly, because each one wanted to rule Egypt alone.

When Ptolemy XIII heard that Caesar was coming, he and his advisers were afraid that Caesar planned to conquer Egypt. "Let's make friends with Caesar instead," Ptolemy's advisers told him. "Caesar's old enemy Pompey is living in Egypt. Let's arrest him and send him to Caesar as a prisoner. Then Caesar will know that we want to be his allies—and he will help us take the throne of Egypt away from Cleopatra."

Ptolemy agreed to this plan. But the men that he sent to arrest Pompey didn't just take Pompey prisoner.

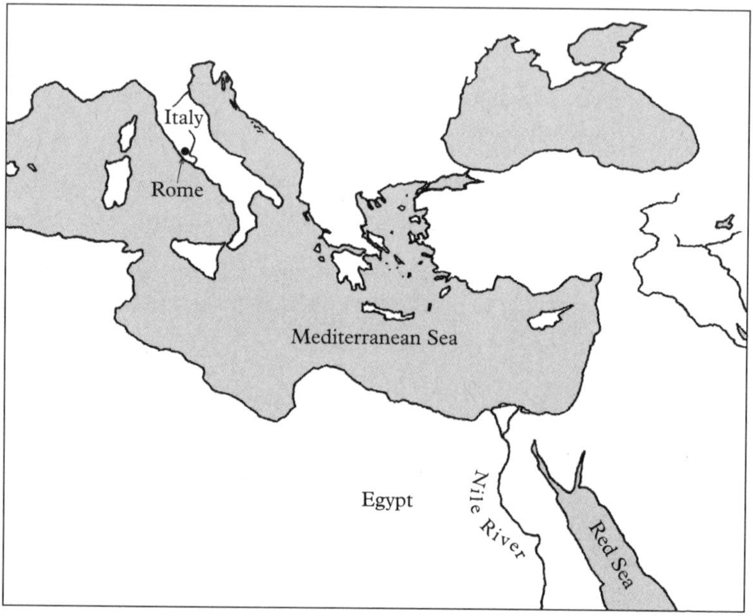

Rome and Egypt

When they found Pompey, one of them stabbed him—and another one cut off his head!

Ptolemy hoped that this would still impress Caesar, so he ordered his advisers to put Pompey's head in a basket and send it to the great Roman warrior. Caesar was startled to get Pompey's head in a basket. And he was sad, too. He and Pompey had once been friends. They had been consuls together for years. And Pompey had been his son-in-law! He hadn't intended to kill Pompey. He just wanted to put him in prison where he couldn't cause any more trouble.

Caesar marched the rest of the way to the Egyptian palace, intending to tell the pharaohs of Egypt how unhappy he was. Meanwhile, though, Cleopatra had an idea. "If I can get Caesar to like me," she thought, "maybe he will help me get rid of my brother Ptolemy! Then I will be the only pharaoh of Egypt!"

So she arranged to meet Caesar all alone. She put on her prettiest clothes and surrounded herself with beautiful treasures of Egypt: gold, spices, monkeys, slaves, and jewelry. When Caesar was shown into Cleopatra's room, he was dazzled by her beauty, and by the riches all around her!

"Caesar," Cleopatra said sweetly, "if you'll help me get rid of my brother, so that I can rule Egypt all by myself, I will share Egypt's riches with you."

Caesar was overcome by Cleopatra. He fell madly in love with her and agreed to do everything she said. He told his army to fight against the Egyptians who were loyal to Cleopatra's brother. The Roman soldiers did as they were told. Cleopatra's brother Ptolemy was killed in the battle, and Cleopatra became the sole ruler of Egypt.

When it was time for Caesar to go back to Rome, he delayed. He didn't want to leave Cleopatra. Instead he stayed in Egypt, keeping his new love company.

But the senators back in Rome still wanted to get rid of Caesar. "This is our last chance," they said to each other. "Let's raise an army of Romans who are loyal to the Senate and try to defeat Caesar, one last time!"

So they gathered together an army and marched down towards Egypt, ready to attack Caesar. Caesar hadn't forgotten how to fight, though. He got his own soldiers together and defeated the Senate army in record time.

Caesar was known for his fast victories. In fact, after one victory, when a friend asked him to describe the battle, he answered, "I can do it in three words: *Veni, Vidi, Vici.*"

In Latin, the language of the Romans, this meant, "I came, I saw, I conquered!"

The Death of Caesar

Caesar finally left Egypt and came back to Rome. No one could fight against him anymore—and the people of Rome loved him. So when he came back to Rome, Caesar was made dictator for life.

A dictator can do whatever he wants. Once Caesar was dictator, he took power away from the Senate. Now, only Caesar could declare war, pass laws, and raise taxes. He started to make money with his own picture on it. He paid for gladiator fighting and chariot racing to amuse the people of Rome.

Everything seemed to be going his way.

But then Caesar did two things that made many people angry. First, he called the Senate together. "I am the dictator of Rome," he told them, "but the kings of other countries will respect me more if you call me 'King Caesar.' So from now on I want you to call me 'king.' Second, I want my nephew Octavian to be king after me. I'm going to adopt him to be my son. I want him to inherit my power too."

The Senate was horrified. They wanted to choose the next leader of Rome. They didn't want another Caesar on the throne, and they didn't want kings of Rome to keep on passing their power on to their sons.

"We have to get rid of Caesar once and for all," said one senator, named Brutus. He had been a friend of Caesar's, but now he too was worried about Caesar's power in Rome.

"Tomorrow is the fifteenth of March. We'll attack him as he enters the Senate and stab him to death!"

Other senators agreed, and the plans were made. Caesar was doomed!

Caesar didn't know anything about the plot to kill him. But a Roman writer named Suetonius tells us that many strange things happened to Caesar leading up to that day. He went out to visit his favorite herd of horses, and found that the horses weren't eating. Instead, they were crying. This made Caesar so nervous that he went to the temple, to ask the gods why his horses were so sad. But while he was in the temple, a fortune teller came up to him and whispered, "Caesar! Caesar! Beware the fifteenth of March!"

When he got home, Caesar told his wife all about the strange things that had happened that day. During the night, she had a terrifying dream. She dreamed that she was holding her husband in her arms, and that he had been stabbed to death. She cried out, "Caesar! Caesar!" and woke up. She sat straight up in bed, and the door of their room flew open—all by itself.

When Caesar got up the next morning, his wife pleaded with him, "Don't go to the Senate today. It's the fifteenth of March. Stay home where it's safe."

"Nonsense!" Caesar said. "Nothing will happen to me." He dressed and headed for the Senate building. He walked up the smooth marble steps. The sun shone on the white stone, and the sky was blue and peaceful overhead. "How silly of me to be nervous!" he thought. "Nothing will go wrong today!"

He went into the room where the Senate met and sat down in his special chair.

"Caesar," said one of the senators, "today I want to ask you to bring my brother back to Rome. He was banished several years ago."

"Let's talk about that later," Caesar said, still thinking about his wife's dream.

The senator leaped to his feet. "Friends!" he shouted, "what are we waiting for!" He ran forward and grabbed Caesar by his purple robe. Brutus and several other senators leaped at him with knives drawn. Caesar fought back, but they stabbed him. He staggered, and fell down at the feet of a statue of Pompey. When he looked up, he could hardly believe that his old friend Brutus had helped plot against him.

"*Et tu, Brute?*" he gasped. In Latin, this meant, "You, too, Brutus?"

And then Caesar died, there on the marble floor of the Senate building. His slaves came and carried his body home. Caesar, the greatest Roman, had been killed by his own friends and countrymen.

Augustus Caesar

After Caesar died, Rome was in an uproar! Who would be in charge of Rome now? The people had loved Caesar. They were angry about his death. Some of the senators were angry about Caesar's death too. Other senators were glad that Caesar was gone. The senators quarreled with each other. The people of Rome were restless. Fights broke out. Rome was in chaos, and no one was in charge.

Caesar's nephew, Octavian, was only nineteen when Caesar died. But he had inherited all of Caesar's money, because he was Caesar's adopted son. He took Caesar's money and threw a big party in memory of Caesar. The party lasted ten days, and the whole city of Rome was invited. Then Octavian gave presents and money to every poor family in Rome. Suddenly Octavian was very popular! The people of Rome loved him because he was generous. The army loved him because he was Caesar's adopted son.

When he saw how popular he was, Octavian went to the Senate and demanded to be made a consul. The Senate didn't want to make Octavian a ruler of Rome. He was too young, and he was too much like Caesar. Once he had power as consul, he could start to work towards becoming a king.

Octavian, Rome's "First Citizen," was renamed Augustus Caesar

But the people of Rome and the army wanted Octavian to be a consul, and the Senate was afraid to say no. So Octavian became a consul of Rome. Just like Julius Caesar, he led the army into nearby countries and conquered them for Rome. Just like Julius Caesar, he made the Roman Empire bigger and richer.

Octavian didn't make the same mistakes that Caesar had made, though. He knew that

Caesar had made the Senate angry when he demanded to be called "king." Octavian wanted to be like Cincinnatus instead. Remember, Cincinnatus was taking care of his grapes when the Senate asked him to be head of the army. But when all the Romans asked him to be king, he gave his power back to the Senate and went back to taking care of his grapes.

One day, Octavian called the whole Senate together.

"I have made Rome bigger and wealthier than ever," he said. "Now there is peace, all over the Roman Empire. No one is fighting. No enemies are attacking us. Rome is strong and healthy. So I have decided to quit my job. I don't need to be consul anymore. I won't lead the army anymore. You can be in charge from now on."

The senators should have been pleased by this. But Octavian had become popular with the people, and they knew that the people would protest if he left the government. They might even riot. And then other ambitious Romans would begin to fight for power. A civil war might break out.

So they protested, "But you brought peace to Rome. If you stop being consul, Rome will fall apart again! Please, stay on and be consul."

"No, no," Octavian said. "Rome shouldn't have a king, and if I stay people will want me to be king. I'm just a Roman citizen like everyone else."

"We won't call you king, then," the senators promised him. "We'll call you the 'First Citizen' instead."

Then the whole Senate met together and voted to make Octavian the "First Citizen" of Rome. In Latin, the word for "first citizen" is *princeps*. Our English word "prince" comes from the word princeps. A prince is the most important citizen in his country. And even though Octavian was called First Citizen, he acted like a prince. He ruled Rome, led the army, and had complete control over the whole Roman Empire. He was actually the first emperor of Rome.

The Senate also gave Octavian a new name. His old name was Octavian Caesar, because he was Caesar's adopted son. But his new name was "Augustus Caesar."

Augustus means "blessed" and "majestic." To show how much they honored Augustus Caesar, the Senate even decided to name a month of the year after him! Can you guess which month of the year is named after Augustus Caesar? The month of August.

They also agreed to name a month of the year after his adopted father, Julius Caesar. Can you guess which month is named after Julius Caesar? The month of July. Julius Caesar and Augustus Caesar lived a very long time ago. But every time we look at a calendar, we are reminded of them.

Note: Cleopatra was born in 69 BC/BCE; she was twenty-one when Caesar arrived in Egypt in 48 BC/BCE (Caesar was fifty-two). Caesar was assassinated on March 15, 44 BC/BCE. Octavian became a consul in 43 BC/BCE, one year after Caesar's death. He remained a consul until 27 BC/BCE, when he assumed the position of emperor and continued to rule until AD/CE 14.

Chapter Thirty-Six
Israel Under Roman Rule

Herod, the "Great"

Augustus Caesar may have been called First Citizen, but he was actually an emperor. He ruled over Rome, and over all the nations that Rome had conquered and made part of the Roman Empire. No one was allowed to question his decrees!

But not all of those nations *wanted* to be part of the Roman Empire. Some of them hated being under Augustus Caesar's rule—and one of the most unhappy countries under Roman rule was the country of the Jews.

We've already learned a lot about the Jewish people. The Jews had been moved around the ancient world for hundreds of years. When the Persian king Cyrus allowed them to return to Israel and rebuild their temple, the Jews hoped that they would finally get to stay in their own country and live in peace.

But then the Persians were conquered by Alexander the Great. And do you remember what happened after Alexander's death? His empire was divided between three of his generals.

The land of Israel became part of the Seleucid Empire. And then the Seleucid Empire was conquered by—the Romans! This ancient land now became part of the Roman Empire.

The Romans installed a king over the Jews and told all of the Jews to obey him. His name was Herod. His father had been a trusted adviser to Julius Caesar, so the Romans also trusted Herod.

Herod had been raised as a Jew, but he was a "client king." That meant that although he could act like a king in Israel, he also had to obey the emperor of Rome without question. He was responsible for making sure that the Jews paid high taxes to Rome and followed all of the Roman laws. And Herod could only stay king of the Jews as long as Augustus Caesar and the Roman Senate approved of the job he was doing.

So it was very important for Herod to show that he was a good king. He could make laws for the people of Israel, but there was a lot that he couldn't do. He couldn't control how much tax his people paid to Rome, or make alliances with other countries, or declare war, like a real king.

Instead, Herod built buildings!

In ancient times, a king's greatness was often measured by how many huge buildings he was able to construct. Buildings took money and manpower. If you could pull off an enormous building project, it showed that you had kingly power.

So Herod poured energy and time into his new building projects. The rebuilt Temple in Jerusalem was small and shabby compared with the original temple, which had been built by the great Jewish king Solomon.Herod wanted to make it twice as large. But the Temple was built on a hill known as the Temple Mount, and there wasn't room on the hill to make the temple wider or longer. So Herod built a wall around the Temple Mount and filled it in with earth so that there was a larger flat space to build a larger

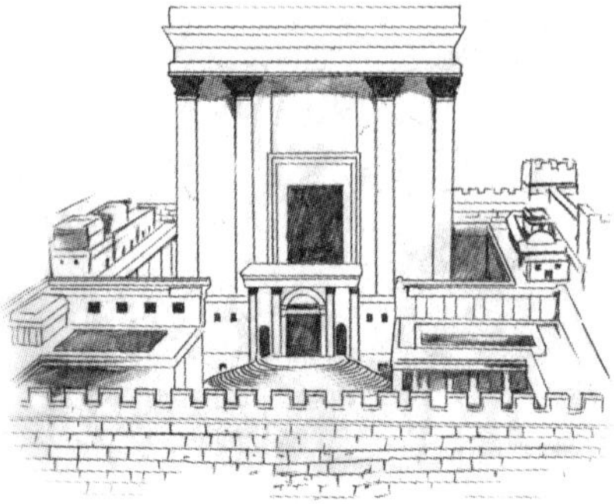
Herod's Temple in Jerusalem

temple on. The final building, huge and elaborate, was known as "Herod's Temple."

Herod also built a wide new harbor so that ships could sail directly to his country and trade with the Jews. And he put up stone fortresses all through Israel.

Because of all of these building projects, Herod came to be known by the Romans as "Herod the Great." But the Jews still hated him! They hated him because he collected taxes from them. They hated him because he spent so much money on his buildings. And they hated him because he was so anxious to make the Romans happy. Even though Herod was a Jew who was supposed to worship only God, Herod was willing to call Augustus Caesar a divine being. He was even willing to put up Roman statues and symbols in the Temple.

When he was close to seventy, Herod grew very ill. He knew that he was dying—and he was sure that the Jews would not miss him. So he told his sister, who was planning his funeral, to invite many distinguished guests to his palace—and then to have them killed. That way, all of their friends and relatives would be weeping during Herod's funeral.

His sister didn't do this! When Herod died, no one wept. The Jews were relieved, and the Romans just put another king in his place.

Today, the only traces that Herod "the Great" left behind him are a few pieces of his great buildings—

including the walls that he built around his temple. If you go to Jerusalem, you can still see them!

A Prophet Named Jesus

Augustus Caesar became famous for keeping the peace all over the Roman Empire. Everywhere in the Roman Empire, Roman law was followed. Roman soldiers kept villages and cities safe from enemy attack. There were no wars anywhere within the Roman Empire.

This time had a name—the *Pax Romana*. In Latin, this means the "Roman Peace." All across the Roman Empire, people could live in safety, without worrying about invasion. They could work out in their fields, raise their animals, travel back and forth between Roman cities, and even sail on the Mediterranean Sea without being attacked.

During the time of this Roman peace, a baby was born in the land of the Jews, which was now under Roman control. This baby would grow up to start a whole new religion. The Bible tells us about this in four books called "the Gospels." Here is the story as it is told in the Gospel of Luke:

> In the days when Augustus Caesar ruled over Rome, a girl named Mary lived in the village of Nazareth. Mary was a Jewish girl who worshipped the God of Abraham. She was engaged to be married to a man named Joseph, but the wedding was still months away.
>
> One day, God sent an angel to Mary to give her a message.

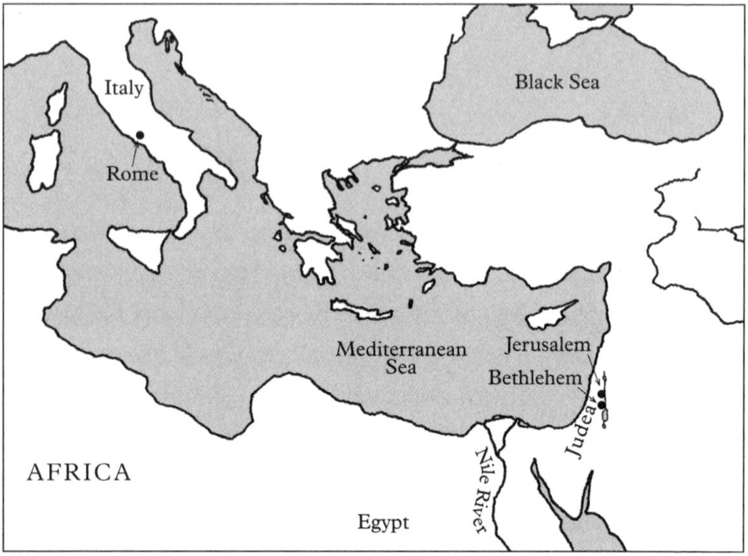

Judea

"Mary, God is with you!" the angel said. "You will have a baby, and you will name him Jesus!"

"But I can't have a baby," Mary said. "I don't even have a husband yet!"

"God will send the baby," the angel answered. "He will be called the Son of God."

When Mary told Joseph about the angel's visit, he was amazed! But he agreed to marry her and help her raise the baby.

Just before Mary's baby was born, Augustus Caesar ordered that everyone in the Roman Empire should be counted. He wanted everyone to go back to the place where their ancestors came from, to make the counting easier. Joseph came from Bethlehem. So, even though Mary was about to have her baby, Joseph and Mary traveled from Nazareth to Bethlehem.

When they arrived in Bethlehem, the village was so full that they couldn't find anywhere to sleep! Finally, they found a cave where animals were kept. Mary had her baby there, in the cave, in the middle of the night. They named the baby "Jesus," just as the angel had said. Joseph wrapped the baby in clean linen cloths, and laid him in the feeding trough where the animals ate.

Now, just outside Bethlehem, there were shepherds spending the night out in the fields, watching over their sheep. When Jesus was born, an angel appeared to the shepherds. The angel shone with light, and the shepherds were afraid.

But the angel said, "Don't be afraid! I bring you good news of great joy. Today, a Savior has been born to you. He is Christ the Lord! You will find him wrapped in linen cloth, lying in a feed trough." Then a great company of angels appeared in the sky over the field where the shepherds were sleeping. "Glory to God in the highest!" they sang. "Peace on earth, good will to men!"

The shepherds were astounded! They hurried to the cave where the baby had been born. And after they saw him, they went out and told everyone what they had seen and heard.

Today, many people celebrate the birth of Jesus on December 25. We call this day "Christmas."

After Jesus was born, he lived among the Jews for thirty years. Then he started to travel around, teaching people what God wanted them to do. His most famous teaching was given on the side of a mountain, so today, people call it the "Sermon on the Mount." Here are some of the things that Jesus taught:

Blessed are the merciful, for they will receive mercy.
Blessed are peacemakers,
for they will be called the children of God.
If someone strikes you on the cheek, don't fight back.
Turn the other cheek instead.
Love your enemies, and pray for those who are mean to you.

The Gospels, in the New Testament, record these and many other teachings of Jesus.

Jesus was very popular with the Jewish people. He was so popular that some of the Jewish religious leaders started to worry that Jesus might begin a rebellion against the Romans. If that happened, Roman soldiers might kill hundreds of Jews.

The death of Jesus

The Romans were worried about Jesus too! So the Romans helped some of the Jewish leaders arrest Jesus. They put him on trial for treason. The penalty for treason was death! Jesus was convicted of treason and put to death near Jerusalem.

The Gospels tell the story of what happened after Jesus' death. Here is what the Gospel of Luke says:

After Jesus died, he was put in a tomb that was like a cave, carved into rock. A huge stone was rolled into place across the entrance to the tomb. His followers and the people who loved him mourned and wept.

Three days after Jesus died, some of the women who followed him went to the tomb where he had been buried. But when they got there, they found that the huge stone at the entrance had been rolled away! And the tomb itself was empty.

"What has happened here?" they asked each other. "What has happened to the body of Jesus?"

Then two angels, dressed in shining clothes, appeared to them. "Why are you looking for Jesus here?" one of them asked. "He is not here. He has risen from the dead!"

The women were terrified! They ran back to tell Jesus' other followers what had happened. But no one believed them!

While his followers were talking about the story the women told, Jesus himself appeared to them. "Peace be with you!" he said. "I am not a ghost! I have risen from the dead." Then he blessed them and said, "Go and tell all nations what you have seen."

The followers of Jesus told this story all around Jerusalem. Then they spread it all the way to Rome itself! More and more people believed that Jesus had been resurrected, or brought back to life from the dead. They were careful to follow the teachings of Jesus. They believed that Jesus was the son of God.

Soon, these people were called "Christians."

The Destruction of the Temple

Augustus Caesar, the First Citizen, was a strict ruler. He didn't allow the nations under Roman control to rebel against him. But he also tried to be fair and just. His people obeyed him, and his army followed his commands. His reign was a good time for the city of Rome, and for the Roman Empire itself.

But after Augustus Caesar died, Rome had other emperors who weren't fair and just. They were cruel to their subjects. They got richer and richer and spent more and more money on themselves, while the people of Rome got poorer and poorer. They killed anyone they suspected of plotting against them—even members of the Roman Senate. The emperor of Rome was supposed to tell the army how to fight, but too many of the emperors after Augustus Caesar were bad generals. Sometimes the army even refused to obey them.

One Roman emperor, named Caligula, even made his horse a consul, and told all the people of Rome to do whatever the horse said. Then, Caligula did something even more harmful. He announced that since he was an emperor of Rome, his subjects should worship him. And he told the Jews that he planned to put a statue of himself up in their temple, so that they could sacrifice to him as if he were a god.

The Jews begged Caligula not to make them do this! Their faith told them to worship only one God—the God of Abraham. But Caligula refused. He ordered them to worship the statue or be punished.

Before Caligula could put the statue in the temple, though, he died. And the emperor who came after him agreed to forget about the statue.

But Roman rule over the Jews was growing more and more harsh. The Jewish people were already paying high taxes. They were already being forced to serve the Romans and follow Roman laws. Now, they knew that it was only a matter of time before they would be forced to break God's laws.

Finally, the Jews refused to obey Rome any longer. A group of Jewish fighters called the Zealots declared war on the Romans. They set fire to the house of their Roman ruler. They fought Roman soldiers in the streets of Jerusalem. The whole city was in an uproar!

When the emperor in Rome heard what was happening, he sent more Roman soldiers with orders to destroy the whole city of Jerusalem. The Roman army swept through the streets of Jerusalem, killing the Zealots and also killing Jews who weren't even fighting against them. They burned the houses and shops in Jerusalem—and they also burned down the Temple.

The Jewish historian Josephus, who lived during the destruction of the Temple, says that the Roman soldiers first set fire to the gates of the Temple, and that the silver decorations and hinges of the gates grew so hot that the silver ran and carried the fire to other parts of the magnificent building. The Jews who were still in the Temple tried to protect it, but the Roman soldiers killed them and heaped their bodies around the sacred altar. Josephus writes that the hill on which the Temple stood itself became "seething hot" and "full of fire."

Finally there was only one small band of Jewish fighters left. They fled to one of the fortresses that Herod the Great had built, and they locked themselves inside.

The fortress was called Masada, and it sat on a steep rocky cliff on the edge of a desert. The Romans were determined to wipe out this last resistance by the Zealots. They began to build a siege ramp up to the walls of the fortress, so that they could use a battering ram to get inside.

The Zealots knew that the Romans would eventually get into Masada. So before the Roman army could break in, they killed themselves rather than surrender.

After the destruction of Jerusalem and the siege of Masada, the Jews had no temple to worship God in, no capital city, and no country of their own. Within a few years, the old nation of Israel would be completely gone. The Romans made it part of a province (an area under the rule of one particular Roman official) called Syria. The Jews scattered throughout all the countries of the ancient world.

They would not return to Jerusalem for centuries.

Note: The actual year of Jesus' birth is probably closer to 3 BC/BCE than to the year AD/CE 1. Caligula ruled as emperor AD/CE 37-41. The Second Temple was destroyed in AD/CE 70. The siege of Masada was AD/CE 72-73.

History-Maker

The Story of Judas Maccabee, Champion of the Jewish People

After the Jews scattered throughout the ancient world, they lived for many centuries without a homeland. They built villages and neighborhoods throughout the lands that would eventually become the countries of France, Germany, Italy, and Poland, Russia and the Czech Republic and Ukraine, Iran and Yemen and Turkey. The Jews still spoke their own language, but they also spoke the languages of the countries where they now lived. There were French Jews and Polish Jews and Russian Jews and Ukrainian Jews and Turkish Jews. They no longer shared a homeland.

But they shared their history!

They kept that shared history alive by telling stories about the great heroes of the past. And one of the greatest of these heroes was named Judas Maccabee.

Judas lived with his five brothers and his father Mattathias, over two hundred years before the destruction of the Temple. Right after the death of Alexander the Great, the land of Israel had been given to Alexander's general Seleucus to rule.

At first, Seleucus and his descendants treated the Jews fairly. But then, a king named Antiochus Epiphanes inherited the Seleucid throne. Antiochus disliked the Jews—and he thought they were planning to be disloyal to him.

So he marched a whole army of Greek soldiers down into Jerusalem and told the Jews that from now on, they would have to worship Zeus, the chief god of the Greeks, inside the Temple of their one God.

The Jews were horrified! They refused to do what Antiochus ordered—so Antiochus declared that Judaism was now illegal. The Jews were no longer allowed to read their sacred scriptures, celebrate their holidays, or observe the Sabbath, their day of rest. Antiochus even ordered his soldiers to sacrifice a pig on the altar in the Temple—the altar that was supposed to be dedicated only to the worship of God.

Judas's father, Mattathias, refused to obey this command.

Instead, Mattathias, Judas, and his four brothers took up swords and declared war against Antiochus and his men. When Mattathias died, Judas stepped up to be the head of the family—and the leader of the battle against Antiochus's cruel orders.

Judas and his brothers went through Israel, calling other Jews to join them. Soon, the band of brothers had six thousand men behind them! Judas led them in a "guerilla" war. Instead of gathering together into a large army and attacking another large army, they banded together into small, fast-moving groups, attacked the Greeks when they least expected it, and then hid again. They burned houses and villages where the Greek soldiers were living. Whenever they found an altar built to a Greek god, they tore it down.

Over many years, Judas and his followers defeated three Greek armies much, much larger than their resistance army! The Greeks were terrified of Judas—and he became a hero to his people. They began to call him "Judas the Hammer," or, in their own language, "Judas Maccabee."

In 164 BC/BCE, Judas Maccabee and his fighters claimed their biggest victory yet. They recaptured the Temple itself!

After Antiochus had ordered that pig sacrificed in the Temple, the Jews had stopped worshipping there. When Judas and his men finally re-entered the Temple, it was deserted and desolate. The gates had been burned down. Thick weeds were growing in the courtyards!

Judas ordered the altar torn down, and a new altar built out of uncut stones. He and his men cleaned the Temple out and scrubbed the sanctuary clean. They rebuilt the gates and hung new curtains. They baked new loaves of sacred bread. Then, Judas told the priests to burn lights in front of the altar for eight days, so that the Temple would be completely purified.

These lights had to use consecrated oil—oil that had been specially dedicated to God. But there was a problem! Here is the story that the Jews told about that problem.

WHEN JUDAS SEARCHED THROUGH THE Temple for the consecrated oil, he discovered that it had all been destroyed—except for one small flask. There was only enough oil to burn for one day.

But Judas knew that the lights needed to burn for eight days! All the way back in the book of Leviticus, when Moses appointed the first priests to serve God, their ceremony of dedication took seven days and seven nights. This rededication needed to last just as long!

"Burn the oil," he said to his men, "and we will start to prepare new holy oil."

Judas Maccabee

It would take days and days for the new holy oil to be ready—but Judas's men obeyed him anyway. They began to burn a light in front of the altar, even though they knew that it would die out in less than a day.

But the next morning, the light was still burning!

Judas and his followers waited for it to die away. And yet it did not. Even though it had no more oil, the light burned for a full seven days and seven nights—right up until the morning of the eighth day!

On the eighth day, the people rejoiced with songs of praise, waving branches, and offerings of ripe fruit. Once again, the Jews could worship in their Temple!

And in recognition of the miracle of the lights, all of the Jews decided to celebrate this festival every year.

The Jews retold this story again and again. The rededication of the Temple represented the triumph of the Jewish faith over their enemies. And even though the Temple was later destroyed, the miracle of the lights showed that God was still with them.

Today, the festival is called Hanukkah, or Chanukkah—the Feast of Lights, or the Feast of the Dedication of the Temple. It is usually observed in November or December. Jews will light eight candles, one more each night, in a special holder called a *menorah*, in memory of the oil lamps originally set in front of the altar by Judas Maccabee.

Chapter Thirty-Seven
Rome and the Christians

Nero, the Evil Emperor

The Roman emperors after Augustus Caesar were not good rulers. But one of the very worst of them was named Nero.

Nero ruled after Caligula. He got drunk every day, and raised taxes so that he could pay for more beer and wine. He ordered his soldiers to murder anyone who disagreed with him. His favorite pastime was playing the lyre; he was a very bad lyre player, but everyone was afraid to tell him so. So they all praised his terrible music. "When I die," Nero used to say, "what a loss I shall be to the art of music!" And the Romans in the royal court all agreed with him, because they were afraid for their lives.

After Nero had been emperor of Rome for ten years, he decided to take a vacation from Rome. He went out to his house in the country and invited his favorite friends to go with him. They had a party that went on for days and days.

Meanwhile, Rome was burning.

The fire began late at night, in a rickety wooden building in a dark and dirty Roman street. No one knows exactly how it started. But the poor families who lived in that part of town often built small fires to keep warm. Perhaps a coal fell out of one of these fires, onto the dry wooden floor. It smoldered away until the floorboard caught fire. The fire spread to a wall, and then to the entire building. And then the flames leapt to the building next door.

Soon a whole section of Rome was on fire. The fire roared along until it came up against a stone wall. The rich people of Rome had built the wall to keep fires from spreading into the wealthy part of town. But this fire was stronger than the wall. The flames leapt right over the wall and kept on burning.

The people of Rome realized that this was the worst fire in Roman history. They sent a messenger to Nero to tell him what was happening. The messenger galloped hard until he reached the country house where Nero and his friends were celebrating.

"Your Majesty!" the messenger cried. "Your city is burning!"

But Nero didn't even answer the messenger. He ordered him taken away, before he ruined the party. And he didn't return to Rome for days more.

When he finally did come back to Rome, he found his people waiting for him. Hundreds of families had been driven out of their homes. Everything they owned had been burned. They were cold and hungry. They begged Nero for help.

"Remember your great ancestor, Augustus Caesar!" they cried. "He gave money to every poor family in Rome! Surely you can help us out of your great wealth!"

Nero did give some money to the poor and the homeless. But he made a big mistake. He announced, "The fire has cleared away ugly, broken-down houses and left space for my new building projects! I will take the land where those houses used to stand and build myself a new and bigger palace."

The people of Rome were furious. Nero had been unpopular even before the fire. Now they hated him even more. Soon, Nero realized that the Romans were on the edge of rebelling and taking his throne away. He had to find someone to blame for the fire—right away.

Nero was an unpopular emperor

"I know who set the fire to Rome!" he told the Romans. "It was those Christians! They set the fire on purpose!"

Of course, the Christians hadn't set the fire. But many people believed Nero's lies. The Romans began to persecute the Christians. Christians were arrested and executed. Some of them were forced to fight in gladiator shows. Others were killed by wild animals. Nero's cruelty to the Christians drew attention away from his own selfishness.

Christians in the Catacombs

The Romans punished runaway slaves, criminals, and Christians by making them fight wild animals. But what was wrong with being a Christian?

The Roman emperors kept control over their people by saying, "Obey us, because we are gods!" The emperors claimed to be descended from Jupiter, the king of the gods. Special feast days were held every year in honor of the emperors. At these celebrations, all Romans were supposed to worship the emperor and promise to obey only him.

But the Jews had refused to do this—and now the Christians also refused.

"We only worship our God!" they told other Romans. "We refuse to bow down to someone who is only a man! The emperor is not God. We will pray for him, but we will not worship him."

The Roman emperors were furious. If the Christians disobeyed them, other Romans might be brave enough to do the same. So the emperors ordered Christians arrested and put in jail. Many Christians were put in prison. Others were forced to fight lions.

The Christians were frightened by this persecution. So they stopped holding their meetings in public. Instead, they dug underground passages beneath Rome and beneath other cities in the Roman Empire. They held their religious meetings in these underground passages, in secret. The passages were called *catacombs*. Down in the catacombs, the Christians also buried their dead. The underground tunnels were dark and damp. Stones lined the floors. They were lit only by torches. Shadows lurked in every corner. But when the Christians were underground, they were safe.

This secrecy soon made people even more suspicious of the Christians. What were they doing down there, underground? Rumors started to fly around. Maybe the Christians were calling down floods and famine on the rest of the Roman Empire. Maybe they were planning to overthrow the government!

"We must wipe out this new and harmful religion," one Roman senator wrote to another. "Otherwise, Romans will cease to worship the emperor."

Of course, the Christians weren't calling down famines or trying to overthrow the government. They were just meeting peacefully together to talk about Jesus and his teachings. They protested to the emperors that they were doing nothing wrong.

But the Roman emperors kept right on throwing them in jail. Soon Christians were even afraid to say to people they didn't know, "I am a Christian! Are you?" If they told the wrong person they were a Christian, they might end up in jail.

So they decided on a secret symbol. It looked like a fish. When a Christian met someone she didn't know, she might draw a fish on a wall, or in the sand at her feet, or on the edge of a piece of paper. If the other person was a Christian, he would draw a fish too. Then both Christians knew that it was safe to talk to each other.

Today, you can still see the catacombs that the Christians dug below the cities of the Roman Empire. Some of the catacombs have tombs of ancient Christians in them. Others have pictures that the Christians drew of Jesus. Archaeologists have found fish carved on the walls as well—secret messages that the Christians sent to each other.

Note: Nero ruled from AD/CE 54–68.

Chapter Thirty-Eight
Rome Begins to Weaken

The British Rebellion

When Julius Caesar and Augustus Caesar were in charge of the Roman Empire, Rome was strong and prosperous. But bad emperors like Nero started to weaken Rome. Even worse, some of the countries that Rome had conquered began to rebel. Like the Jews, they wanted to be free of Roman rule!

The Celts who lived in Britain had never wanted to be part of the Roman Empire. And the Romans had never managed to control all of the British islands. Some of the Celts obeyed Roman laws and paid taxes to the Romans. But others rebelled.

One of these disobedient Celtic tribes was particularly annoying to the Romans—because their leader was a woman! In ancient times, women weren't considered to be brave or strong. Men thought it was very embarrassing to be beaten by a woman.

But the leader of this Celtic tribe was no ordinary woman. She was a powerful warrior queen named Boadicea. A Roman writer named Cassius described Boadicea: She was very tall, taller than a man, and her voice was strong and powerful, loud enough to echo from mountain to mountain. She had fierce, piercing eyes, and long, thick, red-brown hair that hung down past her waist. She wore a billowing tartan cloak and a thick gold collar around her neck.

Boadicea refused to make her tribe part of the Roman Empire. Instead, she led the Celts in raids on the Roman settlements. The Romans seemed powerless to stop them! They even raided the biggest Roman settlement in Britain—Londinium. Later, this Roman settlement became the city of London.

Soon, the Romans in Britain were terrified of Boadicea and her warriors. The Roman citizens who lived in the settlements started telling each other that they had seen strange things, signs that Rome was doomed to be defeated by the Celts. The statue of Victory fell face down without being pushed! A woman claimed that she had seen the sea turn as red as blood. Other people said that they saw a ghost town in ruins near Londinium. And a man insisted that he had heard strange shrieks and yells coming from an empty Roman theater.

Did these strange things really happen? We will never know! But the stories show how nervous the Romans were about Boadicea.

Boadicea collected more and more Celtic warriors around her. Soon there were a hundred thousand British fighters marching down on ten thousand Romans. That means that there was one Roman for every ten British rebels. Just before the final attack, Boadicea rode around and made a famous speech to all her warriors.

"We British are accustomed to having women in command!" she shouted. "The gods will grant us revenge against the Roman invaders! I plan to win this battle—or die trying! Let the men live as slaves to the Romans if they want to—but I refuse to live in slavery!"

Then the Celts attacked. They rode into battle without any plan. They charged in at top speed, each soldier doing exactly what he wanted. But the Romans stayed together. They did what their general said. Even though they were outnumbered, they won!

The victory in Britain was only temporary, though. Eventually, the Romans were forced to leave Britain altogether. Today, in Britain, you can still see the ruins of Roman walls and roads. Those ruins are all that is left of the Roman settlements in Britain.

Rome Divided in Two

The Roman Empire didn't last forever.

Today, if you go to Italy, you will see ruins of old Roman buildings. You will see the remains of old Roman roads. But you won't see any ancient Romans.

What happened to the Roman Empire? The Roman Empire got too big. Its borders were too long for one army to protect. The soldiers of Rome couldn't possibly keep all invaders out of Rome's territory. And more and more invaders started to wander into the Roman Empire.

Ruling Rome was a little bit like having the biggest candy bar in a group of very hungry people. Everyone wanted to take it away. The emperors of Rome had to fight constantly against invaders. These invaders wanted Roman land and Roman wealth. They wanted to use the Roman roads and live in the Roman villages. But they didn't want to obey the Roman emperor or pay taxes to the Roman government. So they attacked Rome's borders with armies, hoping to take Rome's countries away. The Roman emperors had a difficult time keeping invaders out. There was so much Roman land that they couldn't protect all of it at once.

If ruling Rome was like having the biggest candy bar in a group of hungry people, ruling the entire empire was like having a candy bar as big as a car. How could you keep the whole candy bar safe? While you were protecting one side of it, a hungry person could sneak up and take a bite out of the other side. And if you ran around to protect the other side, you would leave the first side without anyone to guard it.

How could you protect such a big candy bar? Do you have any ideas? Here's one idea: You could break the candy bar in half and give the other half to someone you trusted to guard for you.

That's exactly what happened to the Roman Empire. A wise emperor named Diocletian realized that no one ruler could keep all of Rome safe.

"This empire is too big for one man!" he exclaimed. "I will break it into two pieces, and ask someone else to rule the other half."

So Diocletian asked another Roman leader to be his partner. This partner, Maximian, ruled the western part of the Roman Empire. Diocletian ruled the eastern half.

Now Rome had two emperors! Diocletian and Maximian worked hard to protect Rome. Each one had an army, and they recruited more and more soldiers to make their armies bigger. For a while, the Romans held off invaders. The Roman Empire seemed to be doing well.

But something strange began to happen to Rome. The Western Roman Empire grew poorer and poorer, while the Eastern Roman Empire became richer and richer. The people of the West even had trouble finding enough food for themselves. They had to buy food from the East.

And Rome, which had once been the greatest city in the world, was becoming shabby and run-down.

The Western Roman Empire had other problems, too. Invaders from the north kept attacking its borders, and the Western army was too weak to keep these invaders away. The people of the Western Roman Empire called the invaders *barbarians*.

We've met barbarians before! They also invaded the ancient land of Greece. Like the Greeks, the Romans could not understand the language of the newcomers. They sounded as if they were just babbling nonsense: *bar-bar-bar-bar-bar*.

These barbarians seemed able to conquer anything in their path. The armies of the Western Roman Empire tried to fight the barbarians off, but they just kept on coming.

They invaded Britain. They invaded Gaul. They invaded Spain.

And soon, they would invade Italy itself.

The Emperor Is a Christian!

The Roman emperors kept on persecuting Christians until an emperor named Constantine came to the throne.

Constantine was a fair man. He worshipped the Roman god Apollo, but he didn't think it was right to put people in jail because of the god they worshipped. So he ordered all persecution to stop. No one was to arrest Christians for being Christians anymore.

Constantine himself went on worshipping Apollo—until something strange happened to him.

Different ancient writers tell us different stories about Constantine. Some say he had a dream. Others say he had a vision. But whatever Constantine saw, everyone agrees about what happened next: The emperor himself became a Christian!

So what did Constantine see?

One Roman writer tells this story about Constantine's vision:

> CONSTANTINE WAS MARCHING TOWARDS THE most important battle of his life. He had fought the enemy for months now, and had not been able to triumph. The coming battle was his last hope. Would he win? Would the Roman Empire remain safe? Or would his soldiers be defeated, driven backwards by the enemy and forced to surrender?
>
> He would know tomorrow, when they met the enemy at the Milvian Bridge.
>
> He looked behind him at his army. They had fought hard against invaders and won. But now they were so tired they could barely drag themselves along. Their feet hurt; their heels were blistered in their shoes, and their armor was heavy on their shoulders.
>
> Constantine glanced up at the gray, cloudy sky. On top of everything else, he thought, it was going to rain on them. They would be tired, discouraged, and soaking wet. They would have to set up camp in the pouring rain, and no one would sleep well before the next morning's battle.
>
> "Look," the soldier beside him said. "The sun is coming out."
>
> Constantine squinted at the sky. It did look brighter. But —

"That's not the sun," he said. "What is it? It … it looks like a cross!"

Constantine and his soldiers stared with open mouths. Above them in the sky hovered a cross of light, growing larger and brighter by the moment. The golden light from the cross fell across their weary faces until they were forced to blink and shield their eyes with their hands. The grass around them glittered with light!

Underneath the cross, fiery letters burned themselves across the sky. Constantine read them out, one by one: *By this sign you will be victor.*

"It is the cross of Christ!" Constantine gasped.

"What does it mean?" the soldiers asked.

"It means that we must fight for God," Constantine answered. "The God of the Christians!"

When they set up camp that night, Constantine sent out an order to his men. "Every soldier must have the sign of Christ on his shield!" he ordered. "Until that is done, we will not go into battle!"

So each soldier painted onto his shield the Greek letters standing for Christ's name. When they went into battle, Constantine led the charge under a banner bearing the name of the Christian God. And Constantine's army won the Battle of Milvian Bridge.

When he stood victorious on the bridge, Constantine raised his sword to the sky.

"The God of the Christians gave me this victory!" he announced. "From now on, I will always fight under his banner. And I will only worship him!"

Rome and Constantinople

After he won this battle, Constantine became a Christian. He claimed that the Christian God had helped him to beat the enemy. He made Sunday a holiday all over Rome, so that people could go to church. Soon, many more people in the Roman Empire became Christians, following the example of their emperor.

Once he became a Christian, Constantine decided that the new center of the Roman Empire should no longer be in Rome. After all, Rome was an old city, beginning to look shabby and run-down.

Constantine moved the capital of the empire to the eastern part of the empire, to another city that he named after himself: Constantinople. From now on, the eastern Roman city of Constantinople, not the western Roman city of Rome, would be the center of Roman power.

But that power would not last long!

Note: Boadicea's revolt against Rome was in AD/CE 60–61. Diocletian came to the throne in AD/CE 284 and divided the empire in 286. He ruled jointly with Maximian from AD/CE 286–305. Constantine ruled from AD/CE 312–337. Although the emperors between Nero and Constantine had different degrees of severity towards Christianity, before Constantine, Christianity was never tolerated for long.

History-Maker

The Story of Pliny the Younger, Survivor of Mount Vesuvius

In the seventh year of Nero's reign, a baby boy was born in a little town north of Rome.

He belonged to an important family; his grandfather was a Roman senator, and his uncle was a distinguished military commander who had written a best-selling encyclopedia of natural history. And he was given a long important name—Gaius Plinius Caecilius Secundus.

But his family called him Pliny. Because his famous uncle was also named Pliny, the child became known as Pliny the Younger.

Little Pliny's father died when he was still a very small boy, so his uncle Pliny the Elder helped raise him. Pliny the Younger was sent to the best schools. He grew up to become a lawyer and a judge. He held several high positions in the Roman government.

But what we remember the most about Pliny is that he wrote letters—hundreds and hundreds of letters!

Pliny wrote to kings and emperors. He wrote to other Roman officials, to friends and family, and to philosophers and historians that he admired. His letters tell us all about events in the Roman Empire—events that we would know nothing about, if it weren't for Pliny's letters.

One of those letters described something that happened when Pliny the Younger was only seventeen.

His uncle Pliny the Elder was commanding a fleet of ships off the southern coast of Italy. One summer, Pliny the Younger traveled down to a seaside town called Miseno to visit with him. After they spent the afternoon together, Pliny the Elder went back to his ship for the night. Pliny the Younger finished his homework (in the letter, he says, "I completed my studies!"), had dinner, and went to bed.

During the night, Pliny the Younger kept waking up—because the ground was shaking. Loud rumblings and small earthquakes had been disturbing Miseno for weeks. But this was nothing new! Everyone in Miseno knew that the quivering earth and the odd growling noises came from Mount Vesuvius, just down the coast. Pliny could even see Mount Vesuvius, jutting up from the coast, if he walked out on the beach and peered to the east. Mount Vesuvius had been rumbling and shaking for many years. No one was worried about the noise and the quakes.

But this night was different.

Here is how Pliny the Younger described that night, twenty-six years later.

> *The ground had been shaking for many days. This happened all the time—and no one panicked! But during the night, the trembling grew much stronger. The ground began to rise and fall. When the sun rose the next morning, buildings had started to crumble. We were afraid that we would be trapped by falling walls, so we began to make our way out of Miseno.*
>
> *When we reached a flat open space outside of the town, we stopped to rest. But suddenly our carts began to move by themselves, even though we tried to block their wheels with stone. Just beyond, we could see the beach and the sea. The sea was being sucked backwards, leaving sea creatures writhing on the dry sand. Frightening*

The volcano Vesuvius destroyed Pompeii

dark clouds billowed up, pierced by twisted lightning. Below the clouds were huge plumes of flame.

And then a dense cloud swept towards us, like a flood of dirt poured across the land. Darkness came down over us—not like the dark of a moonless or cloudy night, but like the utter blackness of a closed and unlighted room. We could hear the voices of women weeping, children crying, men shouting. Some were calling for parents, others for children or their husbands or wives.

Then ash began to fall on us—a very great weight of ash. We stood up and shook the ash off again and again. Otherwise we would have been covered with it and crushed by the weight. I believed that I was perishing with the world, and the world with me.

Pliny and his friends kept trudging onwards, farther and farther away from the lava and the falling ash. Finally they reached safety.

Pliny had just seen the eruption of Mount Vesuvius—an active volcano that blew up in August of AD/CE 79. Most of the people of Miseno survived. But closer to Mount Vesuvius, the town of Pompeii was buried in twenty feet of ash. Over two thousand people died in Pompeii in that single day. Hundreds of years later, the spaces left by the bodies of Pompeii's victims were discovered, deep under a thick layer of ash that had begun to turn to stone. Archaeologists poured plaster into the spaces and made sculptures of the people in their final moments of life.

A few days after the eruption, Pliny found out that his beloved uncle had been among the victims! Pliny the Elder had seen the black clouds of ash and the tongues of flame shooting up from Mount Vesuvius. One of his friends lived in a villa (a country house) at the foot of the volcano. Pliny the Elder ordered his pilot to sail towards Vesuvius so that he could rescue his friend—even though ash and burning pieces of rock were falling all around them, and the smell of sulfur was washing over them. As they drew closer and closer to the volcano, Pliny the Elder grew ill. Before his ship could take him away from the fumes and heat, the old man died.

Pliny the Younger mourned his uncle's death. But after the eruption of Vesuvius, Pliny finished his education, governed a whole Roman province, and was even elected to the Roman Senate. He wrote plays and poems. He also wrote hundreds more letters about all sorts of Roman events.

But his letters about the eruption of Mount Vesuvius are his most famous writings!

Chapter Thirty-Nine
Troubles in China

The End of the Han Dynasty

The Han emperors had reigned over a unified China for many, many years. But while bad emperors ruled over Rome, China also began to suffer.

Famine wiped out crops in some parts of the vast Han Empire. Other villages and cities were drenched by violent storms; thousands drowned when dams broke and fields and houses were covered with water. Livestock died. Food dwindled. Scores of Chinese farmers had to leave their land and try to find somewhere else for their families. Hungry and desperate, many of them banded together to fight against their local governments. One Chinese historian wrote, "The poor had no way to stay alive. They rose up and became thieves and bandits instead!"

The Han emperors did their best to provide for their people. Throughout the first century AD/CE, the Han rulers tried hard to keep the peace, feed their subjects, and protect the Silk Road.

Slowly, the Han Empire began to recover.

But then, a strange thing happened. Children kept inheriting the throne!

When the Han emperor Zhangdi died, in AD/CE 88, his nine-year-old son inherited his title. This son died in his twenties, when *his* heir was only five months old. And when *that* baby ruler died, his twelve-year old cousin became emperor!

This continued for many years. The next emperors were crowned at the ages of ten, one, seven, and fourteen. All of them died young. For over fifty years, the Han had a child as emperor!

You probably wouldn't be able to rule an entire huge kingdom all by yourself, without the help of any adults. Neither could the young Han emperors. They weren't really running their country. Their uncles, cousins, mothers, and aunts were ruling instead. And not all of those relatives were good people! Many of them were just trying to gain power and wealth for themselves. No one was paying attention to the well-being of the whole Han Empire. Instead, everyone was trying to gather as much land and steal as much tax money as possible.

Meanwhile, the many poor families of China had to work harder and harder to pay higher and higher taxes. Because trade along the Silk Road was so important, hundreds of young men were forced to join bands of soldiers who kept the Silk Road safe from thieves and highwaymen.

Then, more disasters swept over the country.

Horrible epidemics of sickness killed thousands and thousands of people. Floods wiped out more villages and still more farm animals. And then, a wave of locusts—grasshoppers that eat everything in their way—destroyed even more of the crops that the Chinese needed to survive.

The people of Han China were weak, hungry, and hopeless. So in AD/CE 184, a band of warriors who called themselves the Yellow Turbans declared that they were ready to fight back!

They were led by a man named Chang Chueh, who claimed that he was a magician. He promised that he could heal sickness. He told his followers that, if they took his magic medicines, they couldn't be wounded in battle. They could fight against the Han government, and not be afraid.

Of course, Chang Chueh couldn't do anything that he promised. But the Chinese people were angry and desperate. Over 350,000 of them joined Chang Chueh's Yellow Turban rebellion!

At first, the Yellow Turbans lost every battle that they started. The Han armies defeated them easily.

But then, the Han generals started to think to themselves: The Yellow Turbans don't really matter. There are only children in the Han palace. We could take the throne for ourselves!

One of those generals, a man named Dong Zhuo, stopped fighting the Yellow Turbans. Instead, he took his army and marched into the capital city of Han China. He captured the thirteen-year-old emperor and declared himself ruler of the Han. He didn't actually have that many soldiers following him—but every night, he told a hundred or so of his men to sneak quietly out of the city after dark. Then, he had them return during the next morning with flags flying and drums beating. That way, the people of the capital city thought that he was being joined every day by more and more soldiers—when it was actually the same hundred men leaving and coming back into the city over and over again!

Another general, Ts'ao Ts'ao, saw what Dong Zhuo was doing. He said to himself, "Dong Zhuo doesn't even have that many men! If he can make himself emperor, I can claim power for myself as well!"

Soon, Ts'ao Ts'ao got his chance! Another angry war leader assassinated Dong Zhuo. When he heard that Dong Zhuo was dead, Ts'ao Ts'ao marched into the city with his men, took over the royal palace, and forced the young Han emperor to marry his own daughter. Ts'ao Ts'ao didn't try to make himself emperor—but because he controlled his daughter and his son-in-law, he was now the *real* ruler of Han China.

But by then, there was no empire left to rule.

The Yellow Turban rebellion had killed hundreds of thousands of people. The country was still suffering from famine, floods, and sickness. No one really believed that the young emperor was the rightful ruler of China. They all knew that violent generals were in charge instead. The young emperor himself abandoned his throne and spent the rest of his life living quietly.

The time of the Han was over.

The Three Kingdoms, the Jin, and the Sixteen Kingdoms

After the Han emperor gave up his throne, the enormous Han kingdom fractured into three different pieces—the Three Kingdoms.

The Three Kingdoms were called the Cao Wei, the Dong Wu, and the Shu Han. For nearly fifty years, the Three Kingdoms fought with each other. There was no peace in China!

Finally, the strongest of the Three Kingdoms, Cao Wei, conquered the Shu Han and claimed its land. Now there were only two kingdoms—and the Cao Wei was the most powerful.

The king of the Cao Wei, a very young man named Wei Yuandi, was the grandson of a Han dynasty official. The head of the army, a general named Sima Yan, was also the grandson of a Han dynasty official. Wei Yuandi's father and grandfather had been kings of the Cao Wei before him—but Sima Yan's father and grandfather had been generals of the Cao Wei army before him!

After the conquest of the Shu Han, Sima Yan gathered together the soldiers who obeyed him, and told them to follow him. He then buckled on his sword, and went to see the young emperor Wei Yuandi in his throne room.

"Whose efforts have preserved the Cao Wei Empire?" he asked.

Young Wei Yuandi looked around his throne room, and suddenly realized that it was filled with Sima Yan's soldiers.

"Yours have!" he said, nervously. "Your efforts, and the efforts of your father and your grandfather."

"*We* have defended the kingdom," Sima Yan said. "You have not! You should step aside, and give the throne to someone who can fight to protect it. You should give it to me!"

Wei Yuandi realized that he could not resist Sima Yan. So he agreed to abdicate—to give up his claim to be king of the Cao Wei. He climbed down from his throne, bowed down in front of Sima Yan, and said,"Long live the new emperor!" And then he left his palace and gave up his right to rule.

Sima Yan announced, "As your new emperor, I will now be known by the name Jin Wudi. And from now on, this kingdom will be known as the kingdom of the Jin!"

As the first Jin emperor, Sima Yan now decided that he and his army would conquer the last remaining kingdom—the Dong Wu. The best way to attack the capital city of the Dong Wu, Jianye, was by river. So Jin Wudi loaded his men onto ships, and they began to sail down towards Jianye.

When the Dong Wu general realized that the Jin were approaching, he ordered his men to stretch thick iron chains across the river to block the ships. So Jin Wudi and his advisers came up with a new plan. His ships threw down their anchors and stopped. Then, his men went ashore and cut down all of the trees they could find. They made rafts from the trees. They soaked more tree trunks with sap, stacked them onto the rafts, set them on fire, and pushed the rafts into the river.

The blazing rafts drifted down the river, piled up above the chains—and melted them! The chains snapped, and the ships filled with Jin soldiers sailed into the center of the capital city.

The Dong Wu armies surrendered. The Jin emperor now ruled over all of China. The country was united once again.

But this was not a happy ending.

Jin Wudi ruled for twenty-four years. But he had more than one wife—and by the time he died, he had twenty-five sons! All of them began to fight to become the next ruler of the Jin Empire.

The Jin Empire became a patchwork quilt of battling armies, each one supporting a different son of Jin Wudi. No one was protecting the empire's borders.

So barbarians from the north started to raid the Jin lands. Pirates sailed along the coast, burning houses and villages, stealing and kidnapping. The Jin Empire lost everything above the Yangtze River.

All around the shrunken Jin Empire, other warlords pronounced themselves to be kings. There were so many of these little kingdoms around the Jin that the Jin called them the "Sixteen Kingdoms" (even though sometimes there were more than sixteen, and sometimes there were fewer).

The people of the Sixteen Kingdoms adopted Jin customs and the Jin language and the Jin ways of governing. As the years went by, the Sixteen Kingdoms began more and more to think of themselves as, simply, Chinese.

Meanwhile, the embattled Jin kingdom kept insisting that the Sixteen Kingdoms were filled with barbarians. Only the Jin rulers could trace their ancestry back to the royal court of the Han dynasty. Only the Jin people were *truly* Chinese!

Who was right?

Note: The Yellow Turban rebellion lasted AD/CE 184-205. The Han dynasty ended in 220, and the Three Kingdoms period began. Cao Wei conquered the Shu Han in 263; Sima Yan declared himself to be the first Jin emperor, Jin Wudi, in 266. The Jin conquered the Dong Wu in 280. Jin Wudi died in 290, and the Sixteen Kingdoms became more powerful after his death.

History-Maker

The Story of Zhang Heng, Astronomer, Poet, Mathematician, Geographer, and More

IN THE YEARS WHEN CHILDREN WERE INHERITING THE Han throne, a young boy named Zhang Heng was growing up in the north of China.

His father had died when he was only ten, so Zhang Heng had been raised by his mother and his grandmother. Even though he loved them, he wanted to go to Chang'an, one of the greatest cities of the Han.

Zhang Heng longed to learn about everything in the world. He wanted to study poetry and philosophy, the stars and the moon and the sun, the way the earth worked, mathematics, painting, and more. And he knew that the Han dynasty had built a huge college in their capital city. It was called the Taixue. Students came from all over China to study at the Taixue in Chang'an. There, they could read all the great books of the past and learn about the most recent discoveries in math and science. The Taixue had thirty thousand students and teachers! It was like a whole city in itself, all dedicated to learning.

So when Zhang Heng was only sixteen years old, his mother and his grandmother packed him a suitcase, gave him a bag of food and all the money they could spare, and sent him to Chang'an.

Young Heng dove into his studies at the Taixue. He wrote poems and painted pictures. He read scores of books and argued with his friends about the ideas in those books. He studied mathematics. He peered at the heavens and wrote down his observations. He listened to lectures by all of the most accomplished scientists and philosophers at the Taixue.

After five wonderful years of study, Zhang Heng returned home to his mother and grandmother. They were delighted to see him! And they were even happier when Zhang Heng got a job with the local governor of his hometown. His title was Master of the Documents. He was supposed to write all of the official inscriptions and announcements for the governor. He also had to write all of the poems to be performed at official events.

This suited Zhang Heng just fine! He loved writing. He spent many long evenings writing poems that used elaborate, flowery language to praise the rivers and mountains, the villages and cities, and even the trees, birds, and animals of Han China. These poems were called *fu* poems.

Here are a few lines of one of Zhang Heng's *fu* poems about the capital city of Chang'an, the home of the emperor:

> *Fine embroidery of green and gold drape over polished wooden beams.*
> *Blue and scarlet kingfisher feathers,*
> *along with scales of purple amethyst and gold mica,*
> *glitter in the fire,*
> *with shining drops of jade and glowing coral and chalcedony,*
> *all the walls are glorious!*

Zhang Heng wrote many *fu* poems on hundreds of different subjects. But as he grew a little older, he grew more and more interested in astronomy.

He observed the stars and drew pictures of their positions. He studied the mathematics that explained how the stars moved. He read everything about astronomy that he could find. He began to write and publish his own observations on the skies.

More and more people read Zhang Heng's writings. Soon, Zhang Heng was known throughout the Han Empire as one of the greatest students of the stars. And he received a message from the Han emperor: Please, return to the capital and share with the royal court all of your knowledge about the stars.

Zhang Heng decided to go back to Chang'an.

When he arrived, he was appointed Chief Astronomer for the emperor. As Chief Astronomer, Zhang Heng had seventy people working with him to help him study the skies. He listed out 2,500 stars and 124 constellations that could be viewed from the Han lands. He tried to explain the existence of comets, and why the planets give light.

And he was one of the first scientists to propose that the earth might be round like a ball, rather than flat and square. He wrote, "The heavens are like a hen's egg. The earth is like the yolk of the egg, and lies alone in the center. Heaven is large and earth is small!"

Zhang Heng even built an elaborate bronze *armillary sphere*—a model of the earth with the planets and stars around it. Some of the accounts from his time say that this armillary sphere was powered by water, so that the planets and stars actually moved around the earth!

But Zhang Heng had very many other interests as well. He invented an instrument that could detect earthquakes, even those that happened far away. We don't know exactly how this instrument, called a *seismoscope*, worked, but

Zhang Heng's device detected earthquakes

one account says that it was a bronze sphere with eight dragon heads in a circle around the top. Each dragon head represented a different part of the country, and each one had a copper ball in its mouth. When the ground shook, one of the balls would fall out of one of the dragon mouths and be caught by a bronze frog below. Scientists could tell, from which dragon mouth dropped the ball, where the earthquake had occurred!

Zhang Heng also invented a new kind of clock that could keep better time, using dripping water. He drew new, more accurate maps of the Han lands that showed exactly how far apart different cities were. He came up with a new device that could keep track of how many miles a chariot had been driven (an *odometer*). He learned how to paint on silk. And he kept on writing poetry!

Zhang Heng spent his entire life inventing and finding out. Today, we often call people like Zhang Heng *polymaths*. This word comes from two different Greek words: *poly*, which means "much" or "many," and *mathes*, which means "having learned." A polymath is able to learn many different things about many different subjects.

Even though Zhang Heng was offered several more important government positions after he became Chief Astronomer, he turned them down. He wanted to use his time to study the natural world—to keep on being a polymath. When he died, his friend Cui Yuan wrote these words on his tombstone:

> *He solved the riddles of the heavens.*
> *He exhausted the mysteries of the earth.*
> *His talents and his arts*
> *made him seem like a son of the gods.*

Note: Zhang Heng lived AD/CE 78-139. His name is also anglicized as Chang Heng.

Chapter Forty
Lands East of China

The Three Kingdoms of Korea

On the eastern side of China, a whole different people lived on a peninsula that jutted down into the sea.

Today, we call this peninsula Korea. But back in the last days of the Han Empire, the Korean peninsula was home to three different kingdoms. They were called Goguryeo, Baekje, and Silla.

The people in each of the three kingdoms spoke the same language—a language that was very different from Chinese. Their customs were very different from the ways of the Chinese. And the people of the three Korean kingdoms all believed the same myth—that they had been placed on the peninsula by their god Tan'gun, nearly three thousand years before. This was not the same story that the Chinese told at all!

The Han Empire had always wanted to control this peninsula. Before the Han Empire collapsed, the Han Chinese had captured the land in the far north of the Korean peninsula, and had settled Chinese officials and their families there. But the rulers of Silla, Goguryeo, and Baekje didn't want the Chinese in their land! They wanted to drive the Chinese out.

The kingdom of Goguryeo had always been the most troublesome to the Han. In fact, a Chinese account says that the people of Goguryeo are "by temperament ... violent, and take delight in robbery, plunder, and pillage!" That's because the armies of Goguryeo fought hard against the Han cities in the north.

Goguryeo conquered those cities one by one. By the time the Han Empire fell apart, only one city in the north of the peninsula still called itself Chinese. The city was called Wanggomsong. Today, it is called Pyongyang.

When the Han emperor fled, the Chinese in Wanggomsong kept on defending themselves. They kept control of their city for another hundred years—well into the rule of the Jin Empire of China! But finally, in AD/CE 313, an ambitious, energetic Goguryeon king named Micheon managed to march all the way to Wanggomsong. He captured the old Han city, and added it to his own kingdom.

This made Goguryeo the biggest and most powerful of the three Korean kingdoms—and the only one that had a whole city of Han Chinese inside it! The Han Chinese who remained after the conquest continued to speak Chinese and to write in Chinese letters. They taught the Goguryeons around them their ways. Even though the Han Empire was over, Chinese ways were beginning to make their way into Goguryeo.

Now, Goguryeo was three times the size of either Baekje or Silla. And that made the kings of Baekje and Silla nervous.

Neither king was willing to fight against Micheon. He was too strong, and too good a commander. And his army was far too large.

But then King Micheon died, and his son turned out to be a much weaker ruler. He rarely attacked other cities. He couldn't even keep the barbarians out of Goguryeo. The armies of the Sixteen Kingdoms, north of the Jin Empire, invaded Goguryeo over and over again. They took thousands of Goguryeo's people prisoner, and even wrecked the walls of its capital city.

When the king of Baekje saw how weak Goguryeo had become, he sent his son, the crown prince, up to attack his neighbor. The Baekje army killed the weak king of Goguryeo, and claimed most of its land for themselves. Micheon's grandson, a young man named Sosurim, inherited the tiny, battered remnant of Goguryeo. And Baekje now ruled most of the peninsula.

King Sosurim had to figure out how to help his country survive. Most of Goguryeo's army officers and many of his soldiers had been killed in battle. His cities had been burned and destroyed. Many of his officials had fled in fear.

Young Sosurim went to work! He welcomed visitors from China and India who brought teachings from Buddhism and Confucianism—ideas that Sosurim believed could help his country. He rewarded soldiers for joining his army. He strengthened the borders. He rebuilt Goguryeo's damaged cities. And slowly, Goguryeo became stronger and stronger, once again.

In 391, Sosurim's nephew Guanggaeto inherited the throne of Goguryeo. In the very first year of his reign, Guanggaeto decided that it was time to fight back against Baekje.

Do you remember the third kingdom on the Korean peninsula, Silla? Silla was not as warlike as its two neighbors. But the king of Silla was also worried about how strong Baekje was becoming. So he agreed to recognize Guanggaeto as his protector, and to help Guanggaeto fight against Baekje.

The armies of Silla and Goguryeo joined together and stormed through Baekje. Baekje fought back—but the combined armies were too much for Baekje. Finally the king of Baekje was forced to pay homage to King Guanggaeto (he had to say publicly that Guanggaeto was his superior). He also had to send Goguryeo a thousand hostages, as a promise that he would remain loyal! The king knew that if he defied Guanggaeto, those men would be in danger.

The rest of Guanggaeto's rule was spent fighting. He conquered sixty-five cities and fourteen hundred villages! He took back almost all of the northern land that Baekje had seized. He was so successful that he was given the nickname "The Great Expander."

Goguryeo had come the closest of any of the three Korean kingdoms to uniting the peninsula. When Guanggaeto the Expander died, his people carved a tribute to him on his stone monument—the oldest inscription and written history in Korea. It says:

His majestic virtue spread to the heavens,
like a huge willow tree,
and his bravery swayed the four oceans.
The nation was wealthy, the people flourished,
all five grains ripened abundantly in the fields.

The Yamato of Japan

If you put your finger on the map, right in the middle of the Korean peninsula, and then move right (or *east*), you'll cross over the water and come to four long, thin islands in the Pacific Ocean, just east of China. These are the islands of Japan!

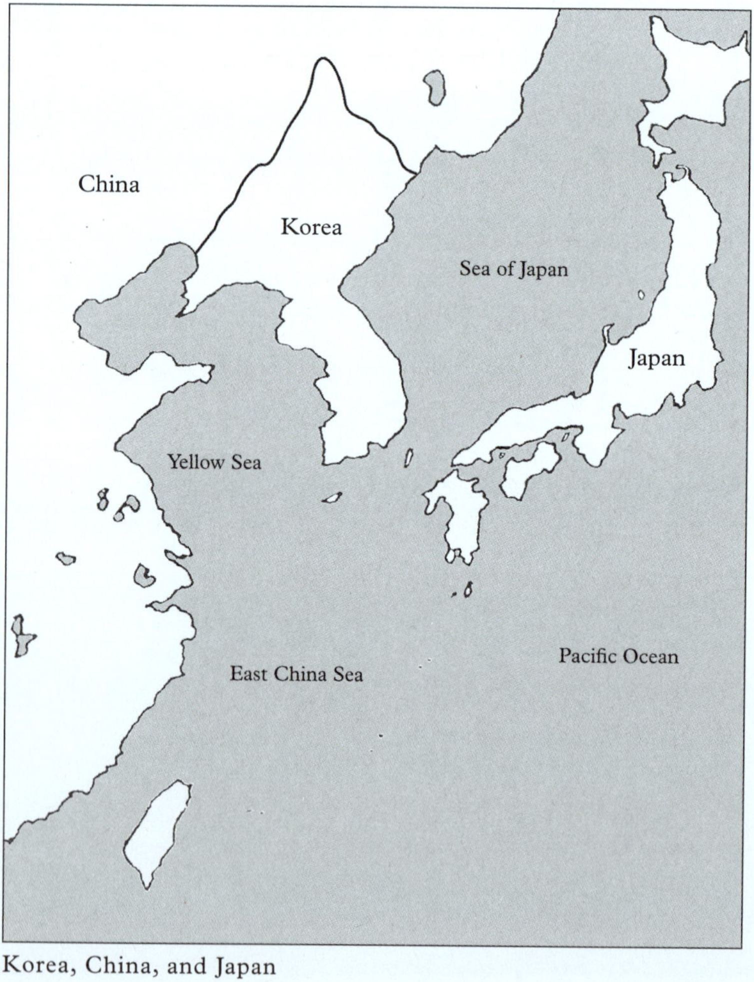

Korea, China, and Japan

Japan isn't very wide, but it is so long that there are frozen plains of snow at the north end of the island—and coral reefs and warm, sunny beaches at the south end. The four big islands that make up Japan have over seven thousand small islands all around them.

In the last days of the Han Empire and the early days of the Jin, Japan was ruled by many different clans, or families. Each clan had its own territory and was ruled by its own warrior chief. But by AD/CE 250, one of those warrior clans had become more powerful than all of the others. This clan ruled from the southern part of the longest Japanese island—an area known as the Nara region. They were called the Yamato.

The first Yamato war leader who called himself a king didn't rule all of Japan. There were too many islands and too many mountains for any single warrior clan to claim the entire country! But this war leader, whose name was Ojin, was the first one to claim the title of "Heavenly Sovereign." He didn't try to control all of the other war leaders. Instead, he told them that he could communicate to the divine on their behalf!

Here is the very ancient story that the Yamato clan told about themselves. These stories announced that the Yamato emperors were living gods, descendants of Amaterasu, the sun-goddess.

In the beginning, the world was full of sky-spirits who created the islands of Japan. These spirits had children of their own. The strongest and most beautiful of the daughters was Amaterasu.

Amaterasu was given the entire sky to rule over. But her brother Susano, who had been given the sea, was jealous. "The sky is larger than the sea!" he complained. So he mounted a war against Amaterasu to throw her out of the sky.

But he lost the fight and had to flee from the sky, down to earth. He ran until he was weary and had to rest by a stream. As he rested, he saw a pair of chopsticks drifting by him on the current. "There must be people around here!" he exclaimed. And he set off upstream to find them.

Soon he heard weeping and wailing. Just around a bend in the stream, he saw an old woman, an old man, and a beautiful young girl on the shore. All three were mourning.

"What's the matter?" Susano asked.

"An evil serpent with eight heads has come to our land!" the old man wept. "Every year for the past seven years, he has eaten one of our daughters. We had eight daughters, but all have been eaten except for our youngest. And today the serpent will come and eat her as well!"

Susano looked at the beautiful girl and fell in love with her at once. "I will save her," he said "if you will give her to me in marriage."

"Anything!" the old man cried.

So Susano turned the lovely girl into a comb and hid her in his hair. Then he laid out eight bowls of rice wine for the serpent, and hid in the bushes. Soon he heard the serpent approaching. It roared and thrashed its eight heads around, looking for its prey. But then it saw the wine. The eight heads

Susano and the serpent

dipped down and drank the eight bowls of rice wine. And then the serpent, full of wine, rolled over and went sound asleep.

Susano came out of the bushes, drew his sword, and chopped the serpent into eighty pieces. Inside the serpent, he found a great magical sword. He sent this sword to his sister Amaterasu for a peace gift. Then he took the comb from his hair and turned it back into the beautiful girl. He built a palace with eight walls and lived there with his lovely wife. Together, they had eighty fine sons.

Their youngest son was named Okuninushi. He settled down in the center of Japan and ruled over a plain covered with reeds. But his kingdom was an unhappy one. All over it, men fought with each other. And Okuninushi's seventy-nine brothers were constantly trying to overthrow his rule. The Reed Plain became so noisy and full of battle that the plants, rocks, and trees started sending up complaints to the heavens!

Up in the sky, Amaterasu heard the complaints. She decided to send her favorite grandson, Ninigi, to bring peace to the Reed Plain. So she called him before her throne and gave him three sacred objects: the string of beads she wore in her hair, the mirror in which she had first seen her own reflection, and the great sword that Susano had found inside the eight-headed serpent.

"Ninigi," she said, "I want you to go down to the islands below and rule there. Establish peace and order, instead of chaos. Your descendants will reign as long as heaven and earth endure!"

So Ninigi went down to the Reed Plain in the center of Japan and began his reign. In time he had children and grandchildren of his own.

His descendants were the Yamatos, and the blood of the goddess Amaterasu runs in their veins.

And when each Yamato emperor comes to the throne, he is given copies of the three sacred objects of Ninigi: the magic sword, the string of beads, and the mirror of Amaterasu.

But Susano retreated into the darkness and chose it as his kingdom. From then on, Susano was the moon-god who ruled the dark, and Amaterasu was the sun-goddess who ruled the day. Because of their old quarrel, the two never met again—just as the sun and the moon never meet in the sky.

The Yamato clan wanted to convince the other clans that they—and only they—had the right to rule all of Japan. And slowly, more and more of the other warrior clans agreed to obey the Yamato.

It would take over two hundred years for the Yamato leaders to rule over all of Japan—but eventually, the Yamato would become the first emperors of Japan.

Note: King Micheon ruled Goguryeo in AD/CE 300-331. Baekje invaded Goguryeo in 371, and Sosurim ruled 371-384. Guanggaeto ruled 391-413.

The traditional dates for Ojin's reign are 270-310, but some historians think that he is legendary, and others believe that he ruled much later.

Chapter Forty-One
The Attacking Barbarians

Stilicho, Roman and Barbarian

All of this time, the Western Roman Empire was under attack!

Remember: the empire had been divided into two parts so that it would be easier for Roman armies to protect it. The Eastern Roman Empire had grown richer and safer—while the Western Roman Empire fought off waves and waves of barbarian invaders. The Visigoths came storming down from around the Danube River. The Huns attacked from the north, from central Asia. And many other tribes tried to break into the Roman lands!

Some barbarians grew to like the Roman way of life. They stopped fighting and settled down in Roman villages. Sometimes, the barbarians even switched sides and fought for Rome.

One barbarian chief who switched sides married a Roman woman and settled down with her. We don't know his name, but we do know the name of his son: Stilicho.

Stilicho grew up with a barbarian father and a Roman mother. But Stilicho thought of himself as all Roman. He was a patriotic man who wanted to fight for Rome and protect Rome's lands from the barbarian invaders. When he was old enough, he joined the Roman army. He was a brave fighter and a loyal servant of the emperor.

Soon the emperor himself took notice of Stilicho. He sent Stilicho on important errands to other countries. And Stilicho fell in love with the emperor's niece, Serena. Finally, they were married. The half-barbarian boy had become part of the emperor's family.

The emperor put Stilicho in charge of the whole Roman army. "Stilicho," he said, "the Visigoths have decided to try and invade the city of Rome itself. I give you the job of keeping them away. Go and destroy the Visigoths! Keep Rome safe."

Stilicho accepted the job. He marched his army out to meet the invading Visigoths. Time after time, the Visigoths and the Romans clashed in battle. Each time, the Visigoths backed away. But the Roman soldiers were never able to destroy the Visigoths completely. After each battle, the barbarians went away, rested, found fresh horses and men, and returned to fight again. Soon the Roman army was exhausted.

Stilicho returned to Rome. "We can never beat the Visigoths," he told the people of Rome. "But if we send them four thousand pounds of gold, they will leave us in peace."

"Four thousand pounds!" the people protested. "We will become even poorer."

"But if we don't send the money," Stilicho said, "the Visigoths will continue to fight us—and soon they will win."

Finally the Roman people agreed. The Visigoths took their gold and retreated from Roman land. But now the Romans were poorer and hungrier than ever. They were angry with Stilicho, because he had not defeated the Visigoths. They resented him because they had been forced to pay gold to drive the Visigoths away.

Soon people began to whisper about Stilicho. "He didn't try hard enough to conquer the barbarians!" they murmured. "He allowed them to escape on purpose! If he really wanted to, he could wipe them out. But he spared them, because he's part barbarian himself! Stilicho is a traitor to Rome! It's his fault that we had to send all that gold to the barbarians!"

Stilicho tried to defend himself. "I did my best," he said. "I am a faithful, loyal servant of Rome. But our armies are weaker than they were in ancient times. No general could defeat the Visigoths. Paying them gold was our only hope!"

But the people of Rome paid no attention. They turned against Stilicho and demanded his execution. Even Stilicho's own army mutinied.

Stilicho was afraid for his life. He ran to a nearby church to hide.

"Come out!" his army told him. "We promise that you will be safe."

So Stilicho came out of the church. But as soon as he appeared, his own soldiers seized him and said, "The emperor has ordered you to be executed."

Stilicho's servants were still loyal to him. "We will fight for you!" they cried.

But Stilicho refused to allow this. "Let us have no more bloodshed," he said. "I will abide by the emperor's command."

So Stilicho was beheaded. After his death, many Romans regretted his execution. "He was a faithful Roman," they said, "and he was our best defense against the barbarians."

The Coming of the Visigoths

Stilicho, the half-barbarian, half-Roman general, did his best to protect Rome from the barbarian invaders. He fought the Visigoths for years. But the Romans executed him because they thought he wasn't doing his best for Rome.

They shouldn't have! Stilicho was the only general who could keep the Visigoths away from Rome. Only two years after Stilicho's execution, the Visigoths finally marched all the way down through Italy and reached the city of Rome itself.

By then, the emperor and his court were already gone! Because of all of the invading barbarians, they had packed up all their belongings and left the city of Rome. They had traveled to a much smaller city called Ravenna. Ravenna sat in the middle of a swamp. The Visigoths couldn't get through the soft, muddy ground of the swamp with their horses, so the emperor was safe.

Now, this tiny, dirty, damp city had become the capital of the Western Roman Empire!

The people who stayed in Rome were terrified. For eight hundred years, the city of Rome had been safe from attack. Its thick walls and world-famous army had protected it from invasion. But now, the army was weak and frightened, and the walls were unprotected.

The people of Rome sent desperate messages to the Eastern Roman Empire. "The Visigoths are coming!" they wrote. "Please, come and help us!"

But the army of the Eastern Roman Empire was afraid to fight the Visigoths. And the Eastern Roman emperor didn't dare send his army away from Constantinople,

The Visigoths invaded Rome

all the way to Rome. If he did, other barbarians might decide to attack his city while it was unprotected.

So no one came to help Rome.

The Visigoths poured through the gates and overwhelmed the soldiers who had remained on duty. The Visigoth commander, Alaric, ordered, "Gather up all the gold you can find! Take Rome's treasures! Now they belong to us!"

The Visigoths were happy to obey. They ripped down Rome's beautiful golden statues and melted them. They stole coins and jewelry.

But because many of the Visigoths had converted to Christianity, they didn't destroy Rome's churches. Instead, they took everything valuable that they could put their hands on, and then marched away.

When they heard the news, people all over the old empire mourned. Over in the Eastern Roman Empire, a monk named Jerome wrote, "Terrifying news has come to us from the West. Rome has been taken by assault. Sobs disturb my every word. The city has been conquered which had once ruled the whole world."

Ancient Rome would never again be a great world power.

Some Romans still lived in the city. But forty-five years after the Visigoth attack, another barbarian tribe invaded the city again. This tribe, called the Vandals, took everything valuable that the Visigoths had left behind. They were even worse than the Visigoths. They captured the frightened people of Rome and led them off to be slaves and hostages. They burned buildings made from wood, and tore bricks and stones out of walls that wouldn't burn. They even peeled the gold decorations off the roofs of Rome's temples! Today, we call someone who destroys things for fun a "vandal," after the Vandals who destroyed what was left of the city of Rome.

The Western Roman Empire still survived, but just barely. Its capital city was gone, and its emperor was ruling in the middle of a swamp.

Soon, the Western Roman Empire would be gone forever.

Attila the Hun

The Visigoths were a powerful barbarian tribe. But so were the barbarians called the Huns.

They swept down on what was left of the Western Roman Empire on strong, fast warhorses, wearing strong armor and shooting deadly arrows from horseback. They drove all their enemies into retreat.

All through the empire, people told terrible stories about the savage Huns. One Roman historian wrote, "They are uglier than any other men on earth. They eat roots that they find in the fields. And they don't even cook their meat. Instead, they put the raw meat between their saddles and the backs of their horses, and ride on it all day. Then they eat it!" The Huns taught their babies to ride horseback even before they could walk. And Hun children didn't go to school; instead, they learned how to shoot arrows at a full gallop.

The most terrifying barbarian of all was Attila, the greatest Hun war leader.

Attila led his Hun army in attacks against both Roman Empires—the East and the West. He was so powerful that the Romans, both West and East, began calling him "The Scourge of God." They thought that God was punishing them by sending Attila the Hun to attack their borders!

The Western Roman emperor and his advisers tried to think of a way to keep Attila away from the ancient city of Rome. But the emperor's sister, Honoria, had different ideas. Honoria was bored with life at the shrunken, dingy Roman court. She was tired of being a great lady. And her

The Area of Attila the Hun's Rule, Before His Attack on Rome

brother, the emperor, wanted her to marry a weak, ugly man whom she didn't love.

"If you don't marry him," he told her, "I'll throw you in jail!"

So Honoria wrote a letter to Attila the Hun.

"Come and rescue me!" she wrote. "If you do, I will marry you!"

She paid a servant to take this letter and her favorite ring to Attila. The servant rode for days and days to reach Attila's army, which was camped at the borders of the Western Roman Empire.

When Attila read Honoria's letter, he thought, "This is my chance to invade the empire and take it for myself!" So he sent a message back to the emperor. The message was: "I am engaged to be married to your sister, Honoria. I want half of your empire as a wedding present. And I'm coming to claim it—now!"

Attila and his men fought their way through Gaul and finally marched down into Italy. They conquered and burned the cities in their path. Finally, the emperor offered to pay Attila a huge amount of money to leave Italy. And he promised to send Attila money every year, if only Attila would leave Italy alone.

Attila agreed to leave Italy, but he warned, "I want Honoria sent to me as my wife, or I will return."

He marched the Huns back out of Italy, planning to come back and claim his wife and his new empire. But before Attila could return to Italy, he died of a nosebleed. He never did marry Honoria, the sister of the emperor.

Attila's followers put his body into a golden coffin. They put the golden coffin into a silver coffin, and the silver coffin into an iron coffin. They buried the iron coffin in the dead of night, and then killed all of the slaves who had helped to dig the grave, so that no one would know where Attila was buried.

To this day, the grave of Attila the Hun has not been found.

Note: Stilicho became regent for the Western Roman Empire in AD/CE 395, after Theodosius. Stilicho drove Alaric away in 397 but fell from favor and was executed in 408. The Visigoths sacked Rome in 410. Attila's birthdate is unknown; he died in 453.

Chapter Forty-Two
The End of Rome

The Last Roman Emperor

The Romans used to rule dozens of other countries. They were the most powerful people in the world.

The Celts who lived in Britain had never wanted to be part of the Roman Empire. And the Romans had never managed to control all of the British islands. Some of the Celts obeyed Roman laws and paid taxes to the Romans. But others rebelled.

But then the empire was divided. The Western Roman Empire grew weaker and weaker, and the Eastern Roman Empire refused to help the West out. The people of the Eastern Roman Empire still called themselves "Romans," but they cared little for the Roman lands around the old capital city of Rome!

The Western Roman Empire still existed. But barbarians had taken over most of its land. And although the Western Roman Empire still had an emperor, he didn't live in Rome, because Rome had been destroyed. He lived in a small, swampy city, hiding from the barbarians.

Finally one of the invaders, named Orestes, decided to drive the Roman emperor out of hiding. He collected an army and marched towards the small, swampy city where the emperor lived.

When the emperor heard that Orestes and his men were coming, he ran away. By the time Orestes arrived, the emperor was long gone.

Orestes decided to make his own son emperor. There was only one problem—his son was just a little boy!

But that didn't stop Orestes. He ordered all his men to obey the new child emperor. And he gave his son a new name, Romulus Augustus. He called him Romulus, because an old legend said that a man named Romulus was the first king of Rome, long, long ago. And he called him Augustus after Augustus Caesar, Rome's most famous emperor.

That was a big name for a little boy! And when the people who were left in the Western Roman Empire heard it, they laughed. "Romulus Augustus!" they said. "What a silly name for a child! We won't call him Romulus—we'll call him Momyllus!"

Momyllus meant "Little Disgrace." The Romans felt insulted, because they were expected to obey the child of a barbarian. But Momyllus didn't get to be emperor very long. Another barbarian captured Momyllus and his father Orestes. Young Momyllus was sent off to live in another city. He was given plenty of money to pay for food and clothes, but he wasn't allowed to rule any more. His crown and scepter were taken to Constantinople.

And that was the end of the Western Roman Empire.

It was full of barbarian kings now, each one ruling his own little kingdom. The lands that used to belong to Rome belonged to them.

The newcomers still used the wide, beautiful Roman roads. Rome's huge buildings still stood, although many were beginning to crumble away. Many people still spoke

Latin, the language of the Romans. And the barbarians had begun to learn Roman ways and Roman customs.

But the Roman Empire itself was gone forever.

Over in the Eastern Roman Empire (which we now call the Byzantine Empire), people mourned. Rome had been a great and beautiful city, but now it was in ruins. As long as an emperor still ruled, there was hope that Rome might be great again. But now the last Roman emperor, a little boy not too much older than you are, had lost his throne.

Rome would never again rule the world.

The Gifts of Rome

The Roman emperor is long gone, and the Roman Empire disappeared long, long ago.

But the Romans gave us words and inventions that we use every single day.

You're using one of them right now! How many books do you have in your house? How often do you use a book?

The Romans were the first people to use books with pages. They figured out how to sew pages together along one side so that you can turn the pages and read both the front and back of each one. Before the Romans, people used *scrolls*—long, long pieces of paper or animal skin, that you had to unroll to read and roll back up whenever you were finished. Can you imagine reading a scroll in bed? Or in the car? Every time you read a book, you're using a Roman invention.

The words you're reading came from the Romans too. We use the Roman alphabet to write our words. Whenever you sing the alphabet song or write a word, you are using the letters that the Romans used.

Do you know the twelve months of the year? Most of those months have Roman names. *January* is named after the Roman god Janus. *March* is named after Mars, the god of war. *June* is named after Juno, the most important Roman goddess. *July* and *August* are both named after Roman heroes: July is named after Julius Caesar, the famous Roman general, and August is named after Augustus, Rome's first emperor.

Do you like to go swimming in the summer? If so, thank the Romans. The Romans built big bathtubs, big enough for twenty or thirty people to wash in at once. These bathtubs were the first swimming pools.

If you look at a United States penny, you'll see that it has the picture of a head on it. The portrait is of Abraham Lincoln, one of the greatest presidents of the United States. The Romans liked to put pictures of their emperors on their coins. Today, we put pictures of our leaders on coins—copying the Romans.

Now look at a dime. On one side of the dime, you can see some tiny words: *E pluribus unum*. Those words are in Latin, the language that the ancient Romans spoke. They mean "Out of many, one." This means that America has many different states in it, but all of the states are united together into one country. The Romans gave us these words to write on our coins.

We live on the planet Earth, but there are seven other planets in our solar system: Mercury, Venus, Mars, Jupiter, Saturn, Uranus, Neptune. Most of our planets have Roman names. They are named after Roman gods and goddesses. Jupiter was the king of the gods. He was a big, important god, and Jupiter is a very big planet. Mars is named after the god of war; Mercury is named after the messenger of the gods, and Venus is named after the goddess of love and beauty. Saturn is Jupiter's father, and Neptune is the god of the sea. Only one planet, Uranus, is named after a Greek god.

Finally, even our words come from Rome! The English language borrowed many, many words from Latin, the language of the Romans. Can you figure out what English words come from these Latin words?

The *frigidarium* was the room where Roman bathers jumped into very cold water. What word sounds like *frigidarium* and keeps things cold? The refrigerator!

A Roman child lived in a *familia* with his mother, father, sisters, and brothers. What is a *familia*? A family.

The Latin word for book was *liber*. What word sounds like *liber* and is a place where books are kept? A library.

In Latin, a ship is a *navis*. Do you know what word comes from *navis*? It means "many ships that sail together." That's right—navy.

Have you ever written "P.S." at the end of a letter? If so, you've used Latin words. "P.S." stands for the Latin words "*post scriptum*," or "after the writing." A "P.S." goes *after* the main *writing* of the letter.

In Rome, a *floris* was a beautiful plant that smelled good. Can you think of a beautiful plant that smells good and sounds like *floris*? Our word "flower" comes from the Latin *floris*.

Even though the ancient Roman Empire is gone, we use the words, inventions, and ideas of the Romans all the time. So, in a way, Rome will never completely disappear. The gifts that the Romans gave to us are still with us today.

Note: Romulus Augustus ruled AD/CE 475–476.

Appendix One
A Chronology of Ancient Times

BC/BCE Dates in Volume 1

(AD/CE dates start on page 391)

9000 BC/BCE	Nomads roam the Fertile Crescent
8000	Stone walls built at Jericho
3500	Climate changes in the Sahara
3000	King Narmer unites Upper and Lower Kingdoms of Egypt
3000–2100	Era of the Old Kingdom of Egypt
3000–1200	Gilgamesh Myth composed
2690	Huang Di rules China
2550	Great Pyramid built (burial place of Cheops)
2334	Sargon becomes king of the city-state of Kish
2200–1450	Peak of Minoan civilization
2040–1720	Middle Kingdom of Egypt
2000–1750	Harappan civilization is at its peak strength
1980–1926	Amenemhet becomes pharaoh of Egypt
1792	Hammurabi inherits the throne of Babylon
1766	T'ang becomes King of China
1766–1122	Shang Dynasty rules
1750	Exodus of Indus Valley
1567	Ahmose expels Hyksos from Egypt
1524	Thutmose I becomes pharaoh

1500	Aryan people enter India
1498–1483	Hatshepsut rules as pharaoh
1450	Mycenaeans settle in Crete
1343	Tutankhamen born
1350–1334	Amenhotep IV rules Egypt as pharaoh
1325	Tutankhamen dies at age 18
1300–1200	Spread of Assyrian Empire
1200–900	Olmec civilization flourishes
1200–700	Height of Phoenician civilization; Greek "Dark Ages"
mid-800s	Greek city-states begin to arise
814	Carthage is first settled
800	Homer lives during this time
800	Shammuramat rules Assyria alongside her son
700	Time of the earliest Persians
668–627	Ashurbanipal's reign as king of Assyria
605–561	Nebuchadnezzar rules as king of Babylon
622-600	Draco and Solon make laws for Athens
563–483	Siddhartha Gautama (the Buddha) lives
559–529	Cyrus the Great rules over Medes and Persians
551–479	Confucius lives
539	Babylon falls to the Persians
535-509	Tarquin the Proud and his wife Tullia rule Rome
500	War against Persia by Greece begins
500	Aryan civilization in India reaches high point

500	"Period of the Warring States" begins in China
492-460	Ajatashatru rules Maghada, helps to collect Buddha's teachings
490	First marathon run by Athenian to announce victory over Persia
480	Battle of Salamis
431–404	War between Sparta and Athens (Peloponnesian War)
338	King Philip of Macedonia conquers Greek city-states
336–323	Alexander the Great rules
320	Mencius writes about virtue
321–185	The Mauryan Empire of India
268–232	Asoka rules India; Mauryan empire begins to disintegrate following his death
264–241	First Punic War fought
264–146	Punic Wars
230	Shi Huangdi (Qin Zheng) begins uniting Warring States of China
221	First united Chinese empire, under Shi Huangdi
218	Hannibal's invasion of Italy
218–202	Second Punic War takes place
214	Construction of Great Wall of China begins
213	Qin Zheng orders book burning
200	Nazca civilization flourishes
164	Judas Maccabee recaptures the Jewish Temple in Jerusalem
138-126	Zhang Qian's expedition to the western borders of China
100	Julius Caesar born

73-71	Spartacus leads a slave rebellion in Italy
69	Cleopatra born
55–54	Caesar's campaigns in Britain take place
48	Caesar arrives in Egypt
March 15, 44	Caesar is assassinated
43	Octavian becomes a consul in Rome
27	Octavian becomes Caesar Augustus, emperor of the Roman Empire
3 BC/BCE	Probable year of Jesus' birth

AD/CE Dates in Volume 1

4 AD/CE	Caesar Augustus dies
54–68	Nero's reign
60–61	Boadicea revolts against Rome
70	The Temple in Jerusalem is destroyed
79	Pliny the Younger sees Mount Vesuvius' eruption; Pompeii is destroyed
100-139	Zhang Heng develops several scientific devices
284	Diocletian comes to the throne in Rome
286	Diocletian divides the Roman Empire
286–305	Diocletian rules jointly with Maximian
312	The Battle of Milvian Bridge
312–337	The reign of Constantine
395	Stilicho, following Theodosius, becomes regent for the Western Roman Empire
397	Stilicho drives Alaric away
408	Stilicho falls from favor and is executed
410	Visigoths sack Rome
453	Attila the Hun dies
475–476	Romulus Augustus rules

Appendix Two
The Geography of Ancient Times

A Listing of Maps in Volume 1

Appendix Three
Pronouncing the Names of Ancient Times

A Pronunciation Guide to the People, Places, and Events in Volume 1

Notes on pronunciation:

1. Chinese pronunciation uses certain diphthongs that do not exist in English. They are represented here by two sounds connected by a hyphen. When these hyphenated sounds appear, they should be pronounced together smoothly as one syllable, not as two.

2. This guide occasionally uses more common, well-known pronunciations—the ones that the child is much more likely to encounter in subsequent life and reading—instead of more technically "correct" ones; for instance, Julius Caesar is rendered here as *JOO lee us SEE zer* instead of the (probably) more accurate *YOO lee oos KAI zar*. This pronunciation guide is meant to help you read the text aloud, not to cover all scholarly disagreements about the pronunciation of ancient names.

Abram. . . . . AY bram
Adad-Nirari . . . . ah DAHD neh RAHR ee
Aegeus . . . . EE jus or EE jee us
Aesop . . . . EE sop
Ahmose . . . . AH mos
Ajatashatru . . . . ah juh tuh SHUH troo
Akhenaten . . . . ah ken AH ten
Akkad . . . . AH kad
Akkadia . . . . ah KAY dee uh
Alaric . . . . ah LAR ic

Alcibiades .... al sih BYE uh deez
Amaterasu .... ah MA teh RA suh
Amenemhet .... AH men EM het
Amenhotep .... AH men HO tep
Amun-Ra .... AH men RAH
Amun .... AH men
Amytis .... uh MYE tis
Anansi .... ah NAN see
Antiochus Epiphanes ... ann TIE uh kuss eh PIFF ah neez
Anu .... AY noo
Anubis .... uh NOO bis
Aphrodite .... A fro DITE ee or AH fro DITE ee
Appian .... AP ee un
Ariadne .... AIR ree ADD nee
Ashurbanipal .... ash ur BAN ih pal
Asia Minor .... AY zhuh MY nor
Asoka .... uh SO kuh
Assur .... AH sur
Assyria .... uh SEE ree uh
Astyges .... uh STIE jeez or uh STEE uh jeez
Aten .... AH tun
Athena .... ath EE nuh
Attila the Hun .... uh TILL uh the HUN
Augustus Caesar .... uh GUS tus SEE zer
Baekje .... behk jeh
Belshazzar .... bel SHAZ er
Bhagiratha .... bah gih RAH thuh
Bimbisara .... BIM bee ser uh
Boadicea .... BO uh dih SEE uh

brahmin	BRAH min
Brutus	BROOT us
Bucephalus	byoo SEH fuh lus or byoo SHE fuh lus
Caesar	SEE zer
Caligula	kuh LIG yoo luh
canopic	kuh NO pick or kuh NAW pick
Cao Wei	tsow way ("ow" should be pronounced as in "crowd")
Capua	KAH poo ah
Carthage	CAR thij
Carthaginian	CAR thuh JIN ee un
Cassius	CASS ee us
Ceres	SEER eez
Chang Chueh	JONG joo-EH
Chang'an	CHONG AHN
chanyu	CHON yoo
Cheops	KEE ops
Cincinnatus	sin sih NAH tus
Claudius Pulcher	CLAW dee us PULL kair
Cleopatra	clee o PAT ruh
Confucius	con FYU shis
Constantinople	CON stan tih NO pul
Cui Yuan	TSWAY yoo-en
Cyclops	SIE clops
Cyrus	SIE rus
Diocletian	DIE o CLEE shun
Diodorus	die oh DOR uhs
Dong Wu	DOHNG woo ("OH" should be pronounced as in "Oh my!")

Dong Zhuo............. dohng joo-WOH ("OH" pronounced as in "oh my!")
Dorians .... DOOR ee uns
E pluribus unum .... EE PLUR ih bus OO num
Enkidu .... en KEE doo or en KIE doo
Eris .... AIR ris
Et tu, Brute? .... Et TOO, BROO tay?
Euphrates .... you FRATE eez
Euripides .... yuh RIP i deez
familia .... fah MEE lee ah
floris .... FLO ris
frigidarium .... frih gih DAR ee um or frih jih DAYR ee um
fu .... foo
Gaius Plinius Caecilius Secundus ..... GUY us PLIN ee us kai KILL ee us seh KUN dus
Ganga .... GANG guh
Gautama .... GOW tuh muh
Gilgamesh .... GILL guh mesh
Goguryeo .... goh goo ryuh
Gordian .... GORE dee un
Guanggaeto .... gwahng geh toh
Gutians .... GOO tee ANS
Hammurabi .... hah mu RA bee
Hannibal .... HAN ih bel
Hanukkah or Chanukah .. HAH nuh kuh
Haran .... hah RAN
Harappan .... huh RAP uh
Harpagus .... har PAG us
Hatshepsut .... hat SHEP soot
Hera .... HEER uh or HAYR uh
Herod .... HAYR uhd

Hieroglyphs .... HIE ro glifs
Honoria .... on OR ee uh
Horus .... HORE us
Huang Di .... hwahng DEE
Hyksos .... HICK sos
imperator .... im PEAR uh tor
Indus .... IN dus
Ishtar .... ish TAR
Isis .... EYE sis
Jakata .... ja KA tah
Janus .... JAY nuss
Jericho .... JAYR ih ko
Jianye .... JEE-en YEH
Jin Wudi .... JEEN woo DEE
Jove .... JOHV
Judah .... JOO duh
Judea .... joo DEE uh or joo DAY uh
Judas Maccabee .... JOO dahs MAK uh bee
Julius Caesar .... JOO lee us SEE zer
Juno .... JOO no
Kahramanmaraş .... kah rah MAHN mah rahsh
Khufu .... KOO foo
Kish .... KISH
Knossos .... NAW sus
Kush .... KUSH (the "u" sounds like the "oo" in "foot")
Lei Zu .... lay TZU
liber .... LEE bear
Licchavi .... lee CHUH vee
Londinium .... lon DIN ee um
Macedonians .... mah suh DO nee unz

Magadha .... MUH guhdh
mahashilakantaka ..... MAH sheel uh kun tuk
Mahayana .... MAH high yah nuh
Marduk .... MAR duke
Mari .... MAH ree
Masada .... mah SAH duh
mastaba tombs .... MAH stuh buh toomz
Mattathias .... maht ah THY us
Mauryan .... MAR ee un
Maximian .... mack SIH mee un
Mayans .... MY unz
Medes .... MEEDZ
Media .... MEE dee uh
Menelaus .... men uh LAY us or men uh LOUSE
Menes .... MEN eez
Mencius .... MEN see us
Meng-tzu .... MUNG tzuh (“uh” as in “uh oh”)
Mesopotamia .... MESS uh puh TAY mee uh
Micheon .... mee chuhn
Milvian .... MILL vee un
Min Lai .... min LIE
Minos .... MY nus or MY nos or MEE nos
Minotaur .... MIN uh tar or MY nuh tar
Miseno .... mee SAY no
Momyllus .... muh MILL us
murex .... MYUR eks
Mycenaeans .... MY suh NEE uns
Narmer .... NAR mare
navis .... NAH vis

Nazca .... NAZ kuh
Nebuchadnezzar ..... NEH buh kud NEH zer
Nefertiti .... NEH fer TEE tee
Nero .... NEER o
Nineveh .... NIN uh vuh
Ningal .... NING gul
Ninigi .... NEE nee ghee
Nubia .... NOO bee uh
Numitor .... NOO mih tor
Octavian .... ock TAY vee un
Odometer .... oh DOM eh ter
Odysseus .... o DIS ee us
Ojin .... OH jin (the "i" in "jin" is sort of like the "i" in "igloo")
Okuninushi .... OH koo nee NOO shee
Olmecs .... OLE mecs
Olympus .... o LIM pus
Orestes .... o REST eez
Osiris .... o SYE rus
Pāli .... PAH lee
Parthenon .... PAR thuh non
Pax Romana .... PACKS ro MAH nah
Peloponnesian .... pel uh puh NEE zhun
Pericles .... PEAR ih cleez
Pheidippides .... fih DIP uh deez or fie DIP uh deez
Pictograms .... PICK toe gramz
Plato .... PLAY toe
Pliny .... PLIN ee
Plutarch .... PLOO tark
Pompeii .... pahm PAY ee
Pompey .... POM pee

Poseidon .... po SYE din
Potiphar .... PAH tih far
princeps .... PRIN keps or PRIN seps
Proserpine .... PRO ser PEE nuh
Ptolemy .... TALL uh mee
Purusha .... POO ruh shuh
Qin .... CHIN
Qin Zheng .... chin ZHUNG
Ra .... RAH or RAY
Rajagriha .... RUHJ GREE huh
rathamusala .... ruh tha moo SAH la
Remus .... REE mus
Romulus .... ROM you lus
Rubicon .... ROO bih con
Sakka .... SACK uh
Sarai .... SAIR eye
Sargon .... SAR gon
Scipio .... SKIP ee o or SIP ee o
scriptum .... SKRIP tum
secutor .... sec YOO tur
seismoscope .... SIZE muh skohp
Seleucids .... seh LOO sidz
Seleucus .... seh LOO cuss
Semiramis .... si MEER uh mis
Servius Tullius .... SER vee us TOO lee us
Seyanaga .... SAY uh nahg uh
shaduf .... sha DOOF
Shammuramat .... shah muhr AH maht
Shamshi-Adad .... SHAM shee ah DAHD
Shandong .... SHAN DOHNG ("OH" as in "oh my!")

Shang .... SHANG
Shi Huangdi .... SHIH hwahng DEE
Shiva .... SHEE vuh
Shu Han .... shoo HON
Siddhartha .... sid ARE thuh
or sih DART uh
Silla .... shil lah
Sima Yan .... SUH ma YEN
("UH" as in "uh oh")
Solon .... SOH lon
Sosurim .... soh soo rim
Sparta .... SPAR tuh
Spartacus .... spart ah kuss
sphinx .... SFINKS
Stilicho .... STILL ih ko
Suddhodana .... SUD ho DAN uh
Suetonius .... soo TOE nee us
Surano .... sue sah NO
Sumer .... SOO mer
Sumerian .... soo MARE ee un
Sutra .... SOO truh
Syrians .... SEER ee enz
T'ang .... TAHNG
Taixue .... TIE shu-EH
Tarquin .... TAR kwin
Terah .... TARE uh
Thebes .... THEEBZ
Theodosius .... thee uh DO shus
Thera .... THAYR uh
Theseus .... THEE see us
Thutmose .... THUT mohs
Tiber .... TIE ber

Tiberius . . . . tie BEER ee us
Tiglathpileser . . . . TIG lath pih LAY zer
Tigris . . . . TIE gris
Tiye . . . . TIE ee
Tripitaka . . . . TRIP ee TAHK uh
Ts'ao Ts'ao . . . . TSOW tsow (the "ow" should rhyme with "cow")
Tullia Minor . . . . TULL ee uh MIN or
Tutankhamen . . . . toot ahng KAH men
Tutankhaten . . . . toot ahng COT en
Tyre . . . . Tire
Ulysses . . . . you LIS eez
Uruk . . . . OO rook
Utnapishtim . . . . ut nah PISH tim
Veni, Vidi, Vici . . . . VAYN ee, VEE dee, VEE chee or WAYN ee, WEE dee, WEE kee
Vesuvius . . . . veh SOO vee us
Visigoth . . . . VIZ ih gawth
Wanggomsong . . . . wahng guhm suhng
Wei Yuandi . . . . WAY yoo-en DEE
Wudi . . . . woo DEE
Xi'an . . . . SHYAN
Xiling Ji . . . . SHEE ling JEE
Xiongnu . . . . SHOHNG new
Yamato . . . . Ya MAH to
Yangtze . . . . YANG see or YANG dzu
Zhangdi . . . . JONG DEE
Zhang Heng . . . . JONG hung
Zhang Qian . . . . JONG CHEE-EN
Zisi . . . . zuh SUH (pronounce SUH to rhyme with the "uh" in "uh oh")
Zou . . . . JOH

Appendix Four
The Abraham Story

A Note for Parents

Biblical commentators agree that Terah's name expresses kinship with the moon-god Sin. Sarai's name is the Akkadian version of "Ningal," the name of Sin's goddess wife. Later in the story, when God renames both Abram and Sarai as part of the covenant, their new names both contain the new syllable ah. This is part of God's own covenant name YHWH, and symbolizes that they have been reclaimed from the worship of the god of Ur, and their ownership has been transferred to YHWH. (See, for example, Victor P. Hamilton, *The Book of Genesis*, Volume I [Eerdmans, 1990], p. 363.)

The Genesis account is ambiguous about Terah's original reasons for leaving Ur. It is not clear whether Abram convinced his father to leave because he heard the voice of God, or whether Terah left the city first; both readings of the text are possible. However, in Terah's day, the southern part of Sumer was suffering from barbarian invasion and war between Ur and the other cities on the plain, while Haran was relatively peaceful.

Index

N

O

P

Q

R

CONTINUE YOUR JOURNEY THROUGH THE ANCIENT WORLD

Some great supplements to accompany
The Story of the World, Volume 1: Ancient Times
25th Anniversary Expanded Edition

FAMOUS FIGURES OF ANCIENT TIMES

978-0-9818566-0-5 | Cathy Diez-Luckie | Well-Trained Mind Press

Creative history for the classical child! Act out the history you've been reading with these movable paper characters - or create new adventures of your own! The book includes 20 historical figures - kings, generals, philosophers, religious leaders, and scholars - in both pre-colored and color-them-in versions, to cut out and assemble into movable action figures.

EGYPTIAN TREASURES: MUMMIES AND MYTHS

978-1-942968-60-3 | Audiobook | Well-Trained Mind Press | Jim Weiss

Thrill to tales of mummies and pharaohs and discover the myths of Egyptian gods and goddesses as you journey through this ancient land.

Timeline: 3000 BCE

GREEK MYTHS

978-1-942968-71-9 | Audiobook | Well-Trained Mind Press | Jim Weiss

Meet mighty Hercules, greedy King Midas, beautiful Arachne, brave Perseus, and dangerous Medusa! These adventurous tales engage children while emphasizing character over violence.

Timeline: 1000 BCE

COURAGE AND A CLEAR MIND: TRUE ADVENTURES OF THE ANCIENT GREEKS

978-1-933339-99-3 | Audiobook | Well-Trained Mind Press | Jim Weiss

Charge into land and sea battles to defend the world's first democracy against a tyrannical empire; attend the original Olympics; hear how the Greeks won a war with the clever trick of the Trojan Horse; share laughter and wisdom with Socrates; and meet artists and authors, as well as typical families, in the rival cities of Athens and Sparta.

Timeline: 1000 BCE to 400 BCE

PHARAOHS AND QUEENS OF ANCIENT EGYPT

978-1-942968-99-3 | Audiobook | Well-Trained Mind Press | Jim Weiss

Travel back to a time of roaring battles, thundering chariot charges, treasure chambers, and secret temples! Meet remarkable rulers (Hatshepsut, Akhenaten, Ramesses II, and more), the Nile River that made it all possible, and the thrilling discovery of King Tutankhamun's treasure-laden tomb.

Timeline: Ancient Egypt

JULIUS CAESAR AND THE STORY OF ROME

978-1-933339-87-0 | Audiobook | Well-Trained Mind Press | Jim Weiss

Meet Julius Caesar - adventurer, conqueror, political genius, author, and famed historical figure. Experience power, ambition, and deadly betrayal in this thrilling version of one of Shakespeare's most famous plays - a great introduction for young listeners.

Timeline - Julius Caesar: 100 BCE-40 BCE

Timeline - Shakespeare: Elizabethan

Find more titles at welltrainedmind.com